Research Linking Teacher Preparation and Student Performance

Teacher Education Yearbook XII

Edited by

Edith M. Guyton and Julie Rainer Dangel

KENDALL/HUNT PUBLISHING COMPANY
4050 Westmark Drive   Dubuque, Iowa 52002

Teacher Education Yearbook XII

EDITORS

Edith M. Guyton, *Georgia State University, Atlanta*
Julie Rainer Dangel, *Georgia State University, Atlanta*

EDITORIAL ADVISORY BOARD

David M. Byrd, *University of Rhode Island, Kingston*
John McIntyre, *Southern Illinois University, Carbondale*
Mary John O'Hair, *University of Oklahoma, Norman*
Sandra J. Odell, *University of Nevada-Las Vegas*
Rudy Mattai, *SUNY College at Buffalo*
Violet Allain, *James Madison University*
Elizabeth Wilkins, *Towson University*
Loren Miller, *Cooper Elementary*
Binyao Zheng, *Kennesaw State University*
Angela Case, *University of Delaware*
Tom Poetter, *Miami University*
Melba Spooner, *University of North Carolina in Charlotte*
Gwendolyn H. Middlebrooks, *Spelman College*
Scott Hopkins, *University of South Alabama*
Linda Quinn, *University of Nevada, Las Vegas*
Alan Reiman, *North Carolina State University*

Gwendolyn T. Benson, *Georgia State University*
Sam Hausfather, *Berry College*

EXECUTIVE DIRECTOR

Ian R. Horen, Association of Teacher Educators, *Reston, Virginia*

Contents

Division 2: Methods of Making Connections between Teacher Education and Student Learning

Foreword

Frances van Tassell is Associate Professor of Teacher Education and Administration at the University of North Texas (Denton, Texas) and is the 2003–2004 President of the Association of Teacher Educators (ATE). Proudly a member of ATE since 1987, Frances has served ATE in many ways. Over these 16 continuous years, she has served as chair or member of several ATE conference planning committees, chair or member of several standing ATE committees, member of one commission, and has been recognized for outstanding service by three ATE presidents.

Teacher Education Yearbook XII: Research on the Effects of Teacher Education on Teacher Performance

It is imperative at this time in the history of public education in the United States of America that those who prepare teachers provide valid evidence of the critical importance of teacher education as it impacts student performance. ATE has evidence of its commitment to quality in teacher education programs, as shown in the outstanding Teacher Educator Standards developed by a commission appointed to examine what it takes to be a highly qualified and highly effective teacher educator. Editors Julie Dangel and Edi Guyton present an outstanding collection of manuscripts to answer questions posed in the call for submissions to this yearbook. They sought manuscripts that would provide research-based evidence of how teacher quality impacts student performance. The authors of the 12th ATE Yearbook provide clear evidence of the importance of quality teacher education. Authors effectively responded to the questions posed for this yearbook, such as, "What role does a teacher's content knowledge play in student performance?" The question, "What models of teacher preparation can be linked to teacher change and student performance?" generated responses from researchers that explored and examined models of teacher education programs and professional development activities that assure teacher knowledge, ability, and disposition as those elements impact student learning and performance.

As the editors wove together the selected manuscripts for this issue of the ATE Yearbook, they effectively clustered the manuscripts into three categories, as follow: 1) models for assessing teacher impact on student learning, 2) methods of making connections between teacher education and student learning, and 3) effects of teacher education interventions on student learning. Readers will find answers to questions about effective models of teacher education and other issues, yet will likely leave the reading of this yearbook with more questions about how to ensure quality teacher education and how to document the impact of teacher education on student learning and performance.

One of the most challenging questions that teacher educators face is how to prepare pre-service and inservice teachers for high stakes testing and personal accountability in an era where parents, legislators, and representatives of business and industry wish to measure teacher effectiveness as it relates to student performance. It is questionable that teacher effectiveness be based solely on student performance, particularly when the one measurement is a standardized test indicator administered on one day in the life of learners who are in school approximately 180 days. What value is there is taking a one-time look at student performance? Should there not be multiple measures for assuring that teachers are accountable for student success? Obviously, there is more than one indicator but too often the public is made aware of only the one high stakes testing indicator. Directly related to this topic is concern about licensing, certification, and accreditation. As states implement more and more means for allowing persons with no background in education to enter the classroom as teachers-of-record, those in educational programs that prepare teachers and school leaders become increasingly concerned about the effectiveness and stability of such teachers and their impact on student learning. That leads to the next question of how teachers may be continuously prepared to effectively and efficiently ensure that students meet learning standards and leave school ready for the work place.

The issue of professional development for educators remains a concern for schools and teacher educators. Teachers often complain about lack of quality professional development offered or mandated by their local district or campus. Equally, teachers frequently complain about the value from their teacher education courses. Some teachers enter their first year of teaching without adequate preparatory experiences in real classrooms, recognizing that student teaching was helpful but not sufficient for knowing all the intricacies of both the art and the science of teaching. Some teachers begin their career believing they have sufficient content knowledge, yet quickly find out that they must learn with their students. Of course, these incidents quickly get the attention of politicians and far too often result in legislation designed to measure teacher effectiveness based solely on one indicator – the standardized test. The reality is that teacher education programs and staff development offerings that educate and prepare teachers to be highly effective abound across this nation. It is the purpose of a publication such as this to document and demonstrate such successful programs.

The public, legislators, and business and industry leaders often complain that high school students enter the workplace without sufficient problem solving skills, adequate basic knowledge, or the ability to get along with others in the work place. It seems that schools have become the one place in the United States where one group of people, the teachers, are expected to provide children and youth with everything from assuring that children are fed to providing counseling and guidance to troubled youth. Teachers are expected to communicate and work with parents to assure student learning and teacher accountability, as they respond to ever-increasing demands for success on high stakes testing. Teachers must provide learners with knowledge that leads to application in order to solve problems in ways never dreamed of even ten years ago. So it is no wonder that teachers must be highly qualified and deeply prepared before they ever enter the classroom! To be so, all teachers must have high quality teacher education and professional development.

The purpose of the divisions in this yearbook is to validate that teacher education does make a difference in the performance of students. The study that reports the effects of empowering beginning teachers to analyze student learning provides evidence from selected student teachers regarding their sense of empowerment (thus success in implementation) to use their knowledge of the teaching-learning setting to meet the needs of all students. These novice teachers learned in their teacher preparation courses and field experiences how to effectively plan and deliver instruction then how to assess student learning in order to improve their teaching. The study that reports the outcomes of a specific project designed to link learning style teacher preparation with student performance outcomes reveals the impact of staff development on middle school teachers' ability to facilitate an increase in student performance in language arts. The statewide professional development program reported in one chapter depicts evidence that a collaborative approach to staff development has effect on student learning.

In response to the ever-increasing growth of enrollment in the population of primary and intermediate grades, educators and legislators are looking for ways to assure that all children can read. As evidenced by the national mandate for reading programs that assure reading competence by the end of third grade, schools and teacher preparation programs are compelled to

examine the effects of preparation for reading instruction, the impact on student growth and literacy of teacher knowledge in the area of reading skills,
and the systems that will assure the success of all learners. Any person
actively engaged in preparing teachers knows that pendulum swings bring
about needed change. At this time in our nation's educational history, it
seems that the pendulum has swung far toward direct instruction, either for
the whole class or small groups, to assure that all children read on grade
level by third grade. Programs such as Dr. Marie Clay's Reading Recovery or
Dr. Gay Su Pinnell and Dr. Irene Fountas' Guided Reading are widely implemented in an effort to assure reading success. Thus, when states such as
Alabama implement a systemic reading initiative, with a goal of 100% of
Alabama students reading on grade level, it is vital that teacher educators
and researchers carefully look at the success and student learning outcomes
associated with such initiatives. The study that reports the Alabama initiative provides evidence of the link between teacher preparation and student
performance.

Even school districts sometimes question the efficacy of teacher preparation programs. In response to that concern, many teacher education programs implemented professional development school (PDS) partnerships in
order to effectively involve schools in the education and training of teachers;
however, there are varying levels of involvement in these partnerships. In
some cases, the model includes as little as expanded field experiences to
assure that pre-service teachers have a stronger knowledge base about how
schools operate and how teachers may be effective, in contrast to traditional
10–12 weeks of student teaching. Other settings offer pre-service teachers'
extensive early field experiences, a full semester of student teaching internship, well-trained mentor teachers, and an unusually strong bond between
the preparation program and the district. In PDS programs where university
faculty are vitally involved in creating and maintaining a partnership with
the school district and campus, teacher learning and student performance
are easily documented to reveal the impact of strong early preparation on
successful teaching. The report on the impact of professional development
schools on student success discusses a design intended to cause educators
and researchers to recognize the necessity of research that focuses on the
children when examining the impact of such partnerships. The study that
reports the link between teacher preparation and student performance as
evidenced by practitioner research in a professional development school
context provides knowledge of how to direct further research to validate the
importance of teacher preparation.

Accrediting agencies, such as the National Council for the Accreditation
of Teacher Education (NCATE), as well as state agencies, hold high stan-

dards for teacher preparation programs in an effort to assure that all children and youth learn to the best of their ability. Professional organizations/associations have developed stringent standards to which teachers should respond, in order to assure that all learners are prepared for effective citizenship and successful work place experiences. NCATE, in particular, spent much time, energy and resources in developing standards for professional development schools. The National Network for Educational Renewal has long provided a framework of success for university/school partnerships where the impact on student learning may be readily documented. The Holmes Partnership group offers models of successful partnerships that assure that teachers are well prepared and successful in the classroom. As teacher education programs engage in these partnership models and examine the effectiveness of such programs, more evidence will evolve to reveal the impact of teacher education on student performance.

Action research has evolved into a verifiable framework under which to document teacher affect on student learning, as implicated in the study reporting the efforts of three teacher preparation programs to examine how teachers document their impact on student learning. Portfolios that depict evidences/teacher work samples to demonstrate the effect of teacher preparation and teacher increased knowledge on student learning are much in vogue in both undergraduate and graduate programs that prepare teachers. The study that examined the use of the Renaissance Partnership Teacher Work Sample provides evidence of the value of teacher work samples as a credible means for verifying candidate performance as teacher education programs seek ways to document their candidates' impact on student learning.

Then there is the issue of how much content knowledge a teacher must have, and to what depth, in order to assure effective teaching in that subject area to result in successful student performance. One answer that the nation seems to have that addresses this issue is the current push to license/certify persons who hold a bachelor's degree in a particular content area, often with little to absolutely no education or training in the art and science of teaching. Beyond the necessity of content knowledge is the need for teacher knowledge of pedagogy. The study that investigated the impact of teacher knowledge related to teaching thinking skills on student performance took a case study perspective. In this study, baseline data revealed a lack of teacher knowledge regarding how to teach thinking skills. Researchers implemented an intervention focused on teaching teachers how to facilitate student decision-making and self-evaluation. A connection was found between the intervention and resulting change in teacher practice and the resulting impact on student performance. Thus, it appears that teacher preparation does make a difference in teachers' knowledge, both for content and pedagogy.

National groups, such as the National Staff Development Council, the Interstate New Teacher Assessment Support Consortium, and the National Board for Professional Teaching Standards, work diligently to assure that new and experienced teachers have the background, experiences, mentoring, staff development, and workplace context necessary to assure quality student performance. The study that presents a theoretical model for the relationship between professional development and improvement in student learning was designed to bring clarity to the examination of the relationship and to offer the means for developing more effective forms of professional development. As teacher education programs and school leaders apply the standards and examine the competencies presented by these national groups, obviously there will become more effective models for assuring that all teacher learning and development result in improvement in student learning.

Ultimately, teacher educators must take the responsibility of documenting and presenting the evidences of the worth of teacher preparation. Reports reveal the anticipated need for a large number of teachers over the next ten years, and research reveals the current impact of preparation, or the lack of, on teacher retention. With these reports in hand, teacher educators and schools must ensure that parents, politicians, and business and industry leaders pay attention to the documented evidence on how critical teacher education is to the successful performance of students in P–12 schools. Without such a zeal for educating our public, we will have little room for complaint when the media charge that there is little value in teacher preparation, as it has been known for decades. As President of ATE, I call on each teacher educator and each teacher preparation program to go busy about the task of documenting the importance of teacher preparation as it relates to student performance, then to present and publicize the findings of such research. What we do is vital to student learning, thus to the enduring growth of our nation. We will not be at risk if teacher educators take the lead in providing the public valid evidence of the need for highly qualified teacher education programs that result in highly qualified teachers for all the nation's children.

Introduction

Edith M. Guyton and Julie Rainer Dangel,
Georgia State University

Edi Guyton is Associate Dean of the College of Education and Professor of Early Childhood Education. She serves as Director of the Metropolitan Atlanta P-16 Council. She is a past president (1999–2000) of the Association of Teacher Educators. She was co-editor of the 1996 *Handbook of Research on Teacher Education* and has published articles in the areas of field experiences, multicultural teacher education and constructivist teacher education.

Julie Rainer Dangel is an associate professor in Early Childhood Education at Georgia State University and currently coordinates the Educational Specialist Program. Her research interests include teacher development and constructivist theory. She has published articles in a variety of journals including *The Journal of Teacher Education, Teaching and Teacher Education and Action in Teacher Education* and edited the recent publication by ATE on *Reframing Teacher Education: Dimensions of a Constructivist Approach.* She is currently a member of NCATE Board of Examiners.

The Yearbook is designed to provide teachers and teacher educators with current research and practical guidelines for implementing research. The conceptual framework of the Yearbook is based on a triadic definition of scholarship: the production of knowledge, the interpretation and synthesis of knowledge, and the application of knowledge. Each year, research reports based on a significant topic to ATE members are solicited for publication in the Yearbook. All research reports are blind reviewed and sand accepted manuscripts are categorized into three or four divisions are published. A responder, a recognized scholar in the field, reacts to the papers selected for each division. The responder synthesizes, interprets, and applies results drawn from the selected research papers.

Current educational discussions focus on how to document the depth of influence that teachers have on their students, in both teacher education and P-12 contexts. This important topic is a complex issue. The chapters in this Yearbook are one effort to address this complexity. They provide some research methods that can be effective in determining what links teacher preparation and student performance and suggest research designs that facilitate answering questions about the linkage between teacher preparation and student performance. The chapters also provide models for conducting this important research and evidence for answering these crucial questions.

This yearbook contributes to the progress being made in teacher education to develop student learning. This connection is ambiguous and it is hard to trace teacher education interventions to student performance in classrooms; many variables can confound the research and its findings. Defining student learning also is problematic; we all know it is more than test scores indicate, yet we are aware of the emphasis on test scores in the teacher education accountability movement. All implications of this research must be viewed with a critical eye, so that we learn more about how to focus on student learning without undue attention to one way of measuring it.

Division

1

Effects of Teacher
Education Interventions
on Student
Learning

Overview and Framework

Alan J. Reiman

Alan Reiman is an Associate Professor of Curriculum and Instruction and former Director of the North Carolina Model Clinical Teaching Network, a consortium of 12 public and private universities committed to research and development related to clinical experiences for teacher candidates. Most recently, he has involved ten school systems and over eighty elementary, middle schools, and high schools in reflective coaching and mentoring that is grounded in contextual-developmental theory. His current research interests include the study of teacher professional judgment and dispositions, developing teachers' ethical judgments and actions, and fostering reflective (epistemological) judgment across the teacher career span.

Introduction

In this introductory section, I describe trends in research that will guide my analysis and interpretation of models for assessing teacher professional development impact and its impact on student learning. Three studies with models for teacher professional development will follow. In the concluding section, I interpret the three studies, attempting to make explicit how the authors findings converge (or diverge) with current research trends in teacher development research. Finally, I raise questions and draw implications for teacher education and teacher development.

The Problem

We do not fully understand professional development. We do not understand how professional development affects student learning. Of course we fill our professional lives with workshops, courses, and the like. We have witnessed a plethora of teacher professional development initiatives since John Dewey. We have insights from qualitative and empirical studies, gleaned from researchers in the last thirty years who began to codify the differences between educative and mis-educative professional development experience. And we have glimmers of more robust models and theories of teacher learning and the relationship to student learning.

But we do not fully understand the complexity of relationships between professional development and student learning. If the mountains represent deep understanding of professional development, we may only now have the foothills in distant sight.

The strange thing about teacher professional development is that everyone thinks they understand it. It seems, of course, relatively simple and straightforward. Teachers participate in educational programming for the purpose of learning more about their subject, or about students, or about classroom management, or about teaching practices. Then they return to their classrooms and attempt to integrate what they have learned into their teaching. But it is never so simple. Obviously, the reality is that teacher development and its relationship to student learning and development is far more complex and far less predictable than we had ever expected, and there is much that we do not understand.

How does one learn to teach? How is learning about content different than learning new instructional approaches? What is the role of teacher conceptual understanding in understanding of students' learning needs? What are the dominant obstacles to optimal professional development programs? These questions can be approached from a diversity of perspectives. But the research is limited, and is so riddled with historical contingency and the vagaries of unfunded political mandates, that it is difficult for most of us to accommodate to a sensible balance. Yet, there are gaps in the research and promising trends in the research evidence that should set a tone for the three papers you will read. How do the findings and proposed models in the three papers converge or diverge with these trends?

Three Gaps in Our Understanding of Teacher Professional Development

At least three gaps are present in research and reviews of research on teacher professional development. These gaps present important challenges for the field, and should inform models of professional development and future research on links between teacher professional development and student learning.

1. Teacher professional development programming continues to be brief, episodic, disconnected to the deeper issues of curriculum and learning, and ignores the processes for producing deeper and more complex learning in students as well as teachers (Cohen & Ball, 2001; Little, 1994).
2. Too little is understood about the relationship between teacher thinking and student learning. Numerous studies have shown that teachers rarely understand the "deeper intent" of professional development reforms. Although reforms call for very deep changes (transformation) in teachers' conceptual understanding of subject matter, teaching, and learning, many teachers' current preferred conceptual understandings are fundamentally conservative and resistant to change. Without understanding the centrality of teacher thinking as the process through which conceptual understanding takes place, reforms will continue to be ineffective (Cohen & Ball, 2001, Sprinthall, Reiman, & Thies-Sprinthall, 1996; Thompson & Zuelli, 1999). Huberman (1995) argues that networks and other forms of professional development are challenged by the "tinkerer" or habits and dispositions of most teachers.
3. Three decades of research has found that only a few professional development interventions have had detectable effects on classroom instruction and student learning and that, when these effects are detected, they rarely last over time (Cohen & Ball, 1999). Where exceptions exist, there has been extraordinary attention to "self-assessment as learning" and careful longitudinal study (Mentkowski and Associates, 2000).

In contrast to these gaps in our understanding of research, there are promising trends as well. It may be premature, however, to suggest anything more than the possibility of a growing consensus.

Promising Trends in Teacher Professional Development

Where professional development interventions have had sustained effects on classroom instruction and student learning, five professional development design conditions have been met.

SUSTAINED AND ACTIVE LEARNING

Active learning accounts for educators' current knowledge, conceptual and reflective capacities, and motivations, and includes complex new and highly engaging experiences such as mentoring, demonstration teaching, observation, self-assessment and reflection, practice in classrooms, review of student work, and presentation of results. Typically, these opportunities for active learning have been enacted continuously over at least three to six months and these practices have been responsive to teacher thinking and conceptual learning (Reiman & Thies-Sprinthall, 1998; Garet, Porter, Desimore, Birman, & Yoon, 2001; Guskey & Huberman,1995).

LEARNER-CENTERED

Effective professional development interventions have framed the intervention around the curriculum and an understanding of student learning (Cohen & Ball, 1999; Guskey, 2002; Kennedy, 1998). The activities connect to teachers' own students. For example, Kennedy reviewed well-designed experimental studies of the relationship between professional development and student achievement in math and science. Professional development that focuses on specific content and how students learn has a larger effect on student achievement outcomes, especially conceptual understanding.

COORDINATION, CONTINUITY, AND CLARITY

Cohen and Ball find coordination, continuity, and clarity to be important prerequisites of effective professional development. Effective coordination in a professional development intervention means the program is coordinated with other programs at the district and school level. As well, program facilitators provide sufficient clarity and elaboration, such that teachers feel confident to enact the innovation (Cohen & Ball, 1999).

SCHOOL-BASED, COLLABORATIVE, AND PARTICIPATORY

Effective professional development is school based, collaborative, and involves teachers in identification of what they need to learn (Hodges, 1996, Little, 1992). Such a focus fosters higher levels of teacher motivation, as well as greater effects on teacher and student learning.

PART OF A COMPREHENSIVE CHANGE PROCESS

Professional development needs to be part of a comprehensive change process (Guskey, 1995). Guskey notes that a quick way to sabotage change efforts is to take on too much at one time. Instead, he recommends thinking big (having a comprehensive plan), but starting small.

The gradual convergence of research of effective teacher professional development illustrates the complexity of the process. My synthesis summarizes the characteristics of professional development that are most likely to lead to improvements in actions of education that contribute to student learning.

Research on Learning

Research on learning has altered our understandings of why and how persons learn. Hawley and Valli (1999) have noted the relevance of this research to our understanding of effective professional development. These understandings are relevant to both student learning and teacher learning. Recently, Alexander and Murphy (1998) have summarized research on learning and identified five learner-centered principles:

- One's existing knowledge serves as a basis for all future learning and it filters all new experiences (The knowledge base principle).
- Reflecting on experience and regulating one's thoughts and behaviors is essential to learning and development (the strategic processing principle).
- Motivational and affective factors, such as intrinsic motivation, emotions, personal goals, as well as the motivational characteristics of the learning tasks, play a significant role in the learning process (the motivation/affect principle).
- Learning proceeds through common stages of development across a series of interdependent domains that are influenced by inherited, experiential, and environmental factors (the developmental principle).

- Learning is as much a socially shared undertaking as it is an individually constructed undertaking (the context principle).

These research-based principles have a number of important implications for professional development. First, they can guide the design of more effective professional development opportunities. And second, they illustrate why so many professional development experiences are ineffective.

Models of Professional Development

Sparks and Loucks-Horsley (1990) summarized five models of professional development. Each model has different assumptions, processes, and outcomes. Unfortunately, too often these models are implemented in ways that ignore research on professional development and/or the learner-centered principles (Hawley & Valli, 1998). The *individually guided model* encourages self-directed professional development activities. Often this model is disconnected from the larger school improvement initiatives. In contrast, the *observer/assessment model* encourages teachers to observe each other and receive feedback on instruction, student learning, and related curriculum issues. To be effective, the model must engage teacher coaches with expertise in conferencing and teaching, and the process must include multiple coaching sessions. The *development/improvement model* engages teachers in the problem solving and thinking about learning, inquiry and self-assessment, curriculum design, and helping activities such as mentoring. Evidence indicates that this model can transform teachers' conceptual understandings of teaching and student learning. However, much of this model's effectiveness depends on well-designed interventions that provide continuous and cumulative experience over at least three-to-six months, and that are responsive to teachers as developing adult learners. The *training model* utilizes an expert who coordinates the content and flow of activities. Because it relies on experts, the model may not be sensitive to contextual issues. As well, the program can ignore the importance of school-based practice. However, evidence suggests that it has the potential to significantly change teachers' beliefs and knowledge as well as the performance of students. The *inquiry model,* sometimes referred to as the teacher as researcher model, prompts teachers to identify a student learning problem, to collect data, to make changes based on the interpretation of the data, and, ideally, to report the findings from their inquiry. However, this model can be disconnected from the larger school improvement process, and the quality of the experience depends on the kinds of questions raised, and the ability of the teacher to interpret the evidence.

Three Research Reports

What follows is a set of three chapters that examine models for teacher professional development and its relationship to student outcomes. The first inquiry, authored by Thomas Guskey and Dennis Sparks, introduces a model for understanding the multi-dimensional relationships between professional development activities for educators and improvements in student learning outcomes. The second inquiry, authored by Mary Little, explores the question of how models of professional development might explain teacher implementation of research-based practices to enhance student performance at a statewide level. The final inquiry, authored by Peter Denner, Antony Norman, Stephanie Salzman, Roger Pankratz, and Samuel Evans, focuses on a multi-university/schools partnerships' investigation of an accountability measure (Renaissance Partnership Work Sample—RTWS) for demonstrating teacher candidates' abilities to meet targeted teaching standards.

REFERENCES

Alexander, P. A., & Murphy, P. K. (1998). The research base for APA's Learner-Centered Psychological Principles. In N. M. Lambert and B. L. McCombs (Eds.), *Issues of school reform: A sampler of psychological perspectives on learner-centered schools.* Washington, D.C.: The American Psychological Association.

Ball, D. L., & Cohen, D. K. (1999). Developing practice, developing practitioners: Toward a practice-based theory of professional development. In L. Darling-Hammond and G. Sykes (Eds.), *Teaching as a learning profession* (pp. 3–32). San Francisco: Jossey-Bass.

Cohen, D. K., & Ball, D. L. (2001). Making change: Instruction and its improvement. *Phi Delta Kappan, 83*(1), 73–77.

Garet, M. S., Porter, A. C., Desimore, L., Birman, B. F., & Yoon, K. S. (2001). What makes professional development effective? Results from a national sample of teachers. *American Educational Research Journal, 38*(4), 915–946.

Guskey, T. R. (1995). *Professional development in education: In search of the optimal mix.* In T. R. Guskey and M. Huberman (Eds.), Professional development in education: New paradigms and practices. New York: Teachers College, Columbia University.

Guskey, T. R., & Huberman, M. (Eds.) (1995). *Professional development in education: New paradigms and practices.* New York: Teachers College, Columbia University.

Guskey, T. R. (2002). Does it make a difference? Evaluating Professional Development. *Educational Leadership, 59*(6), 45–51.

Little, J. W. (1994). Teachers' professional development in a climate of educational reform. *Educational Evaluation and Policy Analysis, 15,* 129–151.

Hawley, W. D., & Valli, L. (1998). The essentials of effective professional development. In L. Darling-Hammond and G. Sykes (Eds.), *Teaching as a learning profession* (pp. 127–150). San Francisco: Jossey-Bass.

Hodges, H. L. B. (1996). Using research to inform practice in urban schools: Ten key strategies for success. *Educational Policy, 10*(2), 223–252.

Huberman, M. (1995). Networks that alter teaching: Conceptualizations, exhanges, and experiments. *Teachers and Teaching: Theory and Practice, 1*(2), 193–211.

Katz, L., & Raths, J. (1985). Dispositions as goals for teacher education. *Teaching and Teacher Education, 1*(4), 301–307.

Keeves, J. P. (1988). Models and model building. In J. Keeves (Ed.), *Educational Research, methodology, and measurement: An international yearbook* (pp. 559–565). New York: Pergasmon Press.

Kennedy, M. M. (1998). *Form and substance in in-service teacher education* (Research Monograph No. 13). Arlington, VA: National Science Foundation.

Mentkowski, M., & Associates (2000). *Learning that lasts.* San Francisco: Jossey-Bass.

Murray, F. (1996). Beyond natural teaching. In F. Murray (Ed.), *The teacher educator's handbook: Building a knowledge base for the preparation of teachers* (pp. 3–13). San Francisco: Jossey-Bass.

Reiman, A. J., & Thies-Sprinthall, L. (1998). *Mentoring and supervision for teacher development.* New York: Longman.

Sparks, D., & Loucks-Horsley, S. (1990). Models of staff development. In W. R. Houston (Ed.), *Handbook of research on teacher education.* New York: Macmillan.

Sprinthall, N. A., Reiman, A. J. , & Thies-Sprinthall, L. (1996). Teacher professional development. In J. Sikula, T. Ballery, E. Guyton, (Ed.) *Second handbook of research on teacher education.* New York: Macmillan.

Thompson, C.L., & Zeulli, J.S. (1999). The frame and the tapestry: Standards-based reform and professional development. L. Darling-Hammond and G. Sykes (Eds.), *Teaching as a learning profession* (pp. 341–375). San Francisco: Jossey-Bass.

Linking Professional Development to Improvements in Student Learning

1.

Thomas R. Guskey and Dennis Sparks

Thomas R. Guskey is Professor of Educational Policy Studies and Evaluation at the University of Kentucky. His major research interests are in educators' professional development, teacher change, assessment, evaluation, and education reform. His books include *Evaluating Professional Development* (Corwin, 2000) and *Professional Development in Education: New Paradigms and Practices* (Teachers College Press, 1995).

Dennis Sparks is Executive Director of the National Staff Development Council. He is also Executive Editor of *The Journal of Staff Development* and has written articles that have appeared in *Educational Leadership, Phi Delta Kappan,* and *The School Administrator.* His most recent book is *A New Vision for Staff Development* (with S. Hirsh, ASCD and NSDC, 2001).

ABSTRACT

This paper describes a theoretical model of the multi-dimensional relationship between professional development activities for educators and improvements in student learning outcomes. The validity and appropriateness of the model are then examined through five in-depth case studies of school-based professional development programs. This model is more comprehensive than previous models and extends the work of current professional development researchers. It is designed to bring added clarity to discussions of this complex relationship and to facilitate the development of more effective forms of professional development.

Recent education reforms brought new prominence to the role of professional development. Recognizing that schools can be no better than the teachers and administrators who work within them, policy makers emphasize professional development as a key component in nearly every education improvement plan. But with this new prominence has come increased demands for evidence on the effectiveness of professional development programs and activities. In particular, policy makers and educational leaders want specific evidence of the impact of professional development activities on well-defined student learning outcomes. While those responsible for professional development have generally assumed a strong and direct relationship between professional development for educators and improvements in student learning, few have been able to describe or demonstrate this relationship precisely (see, for example, Corcoran, 1995; Frechtling, Sharp, Carey, & Baden-Kierman, 1995; Newmann, King, & Youngs, 2000; Wang, Frechtling, & Sanders, 1999).

This paper describes a theoretical model of the multi-dimensional relationship between professional development activities for educators and improvements in student learning. It also examines the validity and appropriateness of the model through five in-depth case studies of school-based professional development programs. The model presented extends the work of current researchers (Cohen & Hill, 1998, 2000; Kennedy, 1998) by considering the relevance of specific contextual factors, as well as content characteristics and process variables. It is also more comprehensive than other models (e.g., Wang, Frechtling, & Sanders, 1999) in that it incorporates significant direct and indirect effects, including that of district and school administrators and parents. This model is designed to bring added clarity to investigations of the complexities of this relationship and, hopefully, will challenge professional development researchers to explore this relationship more thoroughly and with greater precision.

The Model

The proposed theoretical model of the relationship between professional development activities and improvements in student learning is illustrated in Figure 1. It was derived from analytic reviews of research examining this relationship (e.g., Kennedy, 1999; Wang, Frechtling, & Sanders, 1999; Wenglinsky, 2000, 2002) and from qualitative investigations that explored the various dimensions of successful improvement efforts (Killion, 1999, 2002). The premise of the model is that the quality of professional development, or what Cohen and Hill (2000) refer to as "teachers' opportunities to

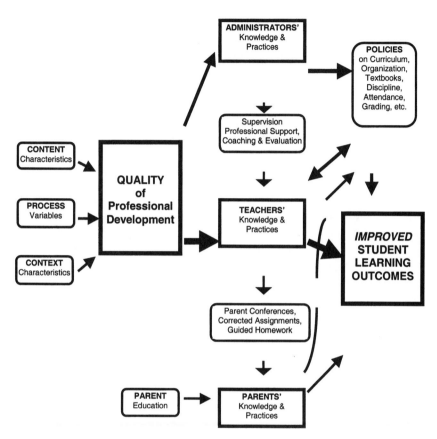

Figure 1. Model of the Relationship Between Professional Development and Improvement in Student Learning

learn," is influenced by a multitude of factors. Those believed to have the most immediate and direct influence, however, can be classified in three major categories: content characteristics, process variables, and context characteristics.

Content Characteristics refer to the "what" of professional development. They concern the new knowledge, skills, and understandings that are the foundation of any professional development effort. Content may include a deeper understanding of specific academic disciplines, how students learn and acquire understanding of those disciplines, and particular pedagogical processes (Shulman, 1986). Professional development activities help educators keep abreast of this emerging knowledge base so that they can continually refine their conceptual and craft skills (Guskey & Huberman, 1995). They also may involve aspects relating to the magnitude, scope, credibility, and practicality of the change required to implement this new knowledge (Fullan, 1993).

Process Variables refer to the "how" of professional development and concern not only the type and forms of professional development activities (Loucks-Horsley, Hewson, Love, & Stiles, 1998; Sparks & Hirsh, 1997), but also the way those activities are planned, organized, carried out, and followed-up. Most of the writing about professional development quality and most professional development research focuses on these variables. Garet, Porter, Desimone, Birman, and Yoon (2002), for example, describe these as professional development's "core features," and stress the importance of "active learning" and "fostering coherence" among various opportunities for teacher learning and development. Other examples include the use of alternative forms of professional development such as coaching, action research, and focused study groups (Joyce & Showers, 1995; Louis & Miles, 1990).

Context Characteristics refer to the "who," "when," "where," and "why" of professional development. They include the traits of the particular group of educators involved in the professional development activities, the environment in which they work, and the students they serve. Context also involves the organization, system, or culture in which professional development takes place and where the new understandings are to be implemented (Huberman & Miles, 1984). Furthermore, context includes the district or school level policies that may impact implementation. An important part of the context, for example, may be the pressure created by a statewide assessment and accountability program or a school district's high expectations for the learning of all students.

Content characteristics, process variables, and context characteristics are all important in determining the Quality of Professional Development, the central component of the model. But professional development programs and activities do not directly or exclusively affect improvements in student learning (Wang, Frechtling, & Sanders, 1999). Rather, their influence on students is accomplished principally through their positive effect on the knowledge and practices of teachers and school administrators.

Teachers' Knowledge and Practices are the most immediate and most significant outcomes of any professional development activity. They also are the primary factors influencing the relationship between professional development and improvements in student learning (Cohen & Hill, 1998, 2000). Clearly if professional development does not alter teachers' professional knowledge or their classroom practices, little improvement in student learning can be expected.

Administrators' Knowledge and Practices are also directly influenced by the quality of professional development activities, although they are often neglected in program evaluations (Guskey, 2000). While administrators typically do not influence student learning directly, their knowledge and practices indirectly influence students in two important ways. The first is in their interactions with teachers, particularly through supervision activities, professional support, coaching, and evaluation procedures. The second way administrators indirectly influence student learning is through their leadership in forming school policies and in establishing elements of the school's community and culture. Teachers' knowledge and practices are influenced by school policies and also affect school policies, especially through lead-teacher programs, shared governance, and school-based decision making (Guskey & Peterson, 1996). Although this influence is direct, its strength depends largely on the degree to which the process for teacher input in policy formulation is routine and formalized (Deal & Peterson, 1994).

Parents' Knowledge and Practices are included in the model as the third primary influence on improvements in student learning. Parents have a direct and powerful effect on student learning, not only through the learning experiences they provide for their children during early years of development, but also by their continuing involvement in school activities and homework assignments (Cooper, 2001; Grolnick & Slowiaczek, 1994).

Parent Education programs designed by educators can provide valuable information and specific strategies to parents in their efforts to help their children succeed in school (Hoover-Dempsey & Sandler, 1995). Although the research evidence on the effectiveness of such programs is mixed, many have proven successful in breaking down the barriers between schools and home, as well as in facilitating communication between teachers and parents (Mattingly, Prislin, McKenzie, Rodriguez, & Kayzar, 2002).

Student Learning Outcomes are broadly defined in the model to include the entire range of student learning goals. Most often they include indicators of student achievement, such as assessment results, portfolio evaluations, marks or grades, or scores from standardized examinations. However, they might also include measures of students' attitudes, study habits, school attendance, homework completion rates, or classroom behaviors. School-wide indicators such as enrollment in advanced classes, memberships in honor societies, attendance rates, dropout statistics, and participation in school-related activities might be considered as well.

We recognize, of course, that some important relationships that can strongly influence both professional development activities and student learning outcomes are not included in the model. Federal and state legislation, state departments of education, and local school boards, for instance, have significant influence on policies that affect student learning. Graduation requirements, school calendars, and assessment and accountability programs are a few examples. Nevertheless, the relationships identified in the model are those that we believe are most direct and most powerful. Furthermore, with the exception of certain context characteristics, these factors are also the most directly influenced by educators and, hence, the most immediately alterable.

Evidence Supporting the Model

To test the model we analyzed reports gathered through the National Staff Development Council's Model School Program (Killion, 1999). These reports consist of five in-depth case studies of school-based professional development programs and activities. The reports are highly detailed and include rich descriptions of the professional development activities within each site over a minimum of three years. Three programs considered "promising" and two considered "insufficient" were randomly selected for analysis. The "promising" programs provided evidence drawn from multiple sources of sustained improvements in students' performance. The "insufficient" programs did not. In other words, although individuals involved in the "insufficient" programs rated highly their professional development experiences and believed they were of excellent quality, no evidence was provided to show that these activities resulted in any change in instructional practices or school procedures, or that they yielded demonstrable improvements in student learning outcomes.

Both authors read the reports independently, analyzing the content in terms of the elements included in the proposed model. Special note also was made of any factors that might have contributed to the results but were not readily classified within a specific model element. These factors were then discussed until consensus was reached about appropriate classification. Relationships between model elements were also considered in the analysis, paying special attention to the reported or implied direction of the relationship.

Our analyses generally confirmed the presence and strong influence of the school-based factors in the model and their relationships. The descriptions of each of the "promising" programs included detailed information about the specific changes in teachers' and administrators' knowledge base, skill level, instructional practices, and school procedures that were believed to have led to the identified improvements in students' performance. Data regarding the implementation of new practices varied from study to study.

In two cases it consisted primarily of self-reports, while the other included evidence from direct observations. Still, model elements and their relationships were supported. Only one of the three program descriptions included information on parent involvement, however, and this evidence was inadequate for judging the validity of this component of the model.

Analyses of the "insufficient" programs offered further supporting evidence. In one case there appeared to be a lack of administrator participation and support. The teachers were involved in professional development activities away from their school and without the involvement of building administrators. There were no follow-up activities on site and no effort was made to ensure appropriate and sustained implementation of the recommended practices. Hence, while administrative support may not be a requirement for improved practices, the lack of such support appears to diminish the likelihood of implementation and continuation.

In the second case a lack of policy consistency seemed to be the most probable factor contributing to the lack of successful implementation and subsequent results in terms of student learning outcomes. The professional development activities emphasized character education and student responsibility and were regarded very favorably by participating teachers. However, no effort was made to offer teachers feedback on the effects of the program and no systematic evidence was gathered regarding relevant student learning outcomes, such as students' involvement in civic activities, their interactions with each other, or incidents of behavioral infractions.

Implications and Conclusions

The proposed model yields three important implications. First, it shows that while the relationship between professional development and improvements in student learning outcomes is complex and multifaceted, it is not random or chaotic. By identifying the major contributing factors in this relationship and offering at least tentative evidence of the direction of interrelatedness among these factors, the model brings a sense of order to efforts to improve the effectiveness of professional development. Obviously the strength of these factors and how they interact will vary from setting to setting. Nevertheless, the model helps make sense of that influence and helps better our understanding of the contribution of these factors to the relationship.

Second, the model offers guidance to those interested in determining what makes professional development effective and in evaluating the effectiveness of professional development programs and activities. Undoubtedly, most educators today would like to be able to measure the impact of professional development in terms of demonstrable improvements in student learning. Recognizing the various factors that influence this relationship, however, will help evaluators not only document results more precisely, but also offer explanations as to why those results occurred.

Third, the model illustrates the importance of a systemic approach to professional development and the need to view professional development reform from a systems perspective (Sparks, 1996). Professional development efforts that do not take into consideration the complex nature of the relationship between professional development and improvement in student learning, or the various factors that impinge on that relationship, are unlikely to succeed. Improvements may be evidenced in some classrooms or in some schools, but it seldom brings improved success at high levels of learning for all students.

Although we believe this model of the relationship between professional development activities for educators and improvements in student learning is a useful tool, we also recognize that any model of such a highly complex process is, in many ways, an over-simplification. Not noted in the model, for example, is the reciprocal influence that exists between administrators and teachers, between teachers and parents, and between students and teachers. The model also does not make clear the effects of improved student learning on teachers' subsequent practices or on the nature of succeeding professional development activities (Guskey, 1991).

Furthermore, the model does not adequately portray the important influence the desired student learning outcomes should have on the content, process, and context of professional development programs and activities. Clearly, student learning outcomes should provide the starting point for all educational improvement efforts and professional development activities (Guskey, 2002).

Still, the model does identify critical factors in the relationship between professional development and improvements in student learning. It also makes clear that these factors can be identified, documented, and assessed. Identifying these factors and providing some indication of their influence, we hope, will lead to higher quality professional development programs and offer guidance to researchers investigating various aspects of this crucial relationship in the educational improvement processes. Teachers, administrators, and parents all have critical roles to play in the improvement of student learning, and their ability to fulfill their responsibilities more effectively will be determined largely by the quality of professional development. We believe this model clarifies those relationships in a way that can assist school leaders in planning, conducting, and evaluating the impact of professional development activities.

REFERENCES

Corcoran, T. B. (1995, June). Helping teachers teach well: Transforming professional development. CPRE Policy Briefs. *New Brunswick, NJ: Consortium for Policy Research in Education, Rutgers University.*

Cohen, D. K., & Hill, H. C. (1998). State policy and classroom performance: Mathematics reform in California. *CPRE Policy Briefs* (RB-23-May). Philadelphia: Consortium for Policy Research in Education (CPRE), Graduate School of Education, University of Pennsylvania.

Cohen, D. K., & Hill, H. C. (2000). Instructional policy and classroom performance: The mathematics reform in California. *Teachers College Record, 102*(2), 294–343.

Cooper, H. (2001). *The battle over homework: An administrator's guide to setting sound and effective policies* (2nd ed.). Thousand Oaks, CA: Corwin.

Deal, T., & Peterson, K. D. (1994). *The leadership paradox: Balancing logic and artistry in schools.* San Francisco: Jossey-Bass.

Frechtling, J. A., Sharp, L., Carey, N., & Baden-Kierman, N. (1995). *Teacher enhancement programs: A perspective on the last four decades.* Washington, DC: National Science Foundation Directorate for Education and Human Resources.

Fullan, M. G. (1993). *Change forces: Probing the depths of educational reform.* Bristol, PA: Falmer Press.

Garet, M. S., Porter, A. C., Desimone, L., Birman, B. F., & Yoon, K. S. (2002). What makes professional development effective? Results from a national sample of teachers. *American Educational Research Journal, 38*(4), 915-946.

Grolnick, W. S., & Slowiaczek, M. L. (1994). Parents' involvement in children's schooling: A multidimensional conceptualization and motivational model. *Child Development, 65*(2), 237–252.

Guskey, T. R. (1991). Enhancing the effectiveness of professional development programs. *Journal of Educational and Psychological Consultation, 2*(3), 239–247.

Guskey, T. R. (2000). *Evaluating professional development.* Thousand Oaks, CA: Corwin Press.

Guskey, T. R. (2002). Does it make a difference? Evaluating professional development. *Educational Leadership, 59*(6), 45–51.

Guskey, T. R., & Huberman, M. (Eds.) (1995). *Professional Development in Education: New Paradigms and Practices.* New York: Teachers College Press.

Guskey, T. R., & Peterson, K. D. (1996). The road to classroom change. *Educational Leadership, 53*(4), 10–14.

Hoover-Dempsey, K. V., & Sandler, H. M. (1997). Why do parents become involved in their children's education? *Review of Educational Research, 67*(1), 3–42.

Huberman, M., & Miles, M. B. (1984). *Innovation up close: How school improvement works.* New York: Plenum.

Joyce, B., & Showers, B. (1995). *Student achievement through staff development: Fundamentals of school renewal* (2nd ed.). New York: Longman.

Kennedy, M. (1998). *Form and substance in teacher inservice education* (Research Monograph No. 13). Madison, WI: National Institute for Science Education, University of Wisconsin-Madison.

Killion, J. (1999). *What works in the middle: Results-based staff development.* Oxford, OH: National Staff Development Council.

Killion, J. (2002). *Assessing impact: Evaluating staff development.* Oxford, OH: National Staff Development Council.

Louis, K. S., & Miles, M. B. (1990). *Improving the urban high school: What works and why.* New York: Teachers College Press.

Loucks-Horsley, S., Hewson, P., Love, N., & Stiles, K. E. (1998). *Designing professional development for teachers of science and mathematics.* Thousand Oaks, CA: Corwin.

Mattingly, D. J., Prislin, R., McKenzie, T. L., Rodriguez, J. L. & Kayzar, B. (2002). Evaluating evaluations: the case of parent involvement programs. *Review of Educational Research, 72*(4), 549–576.

Newmann, F., King, M. B., & Youngs, P. (2000). Professional development that addresses school capacity: Lessons from urban elementary schools. *American Journal of Education, 108*(4), 259–299.

Shulman, L. S. (1986). Those who understand: Knowledge growth in teaching. *Educational Researcher, 15*(2), 4–14.

Sparks, D. (1996, February). Viewing reform from a systems perspective. *The Developer,* pp. 2, 6.

Sparks, D., & Hirsh, S. (1997). *A new vision for staff development.* Alexandria, VA: Association for Supervision and Curriculum Development.

Wang, Y. L., Frechtling, J. A., & Sanders, W. L. (1999). *Exploring linkages between professional development and student learning: A pilot study.* Paper presented at the annual meeting of the American Educational Research Association, Montreal.

Wang, Y. L., Frechtling, J. A., & Sanders, W. L. (1999). *Exploring linkages between professional development and student learning: A pilot study.* Paper presented at the annual meeting of the American Educational Research Association, Montreal.

Wenglinsky, H. (2000). *How teaching matters: Bringing the classroom back into discussions of teacher quality.* Princeton, NJ: Policy Information Center, Educational Testing Service.

Wenglinsky, H. (2002). How schools matter: The link between teacher classroom practices and student academic performance. *Education Policy Analysis Archives, 10*(2). Retrieved May 13, 2002 from *http://epaa.asu.edu/epaa/v10n12/.*

The Renaissance Partnership Teacher Work Sample

Evidence Supporting Score Generalizability, Validity, and Quality of Student Learning Assessment

Peter R. Denner, Antony D. Norman,
Stephanie A. Salzman, Roger S. Pankratz,
and C. Samuel Evans

Peter Denner is Assistant Dean of the College of Education and professor of educational psychology at Idaho State University. His current research interests are focused on standards-based performance assessments of teacher quality. He is both the institutional and assessment coordinator for the Renaissance Partnership work at ISU.

Antony "Tony" Norman is associate professor of psychology in the College of Education and Behavioral Sciences at Western Kentucky University (WKU). He serves as the WKU assessment coordinator for the Renaissance Partnership for Improving Teacher Quality. His scholarly interests include moral development, gifted education, and education reform.

Stephanie A. Salzman is Dean of the Woodring College of Education at Western Washington University. She was formerly the Associate Dean of the College of Education at Idaho State University, where she pioneered the introduction of teacher work sample assessment. Her scholarly interests include standards-based teacher education and assessment.

Roger Pankratz is director of the Renaissance Partnership for Improving Teacher Quality and professor of teacher education in the College of Education and Behavioral Sciences at Western Kentucky University. He is the former executive director of both the governor's Council on School Performance Standards and the Kentucky Institute for Education Research

(KIER). Under his direction, KIER published three annual reviews of research on the Kentucky Education Reform Act of 1990 and more than twenty statewide studies evaluating the results of school reform initiatives.

C. Samuel "Sam" Evans is the Associate Dean for Administration and Graduate Studies in the College of Education and Behavioral Sciences at Western Kentucky University. He serves as the WKU institutional coordinator for the Renaissance Project. His scholarship focuses on affective characteristics of effective teachers and teacher impact on student learning.

ABSTRACT

The Renaissance Partnership Teacher Work Sample (RTWS) was investigated as an accountability measure for demonstrating teacher candidates' abilities to meet targeted teaching standards. The findings support the generalizability of the RTWS ratings. The results revealed high dependability coefficients for panels of three or more trained and experienced raters. Validity evidence for the RTWS was obtained using criteria suggested by Crocker (1997), including the frequency, criticality, necessity, and representativeness of the targeted teaching behaviors to actual teaching practice. The results also affirmed direct correspondence between the targeted RTWS tasks and seven of the ten Interstate New Teacher Assessment and Support Consortium (INTASC) standards. Finally, positive correlations between RTWS performances and independent ratings of the quality of learning assessments indicate that teacher candidates who score well on the RTWS provided better evidence of their impact on student learning than those who scored less well. Collectively, the findings demonstrate teacher work sample performance provides a credible means for teacher education programs to verify teacher candidate performance levels.

Based on the belief that quality teaching results in student achievement, a national trend to improve teacher quality has emerged. Prompted by major works, such as *A Nation at Risk* (National Commission on Excellence in Education, 1983), *Tomorrow's Teachers* (The Holmes Group, 1986), and *A Nation Prepared: Teachers for the 21st Century* (The Carnegie Forum on Education and the Economy, 1986), federal and state policy makers have turned their focus on teachers' ability to positively impact the learning of students. Teaching organizations such as the National Commission for Teaching and America's Future (1996), the National Education Association, and the American Federation of Teachers (Bradley, 1998) have followed suit.

At the same time, a growing body of research confirms the relationship between knowledge of teaching and learning acquired in teacher preparation programs and student achievement. In a study of 900 Texas school districts, Ferguson & Ladd (1996) reported a strong correlation between teacher expertise, measured by licensing exam scores, master's degrees, and years of experience, and student achievement. Other studies (Darling-Hammond, 2000; McRobbie, 2001; Sanders & Rivers, 1996) have reached similar conclusions. Furthermore, this connection persists even when taking into account student poverty and limited English proficiency, as well as selected school resource measures. In every teaching field, stronger preparation resulted in greater success with students and the increased likelihood of continuing in the teaching profession (McRobbie, 2001).

This evidence of the impact of teaching performance on student achievement has prompted various accrediting bodies to create more rigorous standards by which to judge teacher preparation programs and their candidates. Accordingly, the National Council of Accreditation of Teacher Education (NCATE, 2000) requires affiliate institutions to develop assessment systems that document teacher candidates' preparation to meet national or state standards and their impact on P–12 student learning.

In response to the coming changes in accreditation standards, a five year initiative by ten (now eleven) institutions, titled, *"Improving Teacher Quality through Partnerships that Connect Teacher Performance to Student Learning"* (Pankratz, 1999), began with the expressed purpose of advancing "a paradigm shift from a focus on the teaching process to learning results and connecting teacher performance to student learning" (p. 1). These institutions pledged to "implement programs and practices that build their capacity to be accountable for the impact of their teacher candidates and graduates on student learning" (p. 1). As a first action of the initiative, institutional representatives met and jointly identified seven teaching processes as essential to facilitating the learning of all students: (1) using contextual factors to plan instruction, (2) selecting learning goals, (3) developing an assessment plan, (4) designing instruction, (5) making instructional decisions, (6) analyzing student learning, and (7) reflecting on the teaching and learning process.

To measure teacher candidates' abilities regarding these processes, the partnership adapted the Western Oregon University Teacher Work Sample Methodology (Schalock, Schalock, & Girod, 1997). The result has been the development of the Renaissance Teacher Work Sample (The Renaissance Partnership for Improving Teacher Quality, 2001), which consists of seven performance tasks related to each of the above teaching processes. The Renaissance Teacher Work Sample (RTWS) requires teacher candidates to produce a 20-page narrative, plus charts and attachments, that becomes a culminating teaching performance exhibit developed during student teaching (the RTWS assessment may be viewed at: *http://fp.uni.edu/itq/*). Central to this culminating performance is the requirement that teacher candidates demonstrate the end result of their teaching in terms of its impact on student learning. In addition, the partnership institutions collectively have developed scoring guides and rubrics to judge teacher candidates' level of performance on each of the seven teaching process standards, as well as their overall performance.

Although, as a measure of teaching standards, teacher work samples hold great promise, Denner, Salzman, and Bangert (2001) assert that this methodology is not without its critics. Important issues include the validity of teacher work samples as a measure of teaching performance standards and whether the degree of generalizability of scores derived from teacher work samples is sufficient for making high-stakes decisions regarding teaching performance levels with respect to those standards.

Investigation of these issues was the goal of three consecutive partnership meetings (June 2001, January 2002, and June 2002) that included multiple representatives from each of the eleven project institutions. The first purpose of our investigation was to determine score generalizability for the performance scores derived from each of the RTWS scoring rubrics when raters from across the partnership institutions evaluated RTWS performances. The second purpose was to investigate the validity of the RTWS as a measure of actual teaching behaviors and as a measure of national teaching standards. Our third purpose was to evaluate the degree to which performances on the RTWS provided quality assessment evidence for student learning.

Method

TEACHER WORK SAMPLE SETS

The teacher work samples (TWS) evaluated in this investigation were collected from across nine of the universities participating in the Renaissance Partnership to Improve Teacher Quality. The RTWS sets examined in this study were selected from two TWS collections: a collection of N = 110 TWS, gathered in June 2001, and a collection of N = 87 TWS, gathered in June 2002. Both collections contained TWS covering a broad range of subject areas and all grade levels from K to 12. Following a benchmarking process developed by Denner, Salzman and Bangert (2001), each TWS within each collection was assigned to one of four categories along a developmental continuum from beginning to expert level performance. The benchmarking process is described later in the procedures section. After the benchmarking process, smaller sets (n = 10) of TWS were selected for scoring by groups of raters.

From the first RTWS collection, two exemplar sets of TWS, Set A and Set B, were developed. These sets consisted of 10 TWS each. The 10 TWS were chosen from the benchmarked exemplars of each performance category and were randomly assigned by category to the two sets (Set A and Set B). Each TWS exemplar set contained 2 Beginning, 3 Developing, 3 Proficient, and 2 Expert work samples. A third random set, Set C, was also complied containing the same breakdown of beginning to expert TWS. In a later phase of the investigation, a fourth 10 TWS set, Set D, was created from a random selection by category merger of the Set A and Set B work samples. From the second collection of TWS (N = 87) in June 2002, a fifth set, Set E, of 10 TWS was selected. The 10 Set E TWS were chosen at random by category after the entire collection of TWS had been organized into four categories from beginning to expert, following the same benchmarking process as had been used the previous year. Due to an incorrect identification of one of the TWS, the Set E TWS consisted of 1 Beginning, Developing, 4 Proficient, and 2 Expert TWS.

INSTRUMENTS

RTWS Scoring Rubrics. To rate each TWS, two rubrics were developed: the *RTWS Analytic Scoring Rubric* and the *RTWS Modified-Holistic Scoring Rubric.* The rubrics were based on the required components outlined in the RTWS Prompt and assessed the teaching process standards targeted by the RTWS assessment (to view the standards, RTWS Prompt, and analytic rubric go to: *http://fp.uni.edu/itq/*). Both the RTWS prompt and accompanying rubrics were collaboratively developed in an earlier three and a half day meeting of representatives from all partnership institutions. On the modified-holistic scoring rubric, each of the seven targeted standards for the TWS was rated on a 3-point scale: 1 = *Standard Not Met;* 2 = *Standard Partially Met;* and 3 = *Standard Met.* Summing across the seven standards, the total modified-holistic scores could vary from 0 to 21 points. On the analytic scoring rubric, the multiple targeted indicators for each standard were rated on a 3-point scale: 1 = *Indicator Not Met;* 2 = *Indicator Partially Met;* and 3 = *Indicator Met.* Across the seven standards, there were 32 total indicators; therefore, total analytic scores could vary from 0 to 96 points.

Validity Questionnaire. To gather validity evidence, a questionnaire asked a panel of raters (n = 42) about the alignment among the RTWS prompt, the targeted teaching processes (the RTWS standards), and the scoring rubrics on a four point scale: 1 = *Poor;* 2 = *Low;* 3 = *Moderate;* and 4 = *High.* In addition, we applied criteria suggested by Crocker (1997) for judging the content representativeness of performance assessments and scoring rubrics with regard to four criteria: (1) the frequency of the teaching behaviors in actual job performance, (2) the criticality (or importance) of those behaviors, (3) the authenticity (or realism) of the tasks to actual classroom practice, and (4) the degree to which the tasks were representative of the targeted standards. These criteria were rated using a four point scale from 1 = *Not at All* to 4 = *Very,* or in the case of the frequency criterion, a five point scale from 1 = *Never* to 5 = *Daily.* To assess evidence for validity of the RTWS requirements with regards to state and national teaching standards, we chose to focus on the INTASC standards (Interstate New Teacher Assessment and Support Consortium, 1992). The panel of raters were asked to indicate the extent to which the RTWS standards aligned with INTASC standards on a three point scale: 1 = *Not at All;* 2 = *Implicitly;* and 3 = *Directly.*

Quality of Learning Assessment Rating Scale. To independently assess whether RTWS performances reflected a robust representation of teacher impact on student learning that provided quality evidence for student learning, we developed a Quality of Learning Assessment (QLA) rating scale. The QLA scale focused on important criteria for sound student learning assessment, such as whether the learning goals reflected several types of learning and were significant and challenging (see Appendix). The criteria for judging the quality of assessments came from several contemporary textbooks on assessment (Chase, 1999; Gredler, 1999; Stiggins, 2001). Across the items, the criteria were rated as 0 = *Does Not Meet Criterion,* 1 = *Partially Meets Criterion,* or 2 = *Meets Criterion.* Summing the ratings across the items provided a total score. The original scale employed in June 2001 had only 10 items, so scores on the rating scale could vary from zero to 20. When used in June 2002, the scale was modified by the addition of two items. The added items were "assessments were congruent with the targeted learning goals in content and cognitive complexity" and "assessment directions and procedures are clear and would be understood by the students." Scores on the modified scale could vary from zero to 24. The Appendix A presents the full 12-item version of the QLA scale.

TEACHER WORK SAMPLE RATERS

In June 2001, a group of 36 raters from across the Renaissance Partnership institutions assembled in St. Louis, Missouri. The raters included administrators, teacher education faculty members, arts & sciences faculty members, and public school teachers from the regions served by the universities in the partnership. The raters were randomly assigned to groups of six raters to score the Set A, Set B, and Set C TWS using either the modified-holistic rubric or the analytic rubric. In January 2002, two additional groups of raters were selected from the 55 trained raters assembled in St. Louis. The raters for the Set D TWS consisted of 2 administrators, 6 faculty members, and 2 teachers. The ten Set D raters were selected on the basis of their approximation to a scoring criterion after a practice scoring session. The ten raters were randomly assigned by rater type (administrator, faculty member, or teacher) to two groups of 5 raters each. The two groups were then randomly assigned to scoring method (modified holistic versus analytic). In June 2002, six additional raters were asked to score the Set E TWS. The six Set E raters were all teacher education faculty members who had been nominated as experienced raters by their respective institutions.

PROCEDURES FOR SCORING THE TEACHER WORK SAMPLES

RTWS Rater Training. For all TWS raters, the training consisted of two hours of a review of the teaching processes and standards targeted by the RTWS assessment, examination of the relationship between the standards and the RTWS components, instruction on how to use the scoring rubrics to rate TWS performances, and anti-bias training (based on procedures described in Denner, Salzman & Bangert, 2001) during which raters completed a series of activities to uncover and create a reference list of potential sources of scoring bias.

RTWS Benchmarking. After training, groups of raters sorted the TWS gathered in each collection (June 2001 and June 2002) according to a set of holistic category descriptions. The categories described TWS performances along a continuum: 1 = *Beginning,* 2 = *Developing,* 3 = *Proficient,* and 4 = *Expert.* To accomplish this task, the raters were divided into cross-institutional groups of 4 raters each. Each group first performed a quick read of 15 to 20 percent of the work samples. When a group reached consensus on the holistic category, they placed the TWS in that pile. In the afternoon, a different mix of raters were grouped to examine the TWS within each category and to pick category exemplars. Following group discussion, four to six exemplars of performance in each category were identified. As described previously, TWS sets were then created by either randomly assigning the exemplar TWS by category to the TWS sets (Set A and Set B) or selecting TWS at random from within each of the four-benchmark categories (Set C and Set E).

RTWS Scoring. At this stage, all raters scored their assigned set of TWS independently using their assigned scoring rubric (analytic or modified-holistic). As they scored, the raters continued to use their personal lists of biases to remind them to ignore these factors when scoring. They were exhorted to score the TWS on the basis of the standards and the scoring rubrics only. Across all TWS sets, the average grading time per TWS for raters using the analytic rubric was about 28 minutes. The average grading time per TWS for raters using the modified-holistic rubric was about 27.5 minutes.

Validity Ratings. The validity data were gathered in June 2002. The validity assessment panel consisted of 42 representatives from across the 10 partnership institutions. None of the validity assessment panel members had been involved in the TWS development process. Most of the panel members were faculty members from the partnership institutions who were being introduced to the RTWS assessment for the first time. The panel included a mix of administrators, faculty members, and public school teachers. The panel members had received training as RTWS raters (in the same manner as described previously) and had rated at least two work samples prior to completing the validity questionnaire. All panel members independently completed the sections of the content validity questionnaire.

PROCEDURES FOR QUALITY OF LEARNING ASSESSMENT

Expert Raters. Independent panels of experts consisting of 2 to 3 expert raters were asked to evaluate three sets of RTWS (Set A, Set B, and Set E) using the Quality of Learning Assessment (QLA) rating scale. All of the QLA raters had extensive backgrounds in testing and measurement. All were experienced in the development and use of scoring rubrics

Scoring Procedures. Following acquaintance with the RTWS assessment and full rater training, the QLA raters for this study received intensive training that focused on the QLA items and the possible locations and sources of evidence for each item within the various RTWS components. The raters reached consensus regarding key definitions and concepts embedded in the QLA items and practiced locating the evidence using an example TWS. The

QLA raters then independently scored their assigned set of n = 10 TWS. The raters averaged about 20 minutes per work sample to complete their QLA ratings.

Design. To evaluate the reliability of the scores from the RTWS rubrics, we employed a research design from Generalizability Theory (Shavelson & Webb, 1991). A single facet design was used to assess the effect of rater for both the modified-holistic and the analytic scoring methods. This design was analyzed separately for each of the RTWS sets using repeated measures ANOVA. The rater facet served as the repeated-measures factor in each case. Using variance component estimates generated from the ANOVA results, Generalizability Theory permits the calculation of two types of coefficients, depending upon whether the measure is to be used to make decisions about the "relative standing or ranking of individuals" or about "the absolute level of their scores" (Shavelson & Webb, 1991, p. 84). Because the RTWS was designed to measure teacher education candidates' abilities to meet the seven targeted teaching process standards (an absolute decision about performance levels with respect to the standards), the formula presented by Shavelson and Webb (1991) for computing an index of dependability for absolute decisions was employed in this study. An index of dependability indicates the proportion of the score that can be generalized across the raters and reflects the performance level of the candidate. The same formula can be adjusted to provide information regarding the number of raters necessary for making high-stakes decisions about the absolute level of teaching performance of teacher candidates using the RTWS assessment.

Pearson product-moment correlation was used to correlate the RTWS scores with the QLA rating scores. All total scores on all measures were averaged across raters. Percentages were calculated for reporting the responses of the validity assessment panel to the content validity questionnaire. For all statistical analyses, the level of statistical significance was set at $\square$ = .05.

Results

SCORE GENERALIZABILITY

Effect for Raters across TWS Sets. As might be expected, for the initial groups of raters, who had received only minimal training, the effect for rater was found to be statistically significant across all three RTWS sets (Set A, Set B, and Set C). For the groups of six novice raters assigned to the modified-holistic scoring rubric, the effect for rater was statistically significant for the Set A TWS, $F(5, 45) = 6.11$, $MSE = 6.67$, $p < .001$, the Set B TWS, $F(5, 45) =$

3.85, $MSE = 8.18$, $p = .005$, and the Set C TWS, $F(5, 45) = 3.50$, $MSE = 6.20$, $p = .009$. Likewise, for the groups of six novice raters assigned to use the analytic scoring rubric the effect for rater was also statistically significant for the Set A TWS, $F(5, 45) = 4.17$, $MSE = 93.06$, $p = .003$, the Set B TWS, $F(5, 45) = 6.14$, $MSE = 39.78$, $p < .001$, and the Set C TWS $F(5, 45) = 6.00$, $MSE = 78.86$, $p < .001$. Seven months later, following better training, independent groups of five raters, who had been selected on the basis of their ability to meet a scoring criterion, also displayed a statistically significant effect for rater when scoring the Set D TWS for both the modified-holistic scoring rubric, $F(4, 36) = 3.89$, $MSE = 21.71$, $p = .01$, and the analytic scoring rubric, $F(4, 36) = 6.28$, $MSE = 59.21$, $p = .001$. Importantly, after one year, when the partnership institutions nominated six experienced raters to score the Set E TWS using the analytic scoring rubric, the effect for rater was not found to be statistically significant, $F(5, 45) = 1.07$, $MSE = 100.94$, $p = .39$. Together, these findings suggest rater experience may be an important factor influencing score consistency when cross-institutional raters are asked to assess complex teacher work sample performances.

Dependability Coefficients. Table 1 presents the variance components estimates derived from the ANOVA results used in the formulas for computing the dependability coefficients for each of the TWS sets and scoring methods. When groups of novice raters used the modified-holistic rubric to score the Set A, Set B, and Set C TWS, the results yielded six rater coefficients of dependability of .59, .77, and .71 respectively. For the analytic scoring rubric, the six-rater coefficients were computed to be .62 for Set A, .91 for Set B, and .64 for Set C. For raters who were given better training and who were selected on the basis of the degree of match of their practice scores with a scoring criterion, the five-rater coefficients of dependability for the Set D TWS were .74 for the modified-holistic scoring rubric and .88 for the analytic scoring rubric. For the experienced raters, who scored the Set E TWS using the analytic scoring rubric, the six-rater coefficient of dependability was computed to be .87. Together, these coefficients suggest a high proportion of the TWS score differences among teacher education candidates can be generalized across raters.

Adjusting the number of raters included in the formulas revealed that an acceptable level of dependability of .77 to .82 could be achieved with as few as three raters when using the analytic scoring rubric based on the results from the Set D and Set E TWS. Table 2 displays the dependability coefficient estimates for different numbers of raters by scoring method using the results obtained across TWS sets. Overall, the results indicate that scores on the Renaissance TWS performance assessment can be used to make decisions regarding the quality of teaching performance that can be generalized across raters when panels of three or more trained and experienced raters are used.

TABLE 1

Estimates of Variance Components for the Total Modified-Holistic Scores and the Total Analytic Scores across Teacher Work Sample Sets

Estimated Variance Components					
	Modified-Holistic Scores				
Source	Set A (6 raters)	Set B (6 raters)	Set C (6 raters)	Set D (5 raters)	
Person	2.37	5.81	3.13	4.82	
Rater	3.41	2.33	1.55	1.88	
Residual	6.66	8.19	6.20	6.39	
	Analytic Scores				
Source	Set A (6 raters)	Set B (6 raters)	Set C (6 raters)	Set D (5 raters)	Set E (6 raters)
Person	33.55	113.26	35.08	138.38	111.64
Residual	93.06	39.78	78.87	59.21	100.94

VALIDITY

Alignment. For the alignment between the TWS elements presented in the guidelines and the targeted standards, 78.6 percent (f =33) of validity assessment panel members indicated a high degree of alignment, and 21.4 percent (f = 9) said moderate alignment. For the alignment between the TWS task elements and the analytic scoring rubric, 69 percent (f = 29) of the panel members said there was a high degree alignment, 28.6 percent (f = 12) said moderate alignments, and 2.4 percent (f = 1) said low alignment. For the alignment of the analytic scoring rubric with the targeted standards, 73.8 percent (f = 31) said there was high alignment, 23.8 percent (f = 10) said moderate alignment and 2.4 percent (f = 1) said low alignment.

TABLE 2

Dependability Coefficient Estimates by Number of Raters for Each Scoring Rubric

Dependability Coefficient Estimates					
Number of Raters	**Modified-Holistic Rubric**				
	Set A	Set B	Set C	Set D	
6 Raters	.59	.77	.71	.78	
3 Raters	.41	.62	.55	.64	
1 Rater	.19	.36	.29	.37	
Number of Raters	**Analytic Rubric**				
	Set A	Set B	Set C	Set D	Set E
6 Raters	.62	.91	.64	.90	.87
3 Raters	.45	.85	.47	.82	.77
1 Rater	.22	.65	.23	.60	.53

Frequency. Table 3 presents the judgments made by the validity assessment panel with regard to how frequently they would expect a teacher to engage in the teaching behaviors targeted by the RTWS. All the teaching behaviors were considered to be high frequency activities for teachers with 83.3 to 100 percent of the raters indicating "weekly" or "daily" for all but one of the behaviors. The targeted teaching behavior that required teacher candidates to "use assessment data to profile student learning and communicate information about student progress and achievement" was rated "weekly" ($f = 20$) or "daily" ($f = 7$) by only 64.3 percent of the raters.

Criticality. To assess the *criticality* of the tasks performed while completing the RTWS, the validity assessment panel rated the importance of the teaching behaviors required. Table 4 presents the number and percent of the validity panel members indicating the importance to effective teaching (or criticality) of the teaching behaviors targeted by the Renaissance TWS. All

TABLE 3

Number and Percent of Panel Members Indicating How Frequently They Would Expect a Teacher to Engage in the Teaching Behaviors Targeted by the Teacher Work Sample (N = 42)

Teaching Behaviors Targeted By Teacher Work Sample	Never	Yearly	Monthly	Weekly	Daily
Use information about the learning-teaching context and student individual differences to set learning goals and plan instruction and assessments.		2 4.8%	5 11.9%	10 23.8%	25 59.5%
Set significant, challenging, varied, and appropriate learning goals.			5 11.9%	26 61.9%	11 26.2%
Use multiple assessment modes and approaches aligned with learning goals to assess student learning before, during, and after instruction.			2 4.8%	14 33.3%	26 61.9%
Design instruction for specific learning goals, student characteristics and needs, and learning contexts.			1 2.4%	19 45.2%	22 52.4%

(continues on next page)

TABLE 3 (continued)					
Teaching Behaviors Targeted By Teacher Work Sample	**Never**	**Yearly**	**Monthly**	**Weekly**	**Daily**
Use ongoing analysis of student learning to make instructional decisions.				7 16.7%	35 83.3%
Use assessment data to profile student learning and communicate information about student progress and achievement.		1 2.4%	14 33.3%	20 47.6%	7 16.7%
Reflect on instruction and student learning in order to improve teaching practice.		1 2.4%	5 11.9%	5 11.9%	31 73.8%

of the teaching behaviors were considered to be "important" or "very important."

Authenticity. The validity assessment panel judged how authentic the tasks required by the RTWS are to success as a classroom teacher. Table 5 presents the number and percent of the panel members rating each of the nine major TWS tasks as authentic. All tasks required by the RTWS were considered to be authentic or very authentic to success as a classroom teacher by a majority of the panel members. The percentages varied from 61.9 percent for (item # 8) "Teacher uses graphs or charts to profile whole class performance on pre-assessment and post-assessment, and to analyze trends or differences in student learning for selected subgroups" to 97.6 percent for (item #6) "Teacher uses on-going analysis of student learning and responses to rethink and modify original instructional design and lesson plans to improve student progress toward the learning goals(s)."

TABLE 4

Number and Percent of Panel Members Indicating the Importance to Effective Teaching of the Teaching Behaviors Targeted by the Teacher Work Sample (N = 42)

Teaching Behaviors Targeted By Teacher Work Sample	Degree of Importance			
	Not at all Important 1	Some-what Important 2	Important 3	Very Important 4
Use information about the learning-teaching context and student individual differences to set learning goals and plan instruction and assessments.			10 23.8%	32 76.2%
Set significant, challenging, varied, and appropriate learning goals.			4 9.5%	38 90.5%
Use multiple assessment modes and approaches aligned with learning goals to assess student learning before, during, and after instruction.			6 14.3%	36 85.7%
Design instruction for specific learning goals, student characteristics and needs, and learning contexts.			6 14.3%	36 85.7%

(continues on next page)

TABLE 4 (continued)				
	Degree of Importance			
Teaching Behaviors Targeted By Teacher Work Sample	**Not at all Important** 1	**Some- what Important** 2	**Important** 3	**Very Important** 4
Use ongoing analysis of student learning to make instructional decisions.			5 11.8%	37 88.1%
Use assessment data to profile student learning and communicate information about student progress and achievement.			12 28.6%	30 71.4%
Reflect on instruction and student learning in order to improve teaching practice.			4 9.5%	38 90.5%

Representativeness. The validity assessment panel also considered the degree to which the tasks required by the RTWS reflect and represent the targeted standards (See Table 7). Once again, the majority (88.1 to 97.6 percent) of the panel members thought the tasks were "representative" or "very representative" of the targeted standards, with most panel members indicating very representative (59.5 to 73.8 percent).

Match to INTASC Standards. Finally, the panel of experts indicated the extent to which the tasks required for the RTWS reflected the Interstate New Teacher Assessment and Support Consortium (INTASC) standards (Interstate New Teacher Assessment and Support Consortium, 1992). Although not directly designed to assess the INTASC standards, the teaching processes targeted by the RTWS are very similar to those addressed by

TABLE 5

Number and Percent of Panel Members Indicating How Authentic the Tasks Required by the Teacher Work Sample Are to Success as a Classroom Teacher (N = 42)

Tasks Required By the Teacher Work Sample	Degree of Authenticity			
	Not at all Authentic 1	Some-what Authentic 2	Authentic 3	Very Authentic 4
Teacher uses under-standing of student individual differences and community, school, and classroom characteristics to draw specific implica-tions for instruction and assessment.		3 7.1%	15 35.7%	24 57.1%
Teacher sets significant, challenging, varied and appropriate learning goals for student achievement that are aligned with local, state, or national standards.		4 9.5%	13 31.0%	25 59.5%
Teacher designs an assessment plan to monitor student progress toward learning goals, using multiple assess-ment modes and approaches to assess student learning before, during, and after instruction.		6 14.3%	13 31.0%	23 54.8%

(continues on next page)

TABLE 5 (continued)				
	Degree of Authenticity			
Tasks Required By the Teacher Work Sample	**Not at all Authentic 1**	**Some-what Authentic 2**	**Authentic 3**	**Very Authentic 4**
Teacher designs instruction aligned to learning goals and with reference to contextual factors and pre-assessment data, specifying instructional topics, learning activities, assignments and resources.		2 4.8%	17 40.5%	21 50.0%
Teacher designs instruction with content that it accurate, logically organized, and congruent with the big ideas or structure of the discipline.		2 4.8%	15 35.7%	25 59.5%
Teacher uses on-going analysis of student learning and responses to rethink and modify original instructional design and lesson plans to improve student progress toward the learning goal(s).		1 2.4%	17 40.5%	24 57.1%

(continues on next page)

TABLE 5 (continued)				
	Degree of Authenticity			
Tasks Required By the Teacher Work Sample	**Not at all Authentic 1**	**Some-what Authentic 2**	**Authentic 3**	**Very Authentic 4**
Teacher analyzes assessment data, including pre/post assessments and formative assessments, to determine students' progress related to the unit learning goals.		4 9.5%	13 31.0%	25 59.5%
Teacher uses graphs or charts to profile whole class performance on pre-assessments and post-assessments, and to analyze trends or differences in student learning for selected subgroups.	4 9.5%	12 28.6%	15 35.7%	11 26.2%
Teacher evaluates the effectiveness of instruction and reflects upon teaching practices and their effects on student learning, identifying future actions for improved practice and professional growth.		2 4.8%	15 35.7%	25 59.5%

TABLE 6

Number and Percent of Panel Members Indicating the Degree to Which the Tasks Required by the Teacher Work Sample Reflect and Represent the Targeted Standards (N = 42)

Tasks Required By the Teacher Work Sample	Degree of Representativeness			
	Not at all Repre- sentative 1	Some- what Repre- sentative 2	Repre- sentative 3	Very Repre- sentative 4
Teacher uses under-standing of student individual differences and community, school, and classroom characteristics to draw specific implica-tions for instruction and assessment.		2 4.8%	15 35.7%	25 59.5%
Teacher sets significant, challenging, varied and appropriate learning goals for student achievement that are aligned with local, state, or national standards.		1 2.4%	11 26.2%	30 71.4%
Teacher designs an assessment plan to monitor student progress toward learning goals, using multiple assess-ment modes and approaches to assess student learning before, during, and after instruction.		1 2.4%	10 23.8%	30 71.4%

(continues on next page)

	Degree of Representativeness			
		Some-		
Tasks Required By the Teacher Work Sample	**Not at all Repre- sentative 1**	**what Repre- sentative 2**	**Repre- sentative 3**	**Very Repre- sentative 4**
Teacher designs instruction aligned to learning goals and with reference to contextual factors and pre-assess- ment data, specifying instructional topics, learning activities, assignments and resources.		2 4.8%	13 31.0%	27 64.3%
Teacher designs instruction with content that it accurate, logically organized, and congruent with the big ideas or structure of the discipline.		1 2.4%	14 33.3%	27 64.3%
Teacher uses on-going analysis of student learning and responses to rethink and modify original instructional design and lesson plans to improve student progress toward the learning goal(s).		1 2.4%	10 23.8%	31 73.8%

TABLE 6 (continued)

(continues on next page)

TABLE 6 (continued)				
	Degree of Representativeness			
Tasks Required By the Teacher Work Sample	**Not at all Repre- sentative** **1**	**Some- what Repre- sentative** **2**	**Repre- sentative** **3**	**Very Repre- sentative** **4**
Teacher analyzes assessment data, including pre/post assessments and formative assessments, to determine students' progress related to the unit learning goals.		2 4.8%	9 21.4%	30 71.4%
Teacher uses graphs or charts to profile whole class performance on pre-assessments and post-assessments, and to analyze trends or differences in student learning for selected subgroups.	2 4.8%	3 7.1%	12 28.6%	25 59.5%
Teacher evaluates the effectiveness of instruction and reflects upon teaching practices and their effects on student learning, identifying future actions for improved practice and professional growth.		1 2.4%	12 28.6%	29 69.0%

TABLE 7

Number and Percent of Panel Members Indicating the Teacher Work Sample Tasks Matched the Interstate New Teacher Assessment and Support Consortium Standards (N = 42)

INTASC Standards	Not at all	Implicitly	Directly
Knowledge of Subject Matter: The teacher understands the central concepts, tools of inquiry, and structures of the content area(s) taught and creates learning experiences that make these aspects of subject matter meaningful for learners.		13 31.0%	26 61.9%
Knowledge of Human Development and Learning: The teacher understands how students learn and develop, and provides opportunities that support their intellectual, social, and personal development.		16 38.1%	24 57.1%
Adapting Instruction for Individual Needs: The teacher understands how students differ in their approaches to learning and creates instructional opportunities that area adapted to learners with diverse needs.	1 2.4%	7 16.7%	32 76.2%
Multiple Instructional Strategies: The teacher understands and uses a variety of instructional strategies to develop students' critical thinking, problem solving, and performance skills.	1 2.4%	11 26.2%	28 66.7%

(continues on next page)

TABLE 7 (continued)			
INTASC Standards	**Not at all**	**Implicitly**	**Directly**
Classroom Motivation and Management Skills: The teacher understands individual and group motivation and behavior and creates a learning environment that encourages positive social interaction, active engagement in learning, and self-motivation.	10 23.8%	22 52.4%	8 19.0%
Communication Skills: The teacher uses a variety of communication techniques including verbal, nonverbal, and media to foster inquiry, collaboration, and supportive interaction in and beyond the classroom.	4 9.5%	26 61.9%	10 23.8%
Instructional Planning Skills: The teacher plans and prepares instruction based upon knowledge of subject matter, students, the community, and curriculum goals.		5 11.9%	35 83.3%
Assessment of Student Learning: The teacher understands, uses, and interprets formal and informal assessment strategies to evaluate and advance student performance and to determine program effectiveness.		4 9.5%	36 85.7%
Professional Commitment and Responsibility: The teacher is a reflective practitioner who demonstrates a commitment to professional standards and is continuously engaged in purposeful mastery of the art and science of teaching.		16 38.1%	24 57.1%

(continues on next page)

TABLE 7 (continued)			
INTASC Standards	**Not at all**	**Implicitly**	**Directly**
Partnerships: The teacher interacts in a professional, effective manner with colleagues, parents, and other members of the community to support students' learning and well being.	13 31.0%	19 45.2%	8 19.0%

many of the INTASC standards. Table 7 presents the number and percent of responses made by our panel of experts for each of the INTASC standards. The RTWS was seen by a majority of the experts to directly measure seven of the ten INTASC standards. As can be seen from Table 7, the highest rated were those INTASC standards most closely aligned with the seven teaching process standards targeted by the RTWS. Other INTASC standards were judged to be implicitly measured because knowledge and skills related to them might be used in completing a RTWS, even though indicators of these standards are not directly included in the Renaissance scoring rubrics. Of significance is the fact that three of the INTASC standards were not seen as measured by the RTWS and these standards were not targeted by the RTWS.

QUALITY OF LEARNING ASSESSMENT

Effect of Rater. Using repeated measures ANOVA, the effect of rater on the Quality of Learning Assessment (QLA) scores was not statistically significant for the Set A TWS, $F(1, 19) = .85$, $MSE = 5.89$, $p = .38$ or the Set E TWS, $F(2, 18) = .440$, $MSE = 8.40$, $p = .65$, but it was statistically significant for the Set B TWS, $F(2, 16) = 4.07$, $MSE = 5.80$, $p = .04$. The two-rater coefficient of dependability for the QLA scores for the Set A TWS was calculated to be .69. The three-rater coefficients of dependability for the QLA scores for the Set B and Set E TWS were calculated to be .71, and .84 respectively. Together, these findings suggest sufficient inter-rater agreement for the purpose of this investigation.

Correlation with Renaissance TWS Total Scores. Table 8 presents the correlations among the analytic total scores, modified-holistic total scores, and Quality of Learning Assessment (QLA) total scores for the Set A, Set B, and

TABLE 8

**Correlations Among the Total Analytic Scores,
Total Modified-Holistic Scores, and the
Total Quality of Learning Assessment Scores**

	Analytic	Modified-Holistic
Set A Teacher Work Samples (n = 10) Quality of Learning Assessment Analytic	.24	.48 .77*
Set B Teacher Work Samples (n = 10) Quality of Learning Assessment Analytic	.89*	.86* .89*
Set E TWS (n = 10) Quality of Learning Assessment	.70*	

*p < .05

Set E teacher work samples. All total scores were averaged across the raters of each set. As can be seen from Table 8, the correlations for the Set B TWS and Set E TWS were positive and high. These correlations indicate a strong positive relationship between total work sample performance as measured by the analytic and the modified-holistic rubrics and the total scores on the Quality of Learning Assessment measure. Together, these data support the idea that teacher education candidates who scored well on the Set B TWS and the Set E TWS used quality assessments methods to demonstrate their impact on student learning.

Discussion

The Renaissance Teacher Work Sample (RTWS) is an authentic, multifaceted performance assessment completed by pre-service teacher candidates during student teaching to demonstrate their level of teaching proficiency relative to seven targeted teaching standards (The Renaissance Partnership for Improving Teacher Quality, 2001). The seven teaching process standards all address teaching actions influential to student learning. The RTWS was developed to assess teaching performance levels when teacher candidates are asked to show evidence of their impacts on student learning. In this investigation, we examined the generalizability of RTWS scores for two scoring methods (modified-holistic and analytic) when RTWS performances were evaluated by raters from across teacher preparation institutions. In addition, we examined support for the validity of the RTWS for the purpose of making high-stakes decisions about teacher candidates' abilities to meet the targeted teaching process standards. We also examined the link between the targeted standards and national teaching standards as represented by the INTASC standards (Interstate New Teacher Assessment and Support Consortium, 1992). Finally, using groups of measurement experts, we examined whether RTWS performances provided credible evidence for the use of sound assessment practices when teacher candidates' are required to demonstrate their impacts on student learning. Overall, our findings support the RTWS as a method for providing credible evidence of teacher candidate performance.

EVIDENCE FOR SCORE GENERALIZABILITY

A major issue for all performance assessments is the extent to which different raters provide similar judgments with respect to the quality of the observed performances. Applying Generalizability Theory (Shavelson & Webb, 1991), the results revealed significant effects for novice raters using both scoring methods (the analytic rubric and the modified holistic rubric), but not for experienced raters when using the analytic scoring rubric. These findings suggest the training and experience of the raters are important considerations when using the RTWS to make decisions about the quality of teaching performance levels. This finding is consistent with the general findings for other types of performance assessments (Dunbar, Koretz, & Hoover, 1991).

Nevertheless, the important issue for complex performance assessments, like the RTWS, is not whether or not there are scoring differences among the raters, but rather the extent of those differences and the dependability of the score decisions made by the panel of raters. Because performance assessments require the application of professional judgment when scoring, it is natural to expect a certain degree of scoring variability. To determine the degree of consistency in the RTWS scores for making absolute (criterion-referenced) decisions about candidate performance levels, Generalizability Theory (Shavelson & Webb, 1991) was applied to compute dependability coefficients. The formula for computing these coefficients also permitted determination of the required number of raters necessary for making dependable decisions. Based on five-rater and six-rater panels, we found moderate to very high dependability coefficients for scores derived from the RTWS scoring rubrics. This means a large proportion of RTWS scores reflect differences in teacher candidate performances levels (criterion-referenced) that can be generalized across raters.

Dependability coefficients were found to be higher in general for the analytic scoring method than for the modified-holistic scoring method. Coupled with the fact that scoring times were nearly identical for the two scoring methods, the data from this investigation support the use of the analytic scoring method when high-stakes decisions are planned. Adjusting the number of raters in the formulas, we found sufficient dependability could be obtained using the analytic scoring method when panels of three or more experienced raters are used. Collectively, these findings suggest teacher work samples can be administered and scored by raters from across teacher education institutions with sufficient inter-rater agreement to make high-stakes decisions about the performance levels of teacher education candidates with respect to the targeted performance standards. However, multiple scorers remain essential to produce credible measures of performance for high-stakes decisions.

Support for Validity

Contemporary thinking (Joint Committee on Standards for Educational and Psychological Testing of the American Educational Research Association, the American Psychological Association, and the National Council on Measurement in Education, 1999) about validity considers it to be a unitary concept—that is, there are not different types of validity, but rather different types of evidence. Validity does not inhere in the instrument but rather is related to uses of the results for certain purposes. Furthermore, validity is an ongoing argument, combining both logical and empirical elements. This study provides initial support for important aspects of the content validity of the RTWS when used for the purpose of assessing teacher candidates' abilities with respect to seven teaching process standards.

Our empirical findings support the alignment of the RTWS Prompt, the targeted standards, and the RTWS scoring rubrics. We also found support for Crocker's (1997) criteria for judging the content representativeness of performance assessments and scoring rubrics—namely, the frequency, criticality, authenticity, and representativeness of the required RTWS tasks to actual teaching performance. Our findings also yielded evidence of the alignment of the RTWS tasks with national teaching standards in the form of the INTASC standards (Interstate New Teacher Assessment and Support Consortium, 1992). Together, the results support the content validity of the RTWS for the purpose of assessing teacher education candidates' abilities to meet the targeted teaching standards.

Because this study has validated a direct link between the teaching process standards and teaching behaviors measured by the RTWS and the INTASC (1992), the findings of this study are likely to generalize to other teacher education programs whose state and program standards are based on or similar to the INTASC standards. Hence, the RTWS could be considered by other teacher education programs for inclusion as one of their methods for providing evidence of their candidates' abilities to meet such standards as required for unit accreditation (National Council for Accreditation of Teacher Education, 2000).

EVIDENCE FOR QUALITY STUDENT LEARNING ASSESSMENT

Airasian (1999) has expressed concern about the quality of the pre- and post assessments used in teacher work samples. Faced with the demand to demonstrate impact on student learning, there is the possibility teacher candidates' might select only low-level, easy-to-meet learning goals or set easy to meet criteria for their students' responses on the post assessment. Hence, absent explicit evidence for the quality of the assessments, can work samples provide valid and credible evidence of teacher impact on student learning?

The RTWS scoring criteria take into consideration the significance of the learning goals, quality of the assessments, and student performance relative to the chosen learning goals. Hence, teacher impact on student learning is addressed by building explicit criteria relative to these factors into the RTWS scoring rubrics. Thus, the RTWS scores reflect the abilities of teacher candidates to develop quality pre- and post-assessments of student learning aligned with learning goals; to disaggregate assessment data on the pre- and post-assessments to profile student learning; to assess the impacts of their instruction on the learning of their students; and to communicate information about student progress clearly and accurately. The quality and strength of the evidence determines the rating the RTWS receives from the panel of expert raters.

To validate the judgments of the RTWS raters and to address Airasian's (1999) concerns, we had independent measurement experts evaluate the quality of the assessments employed by the teacher candidates in their work samples. Our findings revealed significant high positive correlations between these independent evaluations of the quality of the learning assessments used by the teachers to demonstrate their impact on student learning and the total RTWS performance on the analytic scoring rubric. Although lessened by the lower and nonsignificant correlations for the Set A teacher work samples, these initial findings do provide support for the idea that successful performance on a teacher work sample can be an indication of overall higher quality assessment of student learning. This finding indicates that the approach may provide a way to incorporate impacts on student learning into teaching performance assessments that embody national, state, and institutional standards.

SUGGESTIONS FOR FUTURE RESEARCH

Future research should examine the predictive validity of RTWS performances as teacher education candidates enter the profession and become teachers. McConney et al. (1998) also noted the importance of examining the predictive validity of work sample assessments. Future investigations should also focus on other aspects of score generalizability. One important aspect to consider is the generalizability of performance ratings across different occasions of work sample development by the same teachers or teacher candidates. Future research should also examine the relationship between RTWS performances and student learning when measured by independent achievement assessments, such as high-stakes state mandated achievement tests. In addition, more work needs to be done to find ways to streamline the process and make it more efficient while maintaining high standards of measurement.

Conclusion

The work of the Renaissance Partnership to Improve Teaching Quality presented in this study contributes to a growing body of research (Danielson, 1996; Denner, Salzman, & Bangert, 2001; Denner, Miller, Newsome, & Birdsong, 2002; National Board for Professional Teaching Standards, 2001) that supports the use of complex performance assessments as credible means for documenting candidate performance with respect to national, state, and institutional teaching standards and for linking teacher candidate performance to P-12 student learning. This is important in light of the general concern in the educational community about the use of standardized paper-and-pencil tests for this purpose (see, Darling-Hammond & Snyder, 2000). Specifically, this study has shown that teacher preparation institutions can use an authentic teacher performance assessment in the form of the

Renaissance Teacher Work Sample as they strive to align their programs with performance-based accreditation standards and to meet federal and state mandates for accountability.

Teacher education programs can also learn from the approach described here. The methods followed to establish credibility evidence for the RTWS can be used for other teacher performance assessments that are focused on standards (see, Denner, Miller, Newsome, & Birdsong, 2002 for an application to a case analysis assessment). The process of benchmarking, scorer training, and the procedures for collecting validity and generalizability data can all be applied by teacher education programs to their other performance assessments.

REFERENCES

Airasian, P. W. (1997). Oregon teacher work sample methodology: Potential and problems. In J. Millman (Ed.). *Grading teachers, grading schools: Is student achievement a valid evaluation measure?* (pp. 46–52). Thousand Oaks, CA: Corwin Press.

Bradley, A. (1998). NEA, AFT take up the thorny issues of teacher quality. *Education Week, 18,* p. 6.

Chase, C. I. (1999). *Contemporary assessment for educators.* New York: Longman.

Crocker, L. (1997). Assessing content representativeness of performance assessment exercises. *Applied Measurement in Education, 10,* 83–95.

Danielson, C. (1996). *Enhancing professional practice: A framework for teaching.* Alexandria, VA: Association for Supervision and Curriculum Development.

Darling-Hammond, L. (2000). *Solving the dilemmas of teacher supply, demand, and standards: How we can ensure a competent, caring, and qualified teacher for every child.* New York, NY: National Commission on Teaching and America's Future.

Darling-Hammond, L., & Snyder, J. (2000). Authentic assessment of teaching in context. *Teaching and Teacher Education, 16,* 523–545.

Denner, P. , Miller, T., Newsome, J., & Birdsong, J. (2002). Using complex case analysis to make visible the quality of teacher candidates. *Journal of Personnel Evaluation in Education, 16*(3), 153–174.

Denner, P., Salzman, S., & Bangert, A. (2001). Linking teacher assessment to student performance: A benchmarking, generalizability, and validity study of the use of teacher work samples. *Journal of Personnel Evaluation in Teacher Education, 15,* 287–307.

Dunbar, S. B., Koretz, D., & Hoover, H. D. (1991). Quality control in the development and use of performance assessments. *Applied Measurement in Education, 4,* 289–302.

Ferguson, R. F.& Ladd, H. F. (1996). How and why money matters: An analysis of Alabama schools. In H. Ladd (Ed.), *Holding schools accountable* (pp. 265–298). Washington, D.C.: Brookings Institute.

Gredler, M. E. (1999). *Classroom assessment and learning.* New York: Longman.

Interstate New Teacher Assessment and Support Consortium. (1992). *Model standards for beginning teacher licensing and development: A resource for state dialogue.* Washington, DC: Council of Chief State School Officers.

Joint Committee on Standards for Educational and Psychological Testing of the American Educational Research Association, the American Psychological Association, and the National Council on Measurement in Education. (1999). *Standards for educational and psychological testing.* Washington, D.C.: American Educational Research Association.

McConney, A. A., Schalock, M. D., & Schalock, H. D. (1998). Focusing improvement and quality assurance: Work samples as authentic performance measures of prospective teachers' effectiveness. *Journal of Personnel Evaluation in Education, 11,* 343–363.

McRobbie, J. (2001). *Career-long teacher development: Policies that make sense.* San Francisco, CA: West Education.

National Board for Professional Teaching Standards. (2001). *The effect of National Board Certification on teachers.* Washington, D.C.: National Board for Professional Teaching Standards.

National Commission on Excellence in Education. (1983). *A nation at risk.* Washington, DC: Government Printing.

National Commission on Teaching and America's Future. (1996). *What matters most: Teaching for America's Future.* New York, NY: Author.

National Council for Accreditation of Teacher Education. (2000). *NCATE 2000 unit standards.* Washington, D.C.: Author.

Pankratz, R. (1999). *Improving teacher quality through partnerships that connect teacher performance to student learning.* Unpublished manuscript, Western Kentucky University.

Sanders, W. L., & Rivers, J. C. (1996). *Cumulative and residual effects of teachers on future student academic achievement.* Knoxville, TN: University of Tennessee Value-Added Research and Assessment Center.

Schalock, H. D., Schalock, M., & Girod, G. (1997). Teacher work sample methodology as used at Western Oregon State College. In J. McMillan (Ed.) *Grading teachers, grading schools: Is student achievement a valid evaluation measure?* (pp. 15–45). Thousand Oaks, CA: Corwin Press.

Shavelson, R. J., & Webb, N. M. (1991). *Generalizability theory: A primer.* Newbury Park, CA: Sage.

Stiggins, R. J. (2001). *Student-involved classroom assessment* (3rd ed.). Upper Saddle River, NJ: Prentice-Hall.

The Carnegie Forum on Education and the Economy. (1986). *A nation prepared: Teachers for the 21st century.* New York, NY: The Carnegie Forum on Education and the Economy.

The Holmes Group. (1986). *Tomorrow's teachers.* Lansing, MI: Author.

The Renaissance Partnership for Improving Teacher Quality. (2001). *Teacher work sample: Performance prompt, teaching process standards, scoring rubrics.* Retrieved from *http://fp.uni.edu/itq/ProjectActivities/index.htm.*

Appendix

Quality of Learning Assessment Rating Scale

1. Learning goals reflect several types of learning and are significant and challenging.
2. Learning goals are clearly stated as learning outcomes.
3. Learning goals are appropriate for the development and prerequisite knowledge, skills, and experiences of the students and other student needs.
4. Learning goals are explicitly aligned with national, state, or local standards.
5. Assessments are congruent with the learning goals in content and cognitive complexity.
6. Assessment criteria are clear and explicitly linked to the learning goals.
7. The assessment plan includes multiple assessment modes and assesses student performance throughout the instructional sequence.
8. The assessments appear to be valid measures of the learning goals.
9. Scoring procedures are explained.
10. Assessment items or prompts are clearly written.
11. Assessment directions and procedures are clear and would likely be understood by the students.
12. Evidence of student learning includes data from assessments before and after instruction.

Professional Development to Improve Student Learning
A Systems Approach

Mary E. Little, Ph.D.

Mary E. Little, Ph.D. is an Associate Professor at the University of Central Florida in the Child, Family, and Community Science Department, teaching and advising graduate and undergraduate students in the program area of exceptional education. For the last four years, she has also served as the Principal Investigator of the "Effective Instructional Practices" project (Project CENTRAL), a statewide professional development project funded through the Bureau of Instructional Support and Community Services at the Florida Department of Education. Her research interests include quality implementation of research-based instructional practices through action research and teacher efficacy and retention.

ABSTRACT

Linking professional development and preparation with student performance in classrooms within the context of school reform continues to be a challenge. Given the increasing demand for accountability, implementation of effective instructional practices that improve student learning within all classrooms is critical. This chapter describes the conceptual framework and the specific implementation activities that have been developed within a statewide professional development system focused on improved student outcomes. The specific model and procedures described have been implemented and validated through a systems approach. The resulting model builds upon the collaboration among professionals within the research communities, state departments of education, and local professional developers, administrators, and teachers.

T hrough the history of public education in the United States, there have been many reforms (Cuban, 1996; Fullan, 1999; Sergiovanni, 1999) that focused on standardization, equity, minimum competency, and in more recent years, higher standards of achievement for all students, including students with diverse learning needs. As public education received more federal and state funding, the amount of legislation and involvement from multiple agencies increased dramatically. Commissions published reports, politicians mandated legislation, and researchers validated instructional methods (Carnine, 1999; Fullan, 1993 and 1999).

Within the last twenty years, research has contributed discoveries that advanced the understanding of research-based instructional practices (Carnine, 1999; Forness, Kavale, Blum, & Lloyd, 1997). However, the research to practice gap in education continues (Greenwood & Abbott, 2001; Malouf & Schiller, 1995). Therefore, the most current research-based instructional strategies and interventions are not often implemented within the context of school reforms. The reasons cited are separateness of the legislative, political, research, and practice communities, lack of relevance as perceived by teachers and administrators, and weak professional development opportunities (Fullan, 1993; Greenwood & Abbott, 2001).

The suggested strategies to address these concerns are to bridge the research to practice gap and reform instructional practices for all students, including students with disabilities. Collaboration and partnerships among educational constituents and agencies (teachers, administrators, researchers, state education personnel, etc.) appear to be the common themes to creating and sustaining interactions around issues measuring student outcomes and of effective instructional practices (Espin & Deno, 2000; Gersten, Vaughn, Deshler, & Schiller, 1997).

During the last three years (since 1999 to the present), educators within the state of Florida reviewed the published literature on the topics related to bridging the gap between research and practice, including conceptual models of professional development based on student results. Their goal was to create, implement, and evaluate a statewide research to practice professional development model focused on the implementation of research-based instructional practices to enhance student performance. In this chapter, I first describe a framework of collaboration for school reform (Murphy, 1991) that best addresses the above-described concerns. I then describe the resulting conceptual model for professional development that incorporates Murphy's framework for school reform to enhance student results. Finally, a specific implementation model that addresses research linking professional development of teachers with student performance is described.

Framework for Research to Practice

Much has been written to explain the research to practice gap in special education (Gersten, Woodward, & Morvant, 1992; Malouf & Schiller, 1995) and general education (Fullan, 1993; Goodlad, 1992; Huberman, 1990; Little, 1997). Major themes that explain the apparent lack of specific changes to instruction within the context of school reforms include: (a). separateness of research and practice communities; (b). perceived limited relevance to practitioners; (c). lack of usable innovations for the classroom; and (d). lack of ongoing support (Greenwood and Abbott, 2001). Given these issues within the legal and political context of schools; the relevance, rationale, and potential impact needs to be clearly articulated among various educators to better bridge the gap between research and practice. To address the necessary collaboration among educators responsible for improving student learning, Murphy (1991) developed a conceptual framework that described the components of school reform within three categories: work design, organization and governance, and core technology of instructional practices. The next sections of this paper describe the conceptual framework among each educational constituent.

WORK DESIGN

Work design involves the roles, responsibilities, and relationships of educators within school, district, state, and federal levels of education. School reform activities originate from and impact all levels of the educational system. Therefore, relationships among the members within these various roles, if developed, are complex in nature (Evans, Harris, Adeigbola, Houston & Argott, 1993). Each has specific responsibilities and primary roles within the entire process of school reform. Educational goals are established and mandated at the federal level. Implementation and accountability are the primary focus within the state level, while local school districts support teachers and administrators to achieve these federal, state, and local goals. Teachers and administrators are expected to perform multiple tasks to participate in this total education process (Barth, 1991; Fullan and Miles, 1992), often without benefit of the rationale and full disclosure related to the current mandates and responsibilities. Professional development is designed to support greater accountability for mandates and is a critical component in reform activities to guide effective change in schools (Guskey, 1998). Administrators within school districts make decisions regarding the professional development needs of the teachers to attain the stated goals for their students. However, as discussed earlier, intervention research studies of instructional practices are often not translated into practices for professional development for the teachers and administrators. It is at this juncture that the translation of research into practice needs to be evident. Given the multiple agencies and diverse responsibilities, it appears that issues of separateness and a lack of collaboration are inherent to work design.

However, federal and state education agencies can be collaborative partners in these reform efforts. For example, reform of work design can be reflected as the role of the federal and state agencies shifts from focusing solely on monitoring and assuring compliance with regulation to setting policy directions and providing assistance for implementation of reform efforts. Setting policies with a clear focus on the standards leading to improved outcomes is a primary role of the state education agency. Once the policies are set, states are designing accountability systems to measure progress toward the stated goals. It is incumbent on leadership at the state level to model quality implementation of state standards. Research, development, and dissemination of research-based instructional strategies would support the quality implementation of state standards that align with federal policies and procedures.

ORGANIZATION AND GOVERNANCE

To further address these issues related to work design, recent changes within school organization and governance have occurred. Nationally, major movement in this area has resulted in decentralized school administration (Center for Policy Research on the Impact of General and Special Education Reform, 1996). Decision-making about student outcomes (e.g., instructional decisions) now resides with local school educators and community members. State and district policy makers establish broad outcomes and goals and devise systems to hold schools accountable for achieving the goals (Center for Policy Research on the Impact of General and Special Education Reform, 1996). Therefore, this system of administration provides for more local decision making and accountability at the school and district levels to meet the broader outcomes established. This type of decentralization also supports the movement to a professional work design so teachers also make decisions based on local and classroom needs (David, 1989). Examples of common strategies of reform in organization and structure include school choice, site-based decision making, waivers of state and district policies, and modified union contracts, allowing school-based variance of assigned duties (Evans & Panacek-Howell, 1995). The results of these policy shifts afford local educators ultimately accountable for student learning the opportunities and responsibilities to make instructional decisions based upon the goals and accountability frameworks established by the state and federal educational policy makers.

These shifts also have an impact upon organization and governance of these agencies. Many federal and state education agencies recently have reorganized both their structure and their work to mesh with the shift in organization and governance at the local level. In addition to setting policies, state agencies provide technical support to schools and school districts. States are redesigning professional development structures, providing waivers of current regulations, and deploying staff to provide assistance targeted toward state goals. For example, professional development provided by state agencies is now provided throughout many states by regional resource centers, who respond to local needs of the school districts. The shift in governance finds state agency representatives in a facilitative role with schools and school districts, assisting with reform implementation and resource location.

These reforms within the work design and organization and governance components at both the federal and state levels are a major support for changing the core technology (the last of Murphy's components) in the school and classroom. Issues related to identifying and implementing research-based instructional practices within the schools continue to be a challenge to be addressed. Standards can be established for identifying effective practices for educators. Infrastructure and processes to support implementation and maintenance of the effective practices would ensure ease of access and improved quality of implementation. Reflecting the standards for effective practices and incorporating supporting research into state level activities such as instructional materials adoption, identification of model programs, and awarding special grants and projects sets the tone and expectation for improving the teaching and learning in classrooms (Carnine, 1999). These revisions in policy, organization, and governance impact the third of Murphy's components necessary for effective school reforms, core technology.

CORE TECHNOLOGY

The last component of school reform is one Murphy (1991) labeled core technology. It is defined as the basic work of schools—teaching and learning. Bringing about change in the classroom is extremely difficult . Unless efforts are directed squarely toward reform in the classroom, reform attempts will fall short of improving student outcomes. With the organization and governance policy shifts noted above, this third component of the core technology of the instructional practices within each classroom becomes critically important to the continued changes of school reforms, and directly affects issues related to bridging the research to practice gap.

Addressing these policy shifts necessitates providing professional development of research-based instructional practices that provide new or deeper levels of knowledge and practice. Topics would be related to these policies as well as teaching tools, such as curriculum, textbooks, and intervention resources to improve student learning (Guskey and Sparks, 1996; Hargraves and Fink, 2000). Teachers must use a variety of research-based interventions and instructional strategies to meet all student-learning needs. As accountability demands strengthen, the importance of providing teachers with instructional methods with the strongest research base available to meet these diverse needs also increases (Carnine, 1999). To ensure continued focus on improved outcomes for students with diverse learning needs, a commitment to strengthening the empirical base for research and practice in the field of education is necessary (Carnine, 1999; Kauffman, 1993), as well as bridging the research into practice gap. How are these goals realized, given the concerns and issues reviewed from both the policy and research perspectives?

Coordinating Reforms for Student Success

Incremental, even dramatic, school improvement is not only possible, but also probable under the right conditions. Although the components of change have been described (Fullan, 1999; Guskey & Sparks, 1996; Hargraves & Fink, 2000), reforms at each level must be focused on improved student outcomes. The multiple partners within the educational systems could be each reforming and changing. These changes may not produce the desired results of improved student outcomes if a clearly communicated and implemented vision for school reform has not been articulated among all of the educational partners. Given the complexity of school reform, the multiple educational partners with diverse needs and perspectives must be coordinated around the single focus of improved student outcomes to address the public demand for accountability. Change must be managed, communicated, and coordinated across various stakeholders, issues, resources, and settings to meet the promise of quality education for all students. Given the multiplicity of the issues and stakeholders, is it any wonder why numerous attempts at systemic changes to improve the education and outcomes for all students have not produced the intended results (Elmore, 1990; Elmore & Burney, 1999)?

COORDINATING EFFORTS: A MODEL

Murphy's conceptual framework (1991) of school reform (work design, organization and governance, and core technology) has provided the model for systemic reforms within the state of Florida. Given the impact of each of these components upon school reform, each of the components must be in concert with and communicated among the educational partners. Curriculum, instruction, and assessment for student learning from each of the perspectives of state, district, and classroom must address organization and governance, work design, and core technology (see Figure 1).

Within the state of Florida, revisions in school organization and governance, as well as a redesign of professional development, have been occurring at the policy level. (See previous sections.) The primary focus on learner outcomes for all students within each local school was mandated through revised curriculum changes and statewide accountability measures. Local school improvement plans, mandated to address the state-established curriculum standards are developed by educators, parents, and community members of each school. Successful school improvement is now measured by indicators related to student successes (academics, discipline, attendance, etc.) within each local school for all students. Members of local school advisory committees of site-based management teams are charged with development of action plans (outcomes, professional development, and student outcome measures, etc.) to assure the success of their school as measured through specific student indicators. Regional professional development contacts of the state department (e.g., Area Centers of Educational Enhancement-ACEE; Florida Diagnostic and Learning Resources Systems-FDLRS; Florida Inclusion Network-FIN; Family Network on Disabilities-FND; etc.) provide technical assistance to local schools and districts, regarding policies, mandates, and legislated changes as local implementation occurs. In addition, professional development from regional state personnel immediately communicate policy changes that impact local implementation related to these mandated changes. Roles, responsibilities, and relationships are re-designed within the current structure to one of greater collaboration at the specific schools and districts among the educational partners. School organization and governance and the revision of roles and responsibilities through increased collaboration among the educational partners were two of the three necessary components for school reform.

Curriculum

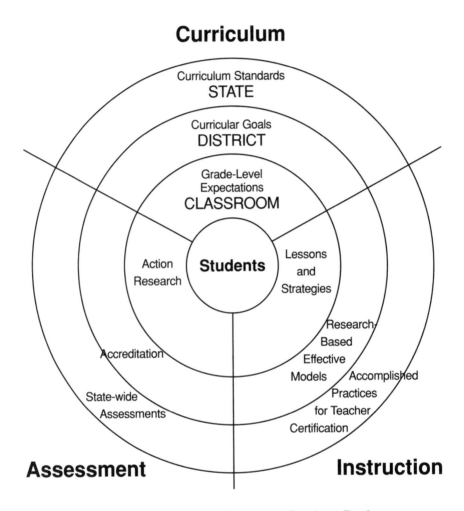

Curriculum Standards
STATE

Curricular Goals
DISTRICT

Grade-Level
Expectations
CLASSROOM

Action
Research

Students

Lessons
and
Strategies

Research-
Based
Effective
Models

Accomplished
Practices
for Teacher
Certification

Accreditation

State-wide
Assessments

Assessment   # Instruction

For School Improvement to Enhance Student Performance

Figure 1. Systems Framework

REFORMING THE CORE TECHNOLOGIES: RESEARCH AND IMPLEMENTATION

To address the need to identify and disseminate effective, research-based instructional practices as the core instructional technology necessary for school reform, the Florida State Department of Education developed a model for professional development through the Effective Instructional Practices (EIP) project. This comprehensive project, Project CENTRAL (Coordinating Existing Networks To Reach All Learners), was designed to identify and disseminate information related to resources, professional development, and research in current and emerging research-based instructional practices. The ultimate vision for this state-sponsored project was to provide professional development, products, and resources to ensure mastery of established outcomes for all students in Florida based upon researched, effective instructional practices delivered through re-conceptualized professional development procedures. The process of teacher development and student performance was conceptualized and delivered within a four-step, continuous improvement model, with specific content related to the needs of the all students, with and without disabilities (see Figure 2).

The four steps included: (a) identification of research-based instructional practices, (b) selection of teams of teachers to attend awareness level professional development, (c) classroom implementation of scientifically-based instructional practice from initial training to quality implementation for all students, and (d) data collection of results of student learning through traditional and action research methodologies. Data collected during implementation further inform the classroom instructional process and the identification and continued dissemination of the specific instructional practice.

This process will be described in general, as well as in some detail, using one of the scientifically based instructional practices (Phonological Awareness) as an example, to provide clarity through specific examples.

Step 1: Identification of research-based instructional practices. To create standards for effective, scientifically based instructional practices to incorporate into professional development (Carnine, 1999), specific criteria were developed as a standard to determine the efficacy of each scientifically based instructional practice in relation to access to the general education curriculum (see Figure 3).

For example, before determining specific reading instructional practices adopted for intensive professional development, graduate students of the EIP project reviewed published literature and materials to locate specific products, methods, and materials that address the standards of the *Level I Criteria* for scientifically based instructional practices. Graduate students participated in a one-day training to learn the components of the *Level I Criteria,* and to identify and review content materials according to criteria. After training, specific materials selected were reviewed by two graduate students independently, with results compared. The reliability of their judgment on the established criteria ranged between 0.85 and 0.92 after training.

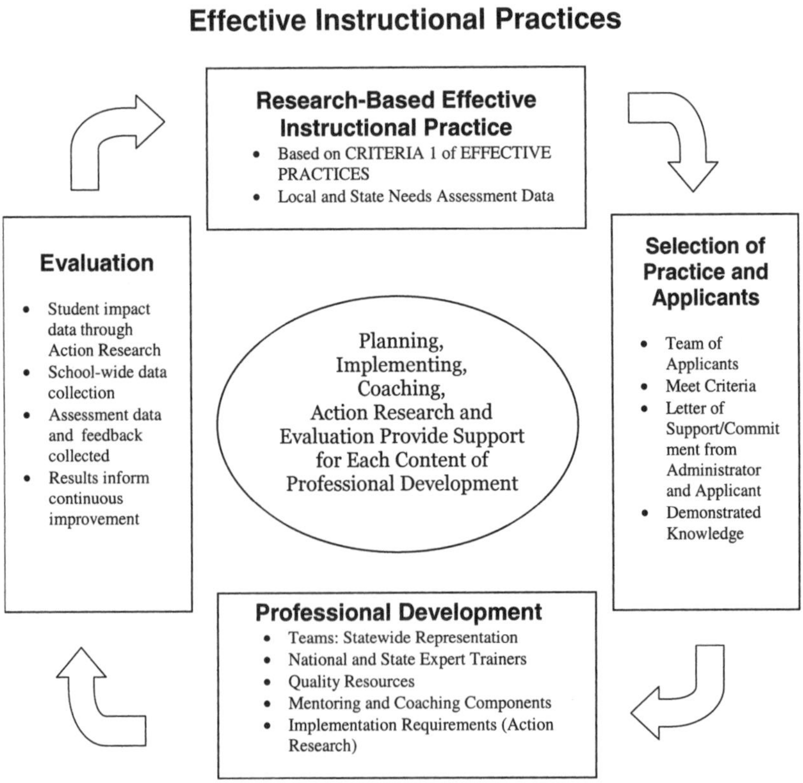

Effective Instructional Practices

Research-Based Effective Instructional Practice
- Based on CRITERIA 1 of EFFECTIVE PRACTICES
- Local and State Needs Assessment Data

Evaluation
- Student impact data through Action Research
- School-wide data collection
- Assessment data and feedback collected
- Results inform continuous improvement

Planning, Implementing, Coaching, Action Research and Evaluation Provide Support for Each Content of Professional Development

Selection of Practice and Applicants
- Team of Applicants
- Meet Criteria
- Letter of Support/Commitment from Administrator and Applicant
- Demonstrated Knowledge

Professional Development
- Teams: Statewide Representation
- National and State Expert Trainers
- Quality Resources
- Mentoring and Coaching Components
- Implementation Requirements (Action Research)

Figure 2. Statewide Model for Professional Development Project

Analyses were completed for each instructional content area (e.g., algebraic thinking, reading, written expression, etc.) of the EIP project. The results of these searches produced research-based information related to the identified curricular content for two purposes. First, these summaries of research-based instructional practices have been disseminated to Florida educators through a project-sponsored web site, and made available as resources for professional development in specific content areas. Second, members of the Advisory Committee for the EIP project (representing state, local, and community partners) considered the results of these analyses to address needs assessment data for professional development throughout the state. This committee recommended national and local consultants,

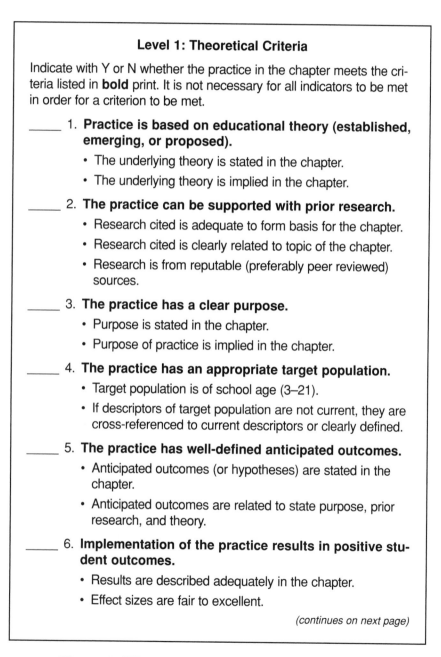

Level 1: Theoretical Criteria

Indicate with Y or N whether the practice in the chapter meets the criteria listed in **bold** print. It is not necessary for all indicators to be met in order for a criterion to be met.

_____ 1. **Practice is based on educational theory (established, emerging, or proposed).**
  - The underlying theory is stated in the chapter.
  - The underlying theory is implied in the chapter.

_____ 2. **The practice can be supported with prior research.**
  - Research cited is adequate to form basis for the chapter.
  - Research cited is clearly related to topic of the chapter.
  - Research is from reputable (preferably peer reviewed) sources.

_____ 3. **The practice has a clear purpose.**
  - Purpose is stated in the chapter.
  - Purpose of practice is implied in the chapter.

_____ 4. **The practice has an appropriate target population.**
  - Target population is of school age (3–21).
  - If descriptors of target population are not current, they are cross-referenced to current descriptors or clearly defined.

_____ 5. **The practice has well-defined anticipated outcomes.**
  - Anticipated outcomes (or hypotheses) are stated in the chapter.
  - Anticipated outcomes are related to state purpose, prior research, and theory.

_____ 6. **Implementation of the practice results in positive student outcomes.**
  - Results are described adequately in the chapter.
  - Effect sizes are fair to excellent.

(continues on next page)

Figure 3. Effective Instructional Practices Criteria

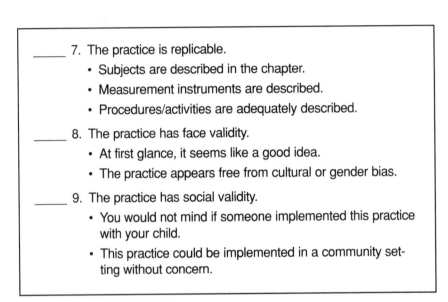

____ 7. The practice is replicable.
   • Subjects are described in the chapter.
   • Measurement instruments are described.
   • Procedures/activities are adequately described.

____ 8. The practice has face validity.
   • At first glance, it seems like a good idea.
   • The practice appears free from cultural or gender bias.

____ 9. The practice has social validity.
   • You would not mind if someone implemented this practice with your child.
   • This practice could be implemented in a community setting without concern.

Figure 3. (continued)

published materials, and instructional practices, based upon the documented local and state needs for professional development of scientifically based instructional practices, in each curricular content area. From these efforts, professional development opportunities of scientifically based instructional practices were scheduled on an annual basis and offered throughout the state of Florida. These instructional practices, materials, and products are the framework for professional development Institutes, ranging from two to five days, depending on content.

Within the content area of phonological awareness, Dr. Joseph Torgesen and Dr. Marilyn Jaeger Adams provided the technical assistance for the resulting three-day Institute. Contents of the Institute included foundational research (Torgesen, 1992), continuum of skills development (Adams, Foorman, Lundberg, & Beeler, 1998), phonemes, (Doyle, 1998), instructional strategies (Adams, et al., 1998), and assessments of phonological awareness (Adams, et al., 1998; Uhry & Shepherd, 1993). Regional mentors were selected due to expertise in speech and language, learning disabilities, and early childhood education.

Step 2: Selection of teams of teachers to participate. As mentioned previously, each scientifically based instructional practice considered for professional development was thoroughly researched. From the annual professional development calendar of various Institutes, local school personnel identified and selected specific practices and/or school-wide initiatives that addressed the specific needs of the students in their schools. Therefore, once the local school personnel identified their needs for professional development, school district personnel nominated teams of educators to address the students' needs by attending and implementing specific professional development deemed necessary within their schools.

Several initial criteria must be met before the nominated applicants are accepted for attendance at the professional development Institute. Teams of applicants, generally consisting of a content area teacher and a special educator, must complete an application detailing their competencies and commitment to implement. Criteria for selection of members of the teams must be met. A letter of support to validate expertise and commitment to classroom implementation from each applicant's administrator must be provided. Applications were screened and evaluated by a panel of content experts. Recommendations were based upon the results of the screening of applications (see Figure #4). Regional applicants with the best summary of scores were recommended to attend the professional development Institute.

Applicants were notified of their acceptance to participate in the initial Professional Development Institute as part of an annual commitment to implement, collect student data, and participate fully with the planned support activities. Therefore, accepted applicants attended a state-sponsored Institute (two to five days) of professional development in a particular content area (e.g., Phonological Awareness, BALANCE reading, algebraic thinking, etc.), received coaching within their school during implementation, and collected data regarding the impact of implementation on students. If professional development is to be re-conceptualized as a process and not an event, it is critical to state clear expectations before the initiation of the professional development.

Accepted applicants for the Phonological Awareness Institute represented teachers of students with and without disabilities throughout the state of Florida in early elementary school classrooms. The teams consisted of kindergarten and early elementary education teachers, special education teachers, speech clinicians, and program specialists who demonstrated awareness level competencies in the area of phonological awareness and had local support for implementation from a local administrator.

Quality implementation and data collection through classroom-based action research were integral components to this research-into-practice professional development model, and comprise the third and fourth steps of this model.

TABLE 4
Team Selection Criteria for "Train the Trainers"

Phonological Awareness					
Eligibility/Criteria	**5** meets criteria beyond expecta-tion	**4** fully meets criteria	**3** meets minimum criteria	**2** does not meet criteria	**1** not included: no mention
1. Member of a 2 person local team (classroom-based/staff development-based)					
2. Documented attendance at overview sessions of Phonological Awareness					
3. Documented implemen-tation of Phonological Awareness					
4. Documented student results of implementa-tion of Phonological Awareness					
5. Successful staff development/training experience					
6. Documented commitment and opportunity for providing further training					
7. Documented personal knowledge and commit-ment to Phonological Awareness					

TABLE 4 (continued)					
Phonological Awareness					
Eligibility/Criteria	5 meets criteria beyond expecta-tion	4 fully meets criteria	3 meets minimum criteria	2 does not meet criteria	1 not included: no mention
8. Documented supervisor support of applicant's knowledge, communication and training					
9. Documented supervisor support of further training opportunities					
10. Packet complete, on-time, well-written					

Step 3: Classroom implementation. National researchers and state and regional content experts/mentors, representing teachers, administrators, curricular specialists, and EIP project staff, developed the Institutes using the knowledge of effective professional development and adult learning theory (e.g., modeling the instructional practice, providing time for processing and practicing, delivering necessary materials.). The emphasis of the resulting professional development Institute is the most current, scientifically based, instructional practices in a specific content area demonstrated with the highest quality materials and practices. At the initial professional development Institute, regional mentors and coaches model and guide the participants through learning the content and discussing its application within their classrooms. At a final action planning session at the Institute, the mentors, coaches, and participants develop specific action plans for implementation and data collection. Electronic and mail networks are created and discussed regarding the long-term follow-up required of the implementation. Each participant leaves with a co-constructed specific plan of action for implementation and student data collection. This plan of action details a

checklist of follow-up activities to complete, criteria to master during coaching sessions, and specific data to collect during implementation. The action plans are developed to insure treatment validity of the scientifically based instructional practices. Participants, regional coaches, and EIP project staff use the same data collection forms during this process.

Research studies in the area of professional development support the need for obtaining a clear picture of the new instructional practice as implemented in the classroom, specific direction and materials for initial implementation, and on-going peer coaching (Fullan, 1993, 1995; Fullan & Hargraves, 1992: Glickman, 1993; Joyce, 1990; Sparks & Loucks-Horsley, 2002). Incorporating peer coaching into the professional development design dramatically increases the implementation of the content of the training (Joyce & Showers, 1988). In a previous investigation of teachers who participated in professional development workshops but did not receive follow-up peer coaching, it was found that only ten percent implemented the instructional strategy (Florida Department of Education, 1999). Therefore, the need to carefully plan the entire process of initiating, implementing, and impacting the results of student learning is very important to this re-conceptualized professional development model.

Project staff, local mentors, and graduate students support and monitor the completion of the agreed-upon implementation plan. Mentors and peer coaches, who have received training in effective cognitive and peer coaching procedures (Garmston, 1987; Joyce & Showers, 1988), meet with and coach the participants early in the implementation process. Feedback is provided, both in person and electronically, to assist problem-solving early implementation issues. Specific support and follow-up sessions, phone calls, and observations occur throughout the next year to support the quality implementation of the initiative. Coaches and project staff observe the teachers in their classrooms and schools to provide support and feedback regarding the implementation of the professional development initiatives. To ensure quality implementation and reliability checks of intervention integrity, observational checklists (see Figure 5) of critical teaching behaviors are used during coaching (Carnine, 1999; Moats, 2002). These checklists have been developed in collaboration with the national and state researchers and outline critical teaching behaviors necessary for high quality implementation during classroom instruction. Through this process, the coaches and mentors insure the quality components of the scientifically based instructional practices are demonstrated.

The integrity of the implementation of the intervention (professional development initiative) is evaluated before student data are collected. Coaching by mentors and EIP staff members occurs and feedback is provided to the teachers. Therefore, quality implementation, as measured

TABLE 5 **Expected Teaching Behaviors**					
Name of Teacher: _____ School: _____ Date: _____ Lesson Topic: _____					
Behavior	**5** excellent	**4** above average	**3** expected behavior	**2** not at expected level	**1** not observed
1. Teach fluently					
2. Start class within 1 minute of tardy bell					
3. Obtain a uniform whole group response when such a response is expected					
4. Correct every error and repeat parts when errors occur					
5. Have a 4:1 ratio of positive comments to reprimands					
6. Get all students immediately on task when direction is given					
7. Use instructional materials, as modeled					
Observer's Name _____ Date Shared with Teacher: _____ Comments: _____ _____					

through direct observations of teacher behavior during coaching sessions using the critical teaching behavior checklists, is demonstrated before the next step in this process.

For example, as part of the implementation requirements of the Phonological Awareness Institute, participants read five research chapters, created an audio-tape of phonemes for coaches, kept anecdotal records of implementation and student results, received feedback through coaching at least three times during initial implementation, recorded specific lessons and activities implemented (from the Institute), and collected and analyzed student impact data using format and procedures received during Institute.

Step 4: Data collection of results of student learning. To positively impact student mastery of the general education curriculum, scientifically-based instructional practices must be implemented well, be relatively few in number, and must address actual learning needs for the students within the classroom. Once there is assurance of quality implementation of the professional development initiative, accurate information and conclusions can be drawn from the student data collected through action research and traditional research methods.

Action research is applied research conducted by teachers who want to study something to improve in their own situation (Little, 2001a). Therefore, the teacher is the decision-maker, data collector, and information source for action research within the classroom. Action research is a continuous process of planned inquiry to determine the effects of the implementation of an instructional practice on the outcomes of the students in a classroom (Calhoun, 1994; Little, 2001a; Sagor, 1992). There are four components in action research, which include:

3. Problem formulation (Identifying classroom needs)
4. Implementation of instructional strategy (Achieving high quality implementation in each classroom)
5. Collect and analyze evidence (Collecting student data)
6. Refine and revise the plan (Updating and sharing the results)

Specific information (process, procedures, results, and samples) about action research is presented with each professional development Institute to assist with this data collection and sharing of results. The issues and concerns confronted in the classroom are the problems to be addressed and changed through this research process. Validated assessment instruments, related to the specific instructional practice, are modeled for the Institute participants, as well as made available for classroom use. For example, in the area of phonological awareness, the Yopp-Singer test has a predictive correlation of 0.74 with reading skills, and a reliability of 0.95, is easily administered within the classroom, and produces specific data related to the content of the instructional practices of phonological awareness (phoneme segmentation, for example). This assessment procedure is included for teachers' use to collect student data within their classrooms. Other curriculum-based assessment measures, both norm-referenced and curriculum-based, are included for teachers' use in assessing impact and effects of their instruction. Multiple measures are requested for triangulation of classroom data.

Data collected through this process are analyzed and reported for two purposes: instructional impact on student outcomes within individual classrooms and impact of professional development through the professional development Institutes. Teachers collect evaluation and student impact data with the support of the coaches and project staff through action research. Classroom implementation, student data, and summaries are submitted to the EIP project staff by participants. In addition, project staff collect data across multiple settings through more traditional research methodologies. Specific questions include the overarching issues such as sustainability of the instructional practice, the student impact using a standardized measure, access to and mastery of general education curriculum by students with disabilities, and changes in teacher efficacy through this professional development process.

As schools continue to define and refine instructional practices to meet the needs of each individual student, dissemination of results is important. By utilizing the principles of school improvement and effective professional development focused on student achievement, student impact data, as collected through action research, traditional research, and data collected from large-scale state assessments and sampling, will continue to show improvements.

One venue to share successful school improvement plans is through demonstration sites. Each school within the state of Florida has the opportunity to share the successful results of their school improvement initiatives by addressing the critical components of a demonstration site. Teachers and administrators must complete the requirements of the specific professional development initiative, demonstrate a commitment to train others, and have the time and resources to mentor and train other educators locally and regionally. Demonstration sites, then, serve as regional and/or school district observation and training sites. Regardless of the professional development initiative, the characteristic of documented student improvement over multiple indicators that can be attributed to professional development, quality implementation, and continued improvement must be described.

Results to Date

This research-into-practice professional development model linked to student performance has completed its third full year of implementation. As previously mentioned, there are specific content areas in various phases of implementation within this re-conceptualized professional development model. Teacher satisfaction results, collected through both questionnaires and focus groups, indicate very positive acceptance of this re-conceptualized professional development model. As collected from participants at each of the Institutes, more than 90% of all respondents are "completely satisfied" with the content and process of the professional development Institutes. Requests for each of the professional development Institutes exceed allocated expectations.

Given another of the goals of this research-into-practice professional development model, current data reflect a substantial increase in the quality implementation of scientifically based instructional practices across the state of Florida. During the last year, over two hundred participants attended the Institutes held in Florida in Phonological Awareness. Implementation of new, scientifically based instructional practices is occurring in more than 80% of the classrooms of those who have attended the Institutes, as determined by self-reports and observations of outside evaluators. In addition, in the Phonological Awareness content area, more than 75% of the participants implemented the instructional practices, used the resources supplied, demonstrated high quality implementation (as determined through observations), and collected student impact data using valid and reliable instruments identified by national researchers. Of those who completed all of the requirements with quality and commitment, there are now seventy-nine state-certified regional and local trainers in this content area within the state.

Surveys are sent to participants within one year after initial professional development. With a return rate of 78%, more than half of the school districts within the state of Florida reported the presence of a state-certified trainer in phonological awareness that was a direct result of this initiative. Almost 20,000 students have been reported as receiving the benefits of this professional development Institute in phonological awareness throughout the state of Florida. These students are reported to be with and without disabilities (learning disabilities, speech and language impaired, and educable mentally handicapped, etc.), as well as students who speak English as a second language and students who are gifted. Instruction is reported within special education classrooms for students with disabilities, as well as general education classrooms. Data of student impact are also collected on a statewide basis for each initiative of the EIP project.

Each of the participants in the professional development Institute of Phonological Awareness completed an action research project. Most of the teachers reported the investigation of the effect of directly teaching activities in phonological awareness on students' phoneme awareness. EIP staff members and regional mentors assisted with the data collection and analysis. Teachers administered the assessments in phonological awareness (e.g., Yopp-Singer Test of Phoneme Segmentation) as part of their action research. Overall, for the children with and without disabilities who were mostly in kindergarten and grade one, the mean growth was impressive at both levels and for both groups. Effect sizes, for fall to spring growth, ranged from 0.67 to 0.89. This corresponds to a significant increase of identification, pronunciation, and segmentation of the forty-four phonemes in various locations by the students from pre-testing to post-testing. The fact that the teachers had actually conducted the research and saw that their instruction in scientifically-based strategies in phonological awareness was helping the students become better early readers seemed to have profound effects on the teachers, as evident in their comments in focus group interviews (Little, 2001b). An overview of the results of another study completed by two participants of a Phonological Awareness Institute through their classroom action research is included.

Discussion

Each of the instructional practices is based upon this re-conceptualized professional development model that links teacher learning to students' performance. Not all of the instructional practices are yielding results at each of these levels, to date. Continuous improvement for this research-into-practice model of professional development is continuing to evolve, both in structure and in practice. These initial results, however, assure us that educational change can occur, when:

1. Change is directly related to issues to solve within the classroom,
2. Support is provided for quality implementation,
3. Scientifically-based instructional practices are introduced using principles of adult learning theory; and
4. Change is directly related to student impact.

Current positive results as reported are due to the collaboration of multiple educators within schools, agencies, and content experts and researchers. Clear goals for the content and the process of professional development are developed, monitored and revised through collaborative process focused on quality implementation of scientifically based instructional strategies to improve achievement for all students. Given the comprehensive and ambitious scope of this project, multiple components directly and indirectly impact its efficiency and effectiveness.

The collaboration among educators from the state department, research communities, regional professional development agencies, and local school districts continues to be critical to the continuing implementation of this project. The knowledge, skills, and perspectives from each of these partners enhance the common vision, necessary support, and unique roles contributed by each collaborator. However, this critical component is also the greatest challenge, as multiple systems often struggle to collaborate within a single system. Responsiveness to identified concerns (e.g., need for validated assessments that could be used in large group settings) is very important to continuing the initiative. At times, skills of problem solving and negotiation are important when discussing issues from multiple perspectives. The overarching question that underlies this framework for collaboration continues, "Will this improve student achievement for all students within our current educational system of this school district and within this state?"

As part of the continuous improvement cycle of this EIP project, an external evaluation has begun. The identified areas for the evaluation include: (a) program improvement, (b) policy decisions, (c) accountability, and (d) public relations. Multi-sourced data will be collected through qualitative and quantitative research methodologies to address the evaluation questions. Ultimately, impacting the outcomes of student learning depends upon the results of the interactions of multiple components; therefore, it is critical to constantly and consistently evaluate both the process and the results of comprehensive school reform that are linked to student outcomes. Results obtained through the multiple data sources (students, parents, teachers, administrators, educational service providers, state department representatives, etc.) will further enhance this professional development model. Research questions regarding sustainability of instructional practices will be addressed with this next annual cycle in this project, as well as teacher efficacy.

As stated by Michael Fullan (1995), "professional development must be re-conceptualized as continuous learning, highly integrated with the moral task of making a difference in the lives of diverse students under conditions of somewhat chaotic complexity" (p. 257). Given the chaotic complexity of creating schools for all students, what better time to re-conceptualize professional development to ensure cognitive access through implementation of scientifically based instructional practices within classrooms?

School reform is achieved through the active participation and collaboration among the multiple educators that are directly responsible for the ultimate outcome: improved student learning for all students. Given the complexity within and among educational systems, the need to develop and implement a common framework based upon mutually agreed-upon standards, outcomes, and competencies must be developed (Fullan, 2000). From this framework, each educational partner contributes expertise to meet the identified standards. The resulting collaborative work design and organizational structures among educators of diverse expertise has produced a very effective professional development framework, as evidenced by the increased implementation of research-based practices in the schools and classrooms, as well as the increased mastery of learner objectives by students. Students across the state of Florida are increasing academic skills, as evidenced through multiple measures (state assessments, curriculum-based measures, informal assessments, etc.). As comprehensive school reform continues, the impact of collaboration among the educational partners will result in improved student learning.

REFERENCES

Adams, M., Foorman, B., Lundberg, I., & Beeler, T. (1998). *Phonemic awareness in young children: A classroom curriculum.* Baltimore, MD: Brookes Publishing Co.

Barth, R., S. (1991). *Improving schools from within.* San Francisco: Jossey-Bass.

Calhoun, E. (1994). *How to use action research in the self-renewing school.* Alexandria, VA: Association for Supervision and Curriculum Development.

Carnine, D. (1999). Campaigns for moving research into practice. *Remedial and Special Education 20*(1), 2–6, 35.

Center for Policy Research on the Impact of General and Special Education Reform. (1996). *Standards-based school reform and students with disabilities* (Issue Brief). Alexandria: Center for Policy Research.

Cuban, L. (1996). Myths about changing schools and the case of special education. *Remedial and Special Education, 17,* 75–82.

David, J. L. (1989). *Restructuring in progress: Lessons from pioneering districts.* Washington, D.C.: National Governors' Association.

Doyle, J. (1998). *Phonemic awareness* (Issue Brief). Florida Department of Education. Tallahassee, FL: Author.

Elmore, R. F. (1990). On changing the structure of public schools. In R. F. Elmore (Ed.), *Restructuring schools Pgs 45–53.* San Francisco: Jossey-Bass.

Elmore, R. F., & Burney, D. (1999). Investing in teacher learning: Staff development and instructional improvement. In L. Darling-Hammond & G. Sykes (Eds.), *Teaching as the learning profession: Handbook of policy and practice* (pp. 236–291). San Francisco: Jossey-Bass.

Espin, CF. A., & Deno, S. L. (2000). Research to practice: Views from researchers and practitioners. *Learning Disabilities Research & Practice, 15*(2), 67–69.

Evans, D. W., Harris, D. M., Adeigbola, M., Houston, D., & Argott, L. (1993). Restructuring special education services. *Teacher Education and Special Education, 16*(2), 137–145.

Evans, D., & Panacek-Howell, L. (1995). Restructuring education: National reform in regular education. In J. L. Paul, H. Rosselli, & D. Evans (Eds.), *Integrating school restructuring and special education reform* (pp. 30–42). Ft. Worth: Harcourt Brace.

Florida Department of Education (1999). *Impact of staff development* (Issue Brief). Florida Department of Education. Tallahassee, FL: Author.

Forness, S., Kavale, K.A., Blum, & Lloyd, J. W. (1997). Mega-analysis of meta-analysis: What works in special education and related services: *TEACHING Exceptional Children, 29*(6), 4–9.

Fullan, M. (1993). *Change forces: Probing the depths of educational reform.* London: Falmer Press.

Fullan, M. (1995). The limits and the potential of professional development. In *Professional development in education: New paradigms and practices.* Guskey, T. & Huberman, M. Eds. New York: Teachers College Press.

Fullan, M. (1999). *Change forces: The sequel.* Bristol, PA: Falmer Press.

Fullan, M. (2000). *Leading in a culture of change.* San Francisco: Jossey-Bass.

Fullan, M., & Hargraeves, A. (1992). *What's worth fighting for? Working together for your school.* Toronto, Ontario: Elementary Teachers Federation of Ontario; New York: Teachers College Press.

Fullan, M.G., & Miles, M. B. (1992). Getting reform right: What works and what doesn't. *Phi Delta Kappan. 73,* 745–752.

Garmston, R. (1987). How administrators support peer coaching. *Educational Leadership, 44*(5), 18–26.

Gersten, R., Vaughn, S., Deshler, D., & Schiller, E. (1997). What we know about using research findings: Implications for improving special education practice. *Journal of Learning Disabilities, 30*(5), 466–476.

Gersten, R., Woodward, J., & Morvant, M. (1992). Refining the working knowledge of experienced teachers. *Educational Leadership, 49*(7), 34–38.

Glickman, C. D. (1993). *Renewing America's schools: A guide for school-based action.* San Francisco: Jossey-Bass.

Goodlad, J. (1998). *How teachers teach*. New York, NY: McGraw Hill.

Goodlad, J. I. (1992). On taking school reform seriously. *Phi Delta Kappan*, 232–238.

Goodlad, J. (1984). *A place called school*. New York, NY: McGraw Hill.

Greenwood, C. & Abbott, M. (2001). The research to practice gap in special education. *Teacher Education and Special Education, 24*(4), 276–289.

Guskey, T. R. & Sparks, D. (1996). Exploring the relationship between staff development and improvements in student learning. *Journal of Staff Development, 17*(4), 2–6.

Guskey, T. R. (1998). The age of our accountability. *The Journal of Staff Development, Fall, 19*, 36–44.

Hargraves, A., & Fink, D. (2000). The three dimensions of reform. *Educational Leadership, 57*(5), 30–33.

Huberman, M. (1990). Linkage between researchers and practitioners: A qualitative study. *American Educational Research Journal, 27*(2), 363–391.

Joyce, B. (1990). *Changing school culture through staff development*. The 1990 ASCD Yearbook. Alexandria, VA: The Association for Supervision and Curriculum Development.

Joyce, B. & Showers, B. (1988). *Student achievement through staff development*. New York: Longman.

Kaufmann, J. M. (1993). How we might achieve the radical reform of special education. *Exceptional Children, 60*(1), 6–16.

Little, J. W. (1997). Teacher's professional development in a climate of educational reform. In Fullan, M. *The challenge of school change*. Eds. Arlington Heights, IL: Skylight.

Little, M. E. (2001a). Successful school improvement using classroom-based research. *Florida Educational leadership, 2*, 41–44.

Little, M. E. (2001b). Summative report of EIP project. *Florida Department of Education*. Tallahassee, FL: Author.

Malouf, D. B., & Schiller, E. P. (1995). Practice and research in special education. *Exceptional Children, 61*, 414–424.

Moats, L. (2002). Reading is rocket science. *Reading Teacher. 37*, 112–118.

Murphy, J. (1991). *The landscape of leadership preparation*. Newbury Park, CA: Corwin Press.

National Association of Secondary School Principals (1996). *Breaking ranks: Changing an American institution*. (Issue brief). National Association of Secondary School Principals. Washington, DC: Author.

Sagor, R. (1992). *How to conduct collaborative action research*. Alexandria, VA: Association for Supervision and Curriculum Development.

Senge, P., Combron-McCabe, N., Lucas, T., Dutton, J., & Kleiner, A. (2000). *Schools that learn*. New York: Doubleday.

Sergiovanni, T. J. (1999). *The lifeworld of leadership: Creating culture, community, and personal meaning in our schools.* San Francisco: Jossey-Bass.

Sparks, D., & Loucks-Horsley, S. (2002). *Five models of staff development for teachers.* Oxford, OH: The National Staff Development Council.

Torgesen, J. (1992). Effects of two types of phonological awareness training on word learning in kindergarten children. *Journal of Educational Psychology, 84,* 364–370.

Uhry, J., & Shepherd, M. (1993). Segmentation/spelling instruction as part of a first-grade reading program: Effects on several measures of reading. *Reading Research Quarterly, 28,* 218–233.

Summary

Alan Reiman

Converging Developments in Professional Development: Implications and Reflections

Throughout my response, I will refer to the three articles you have just read using the name of the authors. I begin by summarizing how findings from the three papers converge with the research presented in the introduction. Additionally, I discuss each of the models for teacher professional development as introduced in the papers. Finally, I raise two questions for further reflection.

CONVERGENCE WITH PRIOR RESEARCH

Guskey and Sparks propose a theoretical model of the relationships between professional development activities for educators and improvements in student learning outcomes. Their model is examined through five in-depth case studies of school-based professional development programs. Consistent with prior research, their model acknowledges that a comprehensive approach to professional development and student outcomes is needed. Likewise, their analysis confirms the importance of programming that is school-based and sustained. The use of case studies is intentional. Guskey and Sparks worked to corroborate the theoretical model with its focus on content, context, and process characteristics. In this regard, it would have been helpful if the authors had made more explicit connections between the case study findings and their posed theoretical model.

Examination of "insufficient" programs offered evidence of lack of administrative support, lack of follow-up, and lack of evidence of "demonstrable improvements in student learning outcomes." These findings converge with prior research which indicates that few professional development interventions have had detectable effects on classroom instruction and student learning. To their credit, Guskey and Sparks focused on changes in student learning outcomes. However, case study data was often insufficient to answer the question of whether there were improvements in student learning. A more extended description of the case studies may have unveiled additional convergence with research trends in the literature. It should be noted as well that a common identified gap in a number of case studies was the lack of careful evaluation. I was reminded of a report by the Association of Teacher Educators entitled: *Distinguished Company* (1991). In this report, the Association reported distinguished school-university professional development initiatives with over 10 years of implementation experience. Although there were many commonalities between these programs and the prior research described (e.g., collaboration, relating theory to practice, active learning focus), the common deficiency of most programs was evaluation.

As the reader should now recognize, there are many ways to construct models of professional development. Guskey and Sparks have chosen an approach that is both comprehensive and expansive. Rather than specifying only processes for professional development, they propose a model that also attends to content and contextual characteristics of the learners, schools, and caregivers. Admittedly, this is an ambitious agenda, yet it does have profound implications for the way professional development is conceptualized and assessed.

The Little paper reports a statewide professional development program that encourages teachers to implement research-based instructional practices in the classroom. Although Little did not initiate and report research evidence per se, she makes use of research findings as a part of the professional development model. As well, Little briefly summarizes evaluation data from the "research-into-practice professional development model." How does this program with its related evidence converge with prior findings on professional development? First, the program has worked to implement more continuous and cumulative forms of professional development. As well, active learning appears to be included in this statewide initiative. The active learning process includes peer coaching and teacher action research. It is laudable that the program emphasizes both teacher demonstration and demonstration sites. "Each school within the state of Florida has the opportunity to share the successful results of their school improvement initiatives by addressing the critical components of a demonstration site." The program also focuses on specific instructional approaches and how practice has a larger effect on student achievement outcomes. However, it is not clear whether the EIP project also examines the role of content knowledge in student achievement. Prior research has underscored that professional development should attend to content knowledge, instructional practice, and teacher cognition. This project is still underway, and more evidence is forthcoming regarding sustainability of the program.

Denner, Norman, Salzman, Pankratz, and Evans report findings from an eleven-university initiative called the Renaissance Partnership. In contrast to the other two papers, which focus on theoretical and conceptual model design, the Denner et al. paper investigates a measure (i.e., teacher work sample) for demonstrating teacher candidates' abilities to meet targeted teaching standards. As such, the authors tackle the empirical challenges of establishing validity, inter-rater reliability, correlations to other measures and standards such as INTASC, and generalizability of an assessment of teacher performance system (Renaissance Teacher Work Sample—RTWS). They argue that teacher education needs more robust systems for assessing relationships between teacher performance and student learning. The RTWS requires teacher candidates to produce a 20-page narrative, plus charts portraying a culminating teaching performance. Drawing on evidence from two large teacher candidate samples (N = 110 and N=87), the study had three goals: (1) to determine score generalizability for the performance scores derived from each of the RTWS scoring rubrics; (2) to investigate the validity of the RTWS as a measure of actual teaching behaviors and as a measure of national teaching standards; and (3) to evaluate the degree to which performances on the RTWS provided quality assessment evidence for student learning. Given these goals, the Denner et al. paper is more narrowly focused on the assessment of culminating professional development for teacher candidates. Finally, it should be noted that our profession needs to see the evolution of more genuine and evidence-based practices. The Little paper describes how such evidence-based practices can be fostered. Consequently, I look forward to the next series of reports on this program.

Perhaps the major point of convergence between the Denner et al. paper and the summary of research trends in professional development is its focus on the relationships between teacher work samples and student learning outcomes. The member institutions pledged to advance a paradigm shift from a focus on the teaching process to a focus on learning results and connecting teacher performance to student learning. Their jointly developed model identifies seven teaching processes as essential to facilitating the learning of all students: (1) using contextual factors to plan instruction, (2) selecting learning goals, (3) developing an assessment plan, (4) designing instruction, (5) making instructional decisions, (6) analyzing student learning, and (7) reflecting on the teaching and learning process. They have begun the painstaking process of examining the strength (or weakness) of relationships between teaching performance work samples and student learning. This is important work for teacher educators, even as it occurs during one of the most puzzling times for teacher education in our country. Though we now have efforts like the Renaissance Group, the National Board for Professional Teaching Standards (NBPTS), and the Interstate New Teacher Assessment and Support Consortium (INTASC) undertaking major research and professional development to make clearer what teaching requires in terms of knowledge, dispositions, and performance, some in the alternative preparation movement have been arguing that a teacher needs little more than a bachelor's degree and a satisfactory score on a test as a "passport" to the school and classroom.

IMPLICATIONS OF MODELS OF PROFESSIONAL DEVELOPMENT

To the credit of all authors, they have presented clear conceptualizations of what teachers need in teacher education and ongoing professional development, and they have begun the next generation of model building and research required to connect theory and practice. In each of the papers there is a deliberative examination of context, knowledge, and process/practice. What can be said about the models presented? Guskey and Sparks propose a theoretical model of the relationships between professional development activities for educators and improvements in student learning outcomes noting "the model presented extends the work of current researchers by considering the relevance of specific contextual factors as well as content characteristics and process variables." It is the most expansive of models, and it incorporates significant direct and indirect effects, including that of district and school administrators and parents. The model is clear in structure and identifies potential causal links.

In contrast to the Guskey and Sparks model which emphasis content, context, and process variables, the EIP model focuses more on context (e.g., research-based effective instructional practices) and process characteristics (e.g., peer coaching and action research). It is most similar to the "observer/assessment" model (Sparks & Loucks-Horsley, 1990). The challenges of this model are the need for high quality teacher demonstration, the need for multiple episodes of coaching, and the need to link the approach to school, school system, and state improvement and contextual issues. Little's commentary suggests that these contextual issues are being addressed. The EIP model does mention selection criteria, state curriculum, district goals, and the need for letters of support/commitment from administrators and applicants, suggesting that the model is responsive to contextual variables. Like the Guskey and Sparks model, Little's model is quite expansive.

However, it gives no attention to the role that policy and parents contribute to our understanding of teacher professional development.

In the spirit of inquiry, I offer two questions for the authors to ponder. The first question is, "Should teacher dispositions be integrated into these models?" In 1998 Edith Guyton wrote an article entitled: "Teacher Cognition, Constructivist Teacher Education, and the Ethical and Social Implications of Schooling" for Teacher Education Yearbook VI. In that work, she insisted that constructivist teacher education must concern itself with how to foster knowledge, performance, and dispositions of teacher candidates. Similar calls have been raised by INTASC and NBPTS, and my own work has examined the role of dispositions in teacher professional judgment and action.

As to the second question, what is the aim of professional development in each model? What do these models intimate about the higher purposes of education? Are they in any way associated to an aim of the development of democratic and ethical character? Thomas Jefferson envisioned democracy and education as interdependent, noting that the mission of publicly supported schools should be to become powerful and proactive citizens of the larger democratic society. Similarly, John Goodlad (1999) has noted that any definition of education invariably contains two components: the individual and the cultural surround. "The self is to develop with responsibility to this cultural surround—civility toward others and support to *civitas* (a body of people constituting a politically organized community)" (p. 1, 1999). As he notes, the moral implications of this mission for educators and their profession abound.

I raise the question of aims because many current discussions about public school and teacher professional development reform omit the most fundamental of reasons for public schools and teacher education programs to exist. Many current policy discussions encourage us to focus on the shortcomings of student performance or the inadequacies of teacher education. Yet, we must remember that all school interactions and all teacher professional development interactions can help or hinder the learning and development of all students, teacher candidates, and professional educators, toward assuming thoughtful and responsible places in society and profession. Learning to teach is a complex undertaking. Facilitating such learning and development through professional programs is an extraordinary challenge. It deserves more than marginal professional preparation or "quick fix" professional development programs. Each of the three papers illustrates the complexity of this enterprise.

REFERENCES

Edelfelt, R. (1991). *Distinguished company.* Reston, VA: Association of Teacher Educators.

Goodlad, J. I. (1999). Educating teachers: Getting it right the first time. In R. Roth (Ed.), *The role of the university in the preparation of teachers* (pp. 1–12). Philadelphia, PA: Falmer Press.

Guyton, E. M. (1998). Teacher cognition, constructivist teacher education, and the ethical and social implications of schooling: Overview and framework. In D. J. McIntyre and D. M. Byrd (Eds.), *Strategies for career-long teacher education* (pp. 1–10). Thousand Oaks, CA: Corwin Press.

Division

2

Methods of Making Connection between Teacher Education and Student Learning

Overview and Framework

Gwendolyn T. Benson

Dr. Gwen Benson is the Associate Dean and Director of Teacher Education at Georgia State University where she is responsible for overall management of the accreditation process and school partnership initiatives. In addition, she serves at the Director for the Alonzo A. Crim Center for Urban Educational Excellence. Her research focus is teaching in urban settings, teacher recruitment and retention and alternative routes to teacher certification.

The long-neglected relationship between K–12 and postsecondary education is beginning to receive merited attention (Maeroff, Callan & Usdan, 2001). There has long been a disconnect between teacher education and student learning at a number of different levels. Generally K–12 teachers and administrators belong to different professional organizations than teacher education faculty and, for the most part, speak a different language. Both sides speak of standards, student achievement, best practices, and school reform but have not been successful in addressing these issues together.

Many public school people feel that university professors do not spend enough time in the schools and thus are not open to learning more about their selected reform initiatives, student demographics, school culture among other variables, yet the same faculty are preparing teachers to work in their schools. Upon entering the classroom, new teachers are shocked when theory collides with practice.

Fraser (2002) suggests the criticism that education programs were long on theory and short on practice has been answered by linking teacher education programs much more effectively to schools through year-long internships and through the development of a clinical faculty of school-based teacher educators who are truly part of the teacher preparation team. He does state that the teacher educator who has not been in a school in years, the one who advocates "multiple modes of instruction" but only lectures in class, and who is just plain boring, are still all too real. Consequently, in many cases, teacher education has not gained the respect of the K–12 community.

Though teacher educators are making significant progress in the development of systemic partnerships with schools, the question remains, "How do we make the connection between research to practice?" Some would suggest the answer to that question would be through revamping university curriculum, professional development schools, action research and other partnership initiatives between universities and K–12 schools (Darling-Hammond, 1994; Cochran-Smith, 2003; Hart & Teeter, 2002).

Colleges of Education have made significant modifications to their teacher education curriculum in the face of new NCATE Standards, changing K–12 Standards, and Program Standards required by State Accreditation Agencies. NCATE began the move to a performance-based system in the mid-1990s when it included specific expectations for candidate performance in its standards. Performance-based accreditation standards set forth expectations for what teacher candidates at accredited institutions should know and be able to do. The institutions must provide compelling evidence that their candidates know the subject matter they plan to teach and how to teach so that students learn (NCATE, 2002).

Although there are many changes taking place to improve teacher education curriculum, diversity is central to today's quest to develop schools that can demonstrate positive outcomes for all students. The changes in the NCATE Standards include explicit references to addressing issues of diversity, specifically in the design and content of the teacher education curriculum, the quality of instruction for teacher candidates, collaborative relationships with the professional community, the composition of the faculty and teacher candidate body and faculty qualifications (NCATE, 2002).

In the design of the curriculum, it is expected that courses and experiences in professional studies incorporate multicultural and global perspectives, thus enabling candidates to develop meaningful learning experiences for students within the context of students' cultures, language backgrounds, socioeconomic status, communities, and families. Additionally, in addressing the quality of instruction, candidates should be able to reflect knowledge about multicultural education, cultural context, exceptionalities, K–12 curriculum design, instruction, and evaluation.

There is also an expectation of teacher preparation programs that course work will be aligned to standards, including learned society standards, K–12 standards, and NCATE standards. Additionally, because in most states, a teacher licensure examination is required for certification, there should also be alignment between the curriculum and the licensure examination.

As the state of public school education is discussed nationally, the pressure for change is more apparent in our colleges of education, especially considering the number of other agencies entering the teacher preparation arena. The time is right for a more systematic and systemic approach to partnership initiatives that result in improved student achievement.

Over the past 10 years, professional development schools have emerged across the country as a compelling new approach to teacher education (Crocco & Schwartz, 2003). Survey data collected by the Clinical Schools Clearinghouse indicate that between 1994 and 1996, more than 84 partnerships between schools and colleges of teacher education exist across 38 states (American Association of Colleges of Teacher Education Web site, *www.aacte.org/glance.html*). The Holmes Group is one of the many organizations that has encouraged establishment of professional development schools, also known as clinical schools, partner schools, and professional practice schools (Abdal-Haqq, 1998). According to Cochran-Smith (1991) professional development schools provide an opportunity to arrange internships so that students, in collaboration with experienced teachers, can learn to "teach against the grain". The phrase "collaborative resonance" is used to describe programs that foster critical inquiry within a culture of collaboration so that "novices and experienced professionals alike work to learn from, interpret, and ultimately alter day-to-day life of schools" (p. 284). As professional development schools have emerged, action research has commonly been promoted alongside the host of nationwide school reform initiatives associated with restructuring schools, especially those centrally concerned with professional development of school faculty (Crocco, & Schwartz, 2003).

A growing body of research suggests that one way to improve teaching and learning in schools is to involve teachers in doing research in their own classrooms (Casanova, 1989; Darling-Hammond, 1996; Herndon, 1994; Lieberman, 1995; Ogberg & McCutcheon, 1987). This moves into the realm of teacher action research and is defined by Lytle and Cochran-Smith (1990) as "systematic, intentional inquiry by teachers" (p. 83). Action research may enable pre-service teachers to reflect on their professional practice with the goal of improving them. Johnson (1995) provided one definition of action research as the teacher's attempt at "learning from one's own work or behavior by critically examining it" (p. 90). Teacher educators involved in doing action research with pre-service and experienced teachers find that both novice and experienced teachers become more reflective, critical, and analytical about their teaching behaviors in the classroom as they engage in the action research process (Cardelle-Elawar, 1993; Carr & Kemmis, 1986; Henson, 1996; Sparks-Langer, Colton, Pasch, & Starko, 1991). Rosaen and Schram (1997) suggested that future research studies should look at the potential for shared inquiry between novice and experienced teachers to promote professional dialogue about teaching and learning and whether it results in greater learning experiences for both sets of teachers. Research should also be conducted to determine the impact of student achievement.

Numerous governmental and private groups have taken up the issue of teacher quality and teacher preparation as a means of improving the nation's schools. We cannot discuss connections between teacher education and student learning without addressing teacher quality. As defined by the No Child Left Behind legislation (2002), a "highly qualified" teacher is a teacher with full certification, a bachelor's degree, and demonstrated competence in subject knowledge and teaching skills. The question remains, how does being a highly qualified teacher translate to being a good teacher and do we know what makes a good teacher? According to Goldhaber (2002), Tennessee is one of the few states with data systems in place that track teachers over time and link them to their students' achievement scores. A closer look at the Tennessee data indicates that the effectiveness of teachers has more of an influence on student achievement than any other schooling factor. Research as far back as the Equality of Educational Opportunity (the "Coleman Report") concluded that among the various influences that schools and policy makers can control, teacher quality was found to account for a larger portion of the variation in student test scores than all other characteristics of a school (Goldhaber, 2002).

School-university partnerships are fertile ground for developing a variety of initiatives that have the potential to significantly impact K–12 student outcomes. Research in school-university partnerships is crucial but challenging when researchers attempt to make a case for linking the work of teacher education with the outcomes of K–12 students. More importantly, research holds partnerships accountable by describing the impact of collaboration on the preparation of new teachers, the continuing professional development of experienced teachers, and the achievement of K–12 students in the schools where the partnerships are formed (Wiseman & Knight, 2003). Current research does not provide a great deal of evidence about what and how specific K–12 teaching and learning behaviors change as a result of partnerships between schools and universities (Abdal-Haqq, 1998, Book, 1996). A small number of studies have regularly been cited as examples of studies that focus on the impact of school-university partnerships activities on student outcome. The four chapters in this section will focus on methods in teacher education that can make legitimate connections between teacher education and K–12 student learning.

REFERENCES

Abdal-Haqq, Ismat. (1998). *Professional development schools: Weighing the evidence.* Thousand Oaks, CA: Corwin Press.

Book, C. L. (1996). Professional development schools. In J. Sikula (Ed.), *Handbook on research on teacher education* (2nd ed., pp. 194–210). New York: Macmillan.

Cardelle-Elawar, M. (1993). The teacher as researcher in the classroom. *Action in Teacher Education, 15,* 49–57.

Carr, W., & Kemmis, S. (1986). *Becoming critical: Education, knowledge, and action research.* London: Falmer.

Casanova, V. (1989). Research and practice: We can integrate them. *NEA Today, 7*(6), 44–49.

Crocco, B. & Schwartz, S. (2003). Inquiring minds want to know: Action research at a New York City professional development school. *Journal of Teacher Education, 54*(1), 19–29.

Crochran-Smith, M. (1991). Learning to teach against the grain. *Harvard Educational Review, 61*(3), 279–310.

Crochran-Smith, M. (2003). Teaching Quality Matters. *Journal of Teacher Education, 54*(2), 95–98.

Crochran-Smith, M., & Lytle, S.L. (1990). Research on teaching and teacher research: The issues that divide. *Educational Researcher, 19*(2), 2–11.

Darling-Hammond, L. (Ed.). (1994). *Professional development schools: Schools for developing a profession.* New York: Teachers College Press.

Darling-Hammond, L. (1996). The right to learn and the advancement of teaching: Research, policy, and practice for democratic education. *Educational Researcher, 25*(6), 5–17.

Fraser, J. (2002). A tenuous hold. *Education Next, 2*(1), 16–21.

Goldhaber, D. (2002). The mystery of good teaching. *Education Next, 2*(1), 50–55.

Hart, P. D., & Teeter, R. M. (2002). *A national priority: Americans speak on teacher quality.* Princeton, NJ: Educational Testing Service.

Henson. K.T. (1996). Teachers as researchers. In J. Sikula (Ed.), *Handbook on research in teacher education* (pp. 53-64). New York: Macmillan.

Herndon, K. (1994, April). Facilitating teachers' professional growth through action research. Paper presented at the annual meeting of the American Educational Research Association, New Orleans, LA.

Johnson, B. (1995). Why conduct action research? *Teaching and Change, 3*(2), 90–104.

Lieberman, A. (1995). Practices that support teacher development: Transforming conceptions of professional learning. *Phi Delta Kappan, 76*(8), 591–596

Lytle, S.L. & Cochran-Smith, M. (1990). Learning from teacher research: A working typology. *Teachers College Record, 92*(1), 83–103.

Maeroff, G., Callan, P., & Usdan, M. (Eds.). (2002). *The learning connection: New partnership between schools and colleges.* New York: Teacher College Press.

National Council for Accreditation of Teacher Education. (2002). Professional standards for the accreditation of schools, colleges, and departments of education. Washington, DC: Author.

Ogberg, A., & McCutcheon, G. (1987). Teachers' experiences doing action research. *Peabody Journal of Education, 64*(2), 116–127.

Rosaen, C., & Schram, P. (1997). Professional development for beginning teachers through practical inquiry. *Educational Action Research, 5*(2), 255–281.

Sparks-Langer, G. M., Colton, A. B., Pasch, M., & Starko, A. (1991, April). Promoting cognitive, critical, and narrative reflective. Paper presented at the annual meeting of the American Educational Research Association, Chicago, IL.

Wisemen, D. & Knight, S. (2002, January). Rethinking teacher education research structures and approaches: Making linkages between school-university partnerships and PK–12 student outcomes. Paper presented at the American Association of Colleges for Teacher Education, New Orleans. LA.

Documenting Positive Impact on Student Learning
A Pre-Service through Professional Continuum

Barbara Sanders, Dennis Sterner, Randall Michaelis, Sharon Mowry, and Linda Buff

Barbara Sanders is Associate Professor, Secondary Coordinator for School of Education, and Director of Assessment at Whitworth College, Spokane, Washington. Dr. Sanders served as chair of a state committee to design a pedagogy assessment instrument for pre-service teachers, and is involved in researching methods to document impact on student learning.

Dennis W. Sterner is Dean of the School of Education at Whitworth College. He served as president of the Washington Association of Colleges for Teacher Education and was on the Board of Examiners for the National Council for the Accreditation of Teacher Education (NCATE). Dr. Sterner is a governor-appointee to the new state Professional Educator Standards Board.

Randall Michaelis is Associate Professor and Chair of the Department of Teacher Education at Whitworth College. His current focus is on the development of long-term K–12 partnerships and their effect on teacher preparation.

Sharon Mowry is Chair of Graduate Studies in Education at Whitworth College. Her current research interests include review of Standards for Principal preparation and certification in Washington State and how these support effective teacher induction.

Linda Buff is a graduate student at Whitworth College. Her research interests include school reform measures in Washington State.

ABSTRACT

Teacher education programs are reforming in response to changing national and state standards. The National Council for the Accreditation of Teacher Education (NCATE) and a growing number of state program approval standards require teacher candidates to demonstrate competency by documenting that their teaching has a "positive impact on student learning." This article describes the evolution of this concept and how three teacher preparation programs are changing in order to satisfy this new requirement at a liberal arts college. The programs studied include a pre-service undergraduate program, a pre-service graduate program, and an in-service continuing certification program. The methods described to document the positive impact of candidates on their students' learning include (a) teacher work sample methodology, (b) action research projects, and (c) positive impact products. The article also discusses some of the concerns raised about the validity and ethics of basing preservice and in-service teacher evaluations on student achievement.

Introduction

Teacher education reform is influenced by both national and state standards; with organizations prescribing specific accountability measures that must be integral to teacher preparation programs (Interstate New Teacher Assessment and Support Consortium, 1992; National Council for Accreditation of Teacher Education, 2002; Washington Administrative Code, 1993). These accountability standards reflect a shift in teacher education. Formerly, standards focused on the candidate's completion of courses and practicum experiences. The new standards emphasize the impact of the candidate's teaching on K–12 student learning.

The impetus for education reform in Washington State occurred with the 1993 legislative mandate (ESHB 1209) and 1997 adoption of new K–12 student learning standards, called Essential Academic Learning Requirements (EALRs). In 1994, the Washington Association of Colleges for Teacher Education (WACTE) was asked by the State Board of Education to revise program approval standards to make them less burdensome and more consistent with K–12 goals (Partnership for Excellence in Teaching, 2000). That effort was the first step in the change process for teacher preparation programs that has included: new standards for residency (initial) certification; new standards for professional (continuing) certification; requirements for candidates to demonstrate a "positive impact on student learning"; performance competencies for all endorsements; teacher testing for basic skills and content; and the collaborative development by all Washington State teacher preparation institutions of a pedagogy assessment instrument.

There was one major organizational change that took place in Washington State as part of the reform of educator preparation standards. The Professional Educator Standards Board (PESB) was created by the legislature and given authority for alternative certification and teacher testing. The board also replaced several advisory committees and is now the sole external advisory body for the State Board of Education on matters related to educator preparation.

The education reforms in Washington State require teacher candidates to document "a *positive impact on student learning* which means that a teacher through instruction and assessment has been able to document students' increased knowledge and/or demonstration of a skill or skills related to the state goals and/or essential academic learning requirements" (Washington Administrative Code 180-7A-00). NCATE Standards have similar language requiring a *positive effect* on student learning. In this article, *impact* and *effect* are used synonymously. Such documentation requires teacher education programs to develop new models of pre-service teacher accountability. In addition, in order for in-service teachers to receive continuing certification (the Professional Certificate) in Washington State, they must provide evidence of their competency, including documentation of positive impact on student learning.

Statement of Purpose

This paper reviews the changing national and state standards that influence teacher education reform, describing the emergence of the requirement for teacher candidates to "document positive impact on student learning." Three models for documenting positive impact are presented: a pre-service undergraduate program, a pre-service graduate program, and an in-service continuing certification program.

Literature Review

POSITIVE IMPACT ON STUDENT LEARNING

In recent decades, education has been restructured to be more student-centered, foster higher-level thinking, address diversity, and consider the holistic needs of students. Conventional methods of teacher evaluation were inadequate to assess the new complexities of teaching (Weiss & Weiss, 1998). In 1987 the National Board for Professional Teaching Standards (NBPTS) was created and produced five propositions to describe good teaching. The Interstate New Teacher Assessment and Support Consortium (INTASC) was a collaborative effort of several states to take the NBPTS propositions a step further. In 1992 INTASC published "model standards" outlining the knowledge, skills and dispositions required for teacher licensing and development. The National Council for the Accreditation of Teacher Education (NCATE) incorporated these ideas in their 2000 Unit Standards (Darling-Hammond, 1999). Teacher certification programs have continually adjusted their programs to adhere to NCATE's performance-based standards.

The standards created by these organizations represent a shift from input-driven evaluation, in which teacher candidates complete prescribed courses, to performance-based evaluation, in which candidates are required to demonstrate competency (Harris, Terrell, & Russell, 1997; Loacker & Mentkowski, 1993; Stiggins, 2001). More recently, the demonstration of competency has expanded to candidates' documenting that their teaching impacts student learning. The origin of the term "positive impact on student learning" is not well documented in the literature. However, it is clear that Washington State was one of the first to use the phrase, that it has been part of the reform movement in the state since the early 1990's, and that the phrase is currently a component of Washington State standards for teachers, administrators and counselors.

The concept of "positive impact on student learning" emerges in the progression to performance-based standards described above. In the NBPTS propositions, it is one implicit facet of many. Key ideas included in the propositions are: a commitment to students and their learning, mastery of subject matter and pedagogy, monitoring student learning, reflectivity, and collegiality (NBPTS, n.d.). The INTASC standards implicitly include positive impact, by requiring the use of various assessments to evaluate learning and adjust instruction accordingly, and by describing the teacher as reflective, self-evaluative practitioner (INTASC, 1992).

The requirement to demonstrate positive impact on student learning is specified explicitly in the NCATE Unit Standards. In Standard 1: *Candidate Knowledge, Skills, and Dispositions—Student Learning for Teacher Candidates,* the rubric target states that candidates should have "a positive effect on learning for all students" (p. 16). The emphasis on student learning is further stressed by NCATE Standard 3, where candidates during field experiences should "collect data on student learning, analyze them, reflect on their work, and develop strategies for improving learning" (p. 26).

METHODS TO DOCUMENT IMPACT

Teacher preparation programs are increasingly utilizing performance-based assessment that focuses on student learning. Wilkerson (2000) describes the paradigm shift in Florida programs "from a focus on 'I taught it' to 'I know they learned it because they have demonstrated it'" (p. 5). The goal of Ohio's Shawnee University is to prepare "learning-centered inquiring professionals prepared to have a positive impact on the learning of all students" (Trube & Madden, 2001, p. 7). Performance assessment is also becoming an emphasis of the K–12 schools in which candidates complete their practica. An added dimension of challenge is for candidates to utilize the performance assessment results of their K–12 students to document the impact of their teaching on student learning.

Oregon has emerged as a leading state in the effort to develop methodology to assess teacher candidates' effectiveness in fostering student learning through development of the Teacher Work Sample Methodology (TWSM). Central elements in Oregon's approach to Teacher Work Sampling include: samples of teacher and student work; targets for learning; measures of learning; descriptors of process; descriptors of context; analyses of learning gains; and reflection and next steps (Schalock & Myton, 2002). The Renaissance Partnership for Improving Teacher Quality, a five year partnership of eleven universities and their partner schools (Pankratz, 1999) established further guidelines for prompts and scoring guides for nine elements in a common TWS.

Renaissance Teacher Work Sampling has been used as "a method for assessing teacher candidates' effectiveness in fostering student learning and for evaluating our teacher education program" by the Idaho State University (Harris, Salzman, Frantz, Newsome, & Martin, 2000, p. 6). Pre-service candidates complete two teacher work samples within the education program, one in a junior-level course based on a semester-long half day practicum in a K–12 school, and the second during a senior-level course taken in conjunction with an 18-week student teaching internship. Candidates utilize a nine-step process to demonstrate the alignment of planning, instruction, and assessment, culminating in a written product that includes a "description of the teaching-learning context, list of the achievement targets, rationale for selection of the achievement targets and learning activities, assessment plan, instructional plans, evidence of student learning, and interpretation and reflection on the success of the teaching- learning sequence with regard to future practice and professional development" (Harris, et al., 2000, p. 7).

Another method of documentation of impact on student learning is action research. Practitioners conducting collaborative inquiry into the process of teaching and learning have been termed *action* or *teacher researchers* (Calhoun, 1994; Sagor, 1992; Stringer, 1996;). The process of action research allows practitioners to identify areas that affect student learning (curriculum, instructional methods, classroom organization), develop a research plan to gather information, analyze collected data, reflect on, and discuss results with peers, and implement changes based on results (Mills, 2000; Robin & Zeichner, 1999). Integrating action research into pre-service education programs has received increased attention in the last decade (Burnaford, Fischer & Hobson, 1996; Hamilton & Pinnegar, 1998). With the increased emphasis on training both in-service and pre-service teachers to conduct action research, models are arising that provide structure for pre-service and in-service higher education programs (Balcerzak, 1998; Cochran-Smith, & Lytle, 1999; Noffke & Stevenson, 1995; Sanders & Cherry, 1999; Sanders, Cherry, & Sterner, 2000).

WASHINGTON STATE EFFORTS

Washington State has been active in the initiative to increase the accountability of pre-service teachers through performance based assessment and documentation of positive impact on student learning (Harding & McLain, 1999). The Washington Administrative Code for Knowledge and Skills of pre-service teachers connects K–12 student learning with beginning teacher standards. "Building on the mission to prepare educators who demonstrate a positive impact on student learning based on the Improvement of Student Achievement Act of 1993" (WAC, 1993), the 25 Knowledge and Skills criteria are organized around three primary standards: Foundational Knowledge, Effective Teaching, and Professional Development. Within the Professional Development standard, state approved teacher education programs must provide an opportunity for candidates to reflect on their teaching and its effects on student growth and learning. In implementing the Knowledge and Skills criteria across all 22 teacher preparation programs in Washington, the State Board of Education required all programs in Spring 2000 to present their response to three key questions, asking how future teachers in the program will:

1. Demonstrate their knowledge of the Essential Academic Learning Requirements (EALRs)?
2. Demonstrate their skill in developing curriculum, instruction, and assessments of K–12 students related to the EALRs?
3. Demonstrate the impact of instruction on K–12 student learning?

This statewide emphasis on programmatic alignment with documenting the positive impact on K–12 student learning was further defined when the State Board adopted the definition of positive impact listed in the introductory section of this paper. Washington State is also using a new set of performance-based standards for state approval of programs. The standards contain the NCATE Standards and rubrics with an addition of a standard focused on the state requirement that programs must utilize Professional Education Advisory Boards (PEABs) made up of K–12 teachers and administrators.

In addition, the state is currently in the process of implementing further accountability measures for pre-service candidates. The Professional Educator Standards Board (PESB) was created by state legislation in June 2000. This board of 19 members includes teachers, educational staff associates, administrators, higher education representatives, a parent, and the Superintendent of Public Instruction (ex officio member) and is charged with overseeing the development of basic skills and content tests for pre-service candidates (Sterner, 2001). A pedagogy assessment, field tested in fall 2002 in all Washington teacher education programs, includes both an observation component during the student teaching practicum, and a unit plan evaluation of candidates' skills in planning and reflection on their impact on student learning (Sanders, 2001). All these changes have resulted in the development of multiple program models to document positive impact on student learning, as described below.

Models for Documenting Positive Impact

The following models were developed at a four-year liberal arts college of approximately 2000 students, located in Washington State. The School of Education houses two different programs by which teachers receive initial (residency) certification: the undergraduate education program (90 candidates per year) and the Master in Teaching (MIT) program (50 candidates per year). Each program developed a different approach to demonstrating "positive impact" on student learning. The undergraduate faculty has adapted for the pre-service level three Positive Impact Products that are similar to those required for continuing (professional) certification. The MIT program, an initial certification and masters degree program, chose an action research model by which to show positive impact.

For continuing (professional) certification, a competency-based program was developed by the Department of Graduate Studies in Education. This program requires candidates to complete a "positive impact plan" as one of the products for certification. This plan provides evidence of how the teacher has enhanced student achievement in the classroom.

UNDERGRADUATE: STUDENT TEACHERS AND POSITIVE IMPACT PLANS

Responding to new Washington State certification standards, the undergraduate teacher education faculty has revised the curriculum to ensure that candidates are prepared in their pre-service program to document positive impact on student learning. These skills are further developed as candidates begin their teaching profession and move towards the second level of certification. In the undergraduate program, candidates learn single-subject research design methods in a newly developed course, *Intervention for Behavior and Motivation.* Candidates are initiated into the concept of "positive impact on student learning" through pairing with students with special needs in the schools. Candidates focus on single-subject intervention and assessment strategies, gathering data regarding the progress special needs students make as a result of intensive tutoring. At the end of the semester-long field experience, candidates present their positive impact documentation to their peers.

During their semester-long student teaching, candidates also develop three products based on the Effective Teaching standard that are included in their final standards-based portfolios. The first product is a *Comprehensive Instructional Plan* that describes the plan for teaching content, assessing student understanding, and reflection regarding the learning of students. In developing the second product, a *Positive Impact Plan,* each candidate pretests the entire class on a specific unit of study based on an EALR. The candidate discusses pretest findings with the cooperating teacher, identifies three students at varying levels of ability, analyzes each student's performance, and then designs instruction to meet the needs of each learner. At the conclusion of the unit of study, the candidate posttests the class and analyzes to what extent the instruction affected the identified students' performances. If appropriate, midpoint assessments also occur. The candidate's findings and reflections on instruction and student learning become part of the plan, which in turn is included in the final portfolio and is discussed with the supervisory cohort at the conclusion of student teaching. The Positive Impact Plan is approved by the college supervisor in consultation with the cooperating teacher and is reviewed by the director of student teaching. The final product, the *Professional Growth Plan (PGP),* documents candidate's strengths and growth areas related to the residency certificate and plans for professional development. Prior to student teaching, faculty and candidate-peer teams assess portfolios for documentation of each standard. At the culmination of student teaching, candidates meet with their supervisory cohort groups and present their three products as evidence for meeting each of the state's standards.

MASTERS IN TEACHING: INTERNS DEMONSTRATE POSITIVE IMPACT THROUGH ACTION RESEARCH

Graduate candidates in the Master in Teaching (MIT) program have used action research to study the impact of their teaching on student learning during their student teaching practica. MIT students complete a three-semester course sequence on action research methodology (Introduction to Research, Research Methods, Data Analysis) taught by one faculty member. In the first summer term, candidates learn about the different types of educational research, review past candidates' research projects, and attend the MIT Research and Development Conference where candidates completing the program present their research in a formal setting to peers, mentor teachers, and K–12 school administrators. During fall semester, each candidate works with a mentor teacher to identify a target EALR for instruction and data collection and completes a research proposal. In order to gather valid data about the impact of the instruction on student learning, the candidate develops, in conjunction with the mentor, three instruments for data collection for each dependent variable (targeted EALR), including surveys, questionnaires, observation guides, scoring rubrics, interview guides, quizzes, and tests. Due to the requirement that candidates must present their study results publicly, and because children are involved in the studies, all candidates complete applications for full review from the college Institutional Review Board (IRB). Candidates also are required to receive parental and student permission prior to collecting and presenting data.

During the spring semester student teaching practicum, candidates and mentors gather data regarding student learning, utilizing pre- and post-assessments, surveys, interviews, review of student work, and observations. Data is collected throughout the 15-week practicum and is analyzed using qualitative and quantitative methodology in the final research course. As candidates analyze their data, they can return to their practicum classrooms to gather more data, or seek clarification of any data collected. Often candidates complete post-study interviews and surveys during this time, since they have completed their full-time instructional responsibilities and have time to work one-on-one with students. After analyzing their data, candidates write up the results of their studies. They include figures and tables presenting the data, and a final section of their research reports that include a discussion of the results, conclusions, and recommendations for their own future teaching, application to other classrooms, and recommendations for further research. The culminating report is termed their Action Research Project and is bound and made available in the college library and on-line at the MIT Journal of Action Research. The action research project is presented at the annual MIT Research and Development Conference, held in July at the college. Mentor teachers and administrators are invited to attend this conference to hear the results of action research studies conducted within their classrooms and districts. After each presentation, time is allotted for discussions with peers, mentor teachers, administrators, and faculty as to the study's impact on student learning. Presenting results of a purposeful study of one's teaching practice provides both an avenue to distribute action research findings to a larger audience, and a forum for continued school improvement.

A shift in the MIT program to incorporating action research within a Teacher Work Sample is currently in progress. Candidates use research literature to inform their unit plan designs and develop assessment plans to evaluate their students' learning during the unit. The TWS provides an alternative vehicle for integration of action research methodology within the instruction of the unit plan.

PROFESSIONAL TEACHING CERTIFICATE: CLASSROOM TEACHERS DEMONSTRATE POSITIVE IMPACT

Due to the new certification requirements, higher education institutions in Washington State are also establishing graduate-level programs for teachers to attain the Professional Teaching Certificate (continuing), which normally is completed within five years of their Residency (initial) certification. A partnership with the pre-service teacher preparation programs helps prepare students to move to this Professional Certificate level by laying foundational instruction, practice, and gathering of data during methods, research, and student teaching courses. Candidates may only apply for the Professional Certificate program when they have secured classroom teaching positions in Washington since the Professional Growth Plan must be based on the candidate's particular classroom context. An essential part of the process is the establishment of a Professional Growth Team for each candidate composed of K–12 educators from the candidate's building/district and a higher education representative.

The Professional Certificate programs have consistent components at higher education institutions across the state so that the programs may have portability. The common components are a Pre-assessment Seminar, instruction on the three standards (Effective Teaching; Professional Development; and Leadership) and candidates' developing individualized *Professional Growth Plans;* the individualized implementation of the plan, including college/university courses, district workshops, conference attendance, and in-service classes; and a Culminating Seminar during which candidates provide the portfolio evidence of their competency in the standards. One of the products mandated in the evidence is the *Positive Impact Plan.* This plan must include a rationale, connections to research, a summary of strategies to invite families/students into the learning process, an evaluation of the efficacy of the plan, demonstrated use of technology, and a reflective analysis of learner assessment data. Components of the reflective analysis focus on student assessment performance, connections to the teacher's impact on student learning, impact on future learning plans, appropriateness and clarity of learning goals, and connection to assessment.

At the in-service, Professional Certificate level, rubrics designed by the college in collaboration with K–12 educators determine whether the candidate has demonstrated competency (Darling-Hammond, 2000; Simpson, 2001). The college will only recommend candidates for the Professional Teaching Certificate when they have clearly demonstrated a positive impact on student learning in their classrooms. A rubric developed by Simpson (2001) is being considered in several Washington State school districts as the formal teacher evaluation model for all teachers. Administrators are being trained in the standards and criteria to give classroom teachers valuable feedback about effective classroom practices based on how well students achieved the intended learning targets.

In 2002, the Washington State Board of Education adopted a new certification system for School Administrators that requires principals to demonstrate how their supervision of teachers has enhanced student learning. They further are required to provide evidence of how their own professional development has led to school improvement and to increased student learning.

QUESTIONS OF RELIABILITY AND VALIDITY

The use of TWS in both Idaho and Oregon for teacher licensure and the mandated requirement in Washington for candidates to demonstrate positive impact on student learning, raise the issues of validity and reliability for this method in assessing teachers based on the learning of the students they teach. To improve inter-rater reliability in scoring of the Renaissance TWS, researchers have identified benchmarks or exemplars of performance along the continuum from pre-service to National Board Certified teachers to use in scoring TWS and have standardized the training of raters (Salzman, Denner, Bangert, Arthur, & Harris, 2001). Research conducted at Western Oregon University in the last decade indicated that inter-rater reliability of 81–98% can be achieved between college and school supervisors (Girod, 2002). In addition, extensive research on validity of TWS has resulted in high resolution of face and content validity, indicating that the TWS tasks appear "relevant, familiar, reasonable, and clear to those who complete them" (p. 79), and "the tasks reflect well the domain of knowledge and skills that make up teaching" (p. 80). In addition, construct, consequential and professional validity had partial resolution and indicated that the TWS tasks are "consistent with the roles and responsibilities of teachers and learners . . . result in internalization of the methodology past student teaching . . . and adds to the conception of teachers as professionals" (p. 80–81). An area of validity that requires more investigation is predictive validity, the potential to forecast performance in other settings or at other times.

ETHICAL IMPLICATIONS FOR TEACHER EVALUATION

The practice of documenting positive impact on student learning leads naturally to evaluating teachers based on student achievement instead of teacher behaviors. Although TWS methodology is being adopted by many teacher preparation programs to document impact on student learning, more research is needed to connect pre-service teacher performance and student learning before being utilized in high stakes assessment and program accountability (Denner, Salzman, & Harris, 2002). Several states are measuring teacher quality based on student achievement, termed "Value-Added" assessment systems. The National Education Association is opposed to using measures of student learning for in-service teacher evaluations (Tucker & Stronge, 2001). The issue of linking teacher quality to impact on student learning for purposes of evaluation and accountability will continue to focus attention on pre-service and in-service programs methods of documenting impact on student learning.

Conclusion

FUTURE CHALLENGES

Questions and challenges remain as to the most efficient way to train future teachers to be reflective gatherers and users of student performance data. The three models presented in this paper provide frameworks from which other programs may be developed. Each model requires a paradigm shift changing the focus from the coursework of candidates to the learning of K–12 students. This shift is also necessary for cooperating teachers who were not trained under these models. These mentors will need professional development to assist them in understanding how new teachers gather and use student achievement data to make teaching decisions. College supervisors of pre-service candidates must also be trained to evaluate and make recommendations on candidates' positive impact plans. Thus, teacher preparation programs must include supervisors in professional development. The conversation about documenting positive impact on student learning must expand to include all stakeholders—pre-service and in-service practitioners, higher education faculty, and supervisors.

The changes in teacher preparation described in this paper come with considerable costs for candidates, programs, and the statewide system. Candidates have increased demands on them to collect and analyze data regarding the impact that their teaching has on their students and to provide documentation and evidence that they have met each of the state standards. This is a daunting task for novice teachers trying to complete all of the requisite demands of student teaching. To prevent overloading candidates, faculty members must reconsider the requirements in place to see where adjustments can be made prior to and during student teaching. Similarly, beginning teachers are now required to develop professional growth plans and participate in a high stakes process to acquire the Professional Certificate. This is a new layer of responsibility for the teacher in her/his first five years of experience.

From a systems viewpoint, the requirements placed on faculty in schools, colleges, and departments of education for assessing all of the data being collected by candidates as well as providing training for college supervisors and cooperating teachers has significant resource implications. The Professional Certificate process in Washington State also requires that Professional Growth Teams be in place for each candidate. These teams need to be staffed with higher education and K–12 faculty, with no increase in state funding for K–12 or higher education for the program. Finally, as the level of accountability is increased and "the bar is raised" for people to enter the profession, there is a risk of aggravating the need to prepare more teachers for the schools. The cumulative effect of the changes described above has implications for higher education and K–12 with the possibility of system-wide overload to the extent that the reforms themselves are threatened. Shortly before this article was written, the Washington Education Association submitted a lengthy letter of concern regarding the Professional Certificate process that called for a halt to that process until more resources are provided.

New Responsibilities for
Teacher Education Programs

NCATE standards require teacher education programs to prepare future teachers to conduct reflective, intentional study of the impact of their teaching on student learning. Teacher education programs must re-vision their importance as both training agents and supportive collaborators in preparing graduates to document positive impact. Graduate level continuing certification programs need to align their curriculum and assessments around K–12 student performance, preparing in-service teachers to monitor and adjust their teaching based on student learning. Collaboration is needed among educators at all levels of service to provide a united front of professional development. In this way, a common language and concept of effective teaching will be developed, and *all* teachers will be equipped to study teaching and its impact on learning.

REFERENCES

Balcerzak, P. (1998). *The benefits and challenges of teaching action research to pre-service teachers.* Paper presented at American Educational Research Association, San Diego, CA.

Burnaford, G., Fischer, J., & Hobson, J. (Eds.). (1996). *Teachers doing research: Practical possibilities.* Mahwah, New Jersey: Lawrence Erlbaum Associates.

Calhoun, E. F. (1994). *How to use action research in the self-renewing school.* Alexandria, VI: Association for Supervision and Curriculum Development.

Cochran-Smith, M., & Lytle, S. (1999). The teacher research movement: A decade later. *Educational Researcher, 28*(7), 15–25.

Darling-Hammond, L. (1999). *Reshaping teaching policy, preparation, and practice. Influences of the National Board for Professional Teaching Standards.* New York: American Association of Colleges for Teacher Education.

Darling-Hammond, L. (2000). Teacher quality and student achievement: A review of state policy evidence. *Educational Policy Analysis Archives, 8*(1). Available: *http://www.epaa.asu.edu/epaa/v8n1.*

Denner, P. R., Salzman, S. A., & Harris, L. B. (2002). *Teacher work sample assessment: An accountability method that moves beyond teacher testing to the impact of teacher performance on student learning.* Symposium presented at the American Association of Colleges for Teacher Education. New York. Eric Document Reproduction services No. 463 285.

Girod, G. R. (Ed.) (2002). *Connecting teaching and learning: A handbook for teacher educators on Teacher Work Sample Methodology.* Washington DC: Western Oregon University, AACTE Publications.

Hamilton, M. L., & Pinnegar, S. (1998). Reconceptualizing teaching practice. In M. L. Hamilton (Ed.), *Reconceptualizing teaching practice: Self-study in teacher education* (pp. 1–4). London: Falmer Press.

Harding, E., & McLain, B. (1999, August). *Teacher preparation and development.* Olympia, WA: Washington State Institute for Public Policy.

Harris, L. B., Salzman, S., Frantz, A., Newsome, J., & Martin, M. (2000). *Using accountability measures in the preparation of pre-service teachers to make a difference in the learning of all students.* Paper presented at the Annual Meeting of the American Association of Colleges for Teacher Education, Chicago, IL. Eric Document Reproduction Service No. 440 926.

Harris, L. B., Terrell, S. M., & Russell, P. W. (1997). *Using performance-based assessment to improve teacher education.* Paper presented at the 77th Annual Conference of the Association of Teacher Educators, Washington, D.C. Eric Document Reproduction Service No. 406 346.

Interstate New Teacher Assessment and Support Consortium (1992). *Model standards for beginning teacher licensing and development: A resource for state dialogue.* Washington, D.C.: Council of Chief State School Officers. Eric Document Reproduction Service No. 369 767.

Loacker, F., & Mentkowski, M. (1993). Creating a culture where assessment improves learning. In Banta and Associates. *Making a difference: Outcomes of a decade of assessment in higher education.* San Francisco, CA: Jossey-Bass.

Mills, G. E. (2000). *A guide for the teacher researcher.* Upper Saddle River, NJ: Merrill.

National Board for Professional Teaching Standards. (n.d.). *What teachers should know and be able to do.* Detroit, MI: Author.

National Council for Accreditation of Teacher Education. (2002). *Professional standards for the accreditation of schools, colleges, and departments of education: 2002 edition.* Washington, D.C.: Author.

Noffke, S. E., & Stevenson, R. B. (Eds.). (1995). *Educational action research: Becoming practically critical.* Columbia University: Teachers College Press.

Pankratz, R. (1999, Feb.). *Becoming accountable for the impact of graduates on students and schools: Making operational the shift from teaching to learning.* Concept Paper for Presentation at The American Association of Colleges for Teacher Education Annual Meeting. Washington, D.C..

Partnership for Excellence in Teaching. (2000, Oct.). *The status of teaching in Washington State.* Olympia, WA.: Office of Superintendent of Public Instruction.

Robin, M., & Zeichner, K. (1999). *Guide to practitioner research resources in North America.* Washington, D.C.: National Partnership for Excellence and Accountability in Teaching.

Sagor, R. (1992). *How to conduct collaborative action research.* Alexandria, VA: Association for Supervision and Curriculum Development.

Salzman, S. A., Denner, P. R., Bangert, A. W., & Harris, L. B. (2001). *Connecting teacher performance to the learning of all students: Ethical dimensions of shared responsibility.* Paper presented at the Annual Meeting of the American Association of Colleges for Teacher Education, Dallas, TX. Eric Document Reproduction Services No. 451 182.

Sanders, B. J. (2001, Oct. 5). *Pre-service teacher pedagogy assessment.* Paper presented at the Professional Education Advisory Board Conference: Challenges and Opportunities. Wenatchee, WA.

Sanders, B. J., & Cherry, D. (1999, Fall). Collaborative action research: Pre- and in-service teachers. *AILACTE Views and News,* p. 9–11.

Sanders, B. J., Cherry, D., & Sterner, D. (2000, Feb.). *Accounting for K–12 student learning: Teachers with a vision who study their own practice.* Paper presented at the Association of Independent Liberal Arts Colleges for Teacher Education Annual Meeting. Chicago, IL.

Schalock, H. D., & Myton, D. (2002). Connecting teaching and learning: An introduction to Teacher Work Sample Methodology. In G. R. Girod (Ed.), *Connecting teaching and learning: A handbook for teacher educators on Teacher Work Sample Methodology* (pp. 5–32). Washington, D.C.: AACTE Publications.

Simpson, M. L. (2001, Jan.). *The art and science of professional teaching: A developmental model for demonstrating positive impact on student learning.* Career Standards and Evaluation Project. Office of Superintendent of Public Instruction: Olympia, WA.

Sterner, D. (2001–02, Fall/Winter). The two Washingtons: Accountability in teacher education—New federal and state requirements. *Curriculum In Context: Journal of the Washington State Association for Supervision and Curriculum Development, 28*(2), 5–6.

Stiggins, R. J. (2001). *Student-involved classroom assessment* (3rd ed.). Upper Saddle River, NJ: Merrill Prentice Hall.

Stringer, E. (1996). *Action research: A handbook for practitioners.* Thousand Oaks, CA: Sage Publications.

Trube, M. B., & Madden, P. M. (2001, March). *National standards, state goals, and the university's vision align to provide a framework for the pre-service teacher portfolio.* Paper presented at the Annual Meeting of the American Association of Colleges for Teacher Education. Dallas. TX. Eric Document Reproduction Service No. 454 169.

Tucker, P. D., & Stronge, J. H. (2001, September). Measure for measure. Using student test results in teacher evaluations. *American School Board Journal, 188*(9), 34–37.

Washington Administrative Code. (1993). Office of Superintendent of Public Instruction. Olympia, WA.

Weiss, E., & Weiss, S. (1998). *New directions in teacher evaluation. ERIC Digest, 97*(9), 3–4. Eric Document Reproduction Service No. 429 052.

Wilkerson, J. R. (2000, February). *Standards-based accountability as a tool for making a difference in student learning: A state and an institutional perspective on standards-based accountability.* Paper presented at the Annual Meeting of the American Association of Colleges for Teacher Education. Chicago, IL. Eric Document Reproduction Service No. 440 067.

5.

Teachers' Mathematics Preparation and Student Learning of Elementary School Mathematics*

Frank. B. Murray, James Raths, and Yanwei Zhang

Frank B. Murray is H. Rodney Sharp Professor in the School of Education and Department of Psychology at the University of Delaware where he served as dean of the College of Education. He is also President of the Teacher Education Accreditation Council (TEAC) in Washington, DC.

James Raths, former dean of education at the University of Vermont, is a professor at the University of Delaware.

Yanwei Zhang is a doctoral student in the School of Education at the University of Delaware.

We know that elementary teachers vary in their backgrounds in mathematics, with some elementary teachers having solid preparation in mathematics, ranging from an undergraduate major in mathematics for some, to only a few courses in mathematics in high school or college for others. We know also that elementary school students vary significantly in their mathematics achievement, but we don't know whether there is a link between the strength of teachers' preparation in mathematics and their students' achievement in elementary mathematics.

*Primary funding for this study came from the Office of Educational Research and Improvement, U.S. Department of Education, under contract number RD97124001. The opinions expressed herein may not necessarily reflect the positions or policies of the Association of Teacher Educators.

Such a link has been asserted in the recently enacted *No Child Left Behind Act* (2001) as the primary purpose of teacher education. In the language of this act, one of the salient characteristics of a qualified teacher is the passing of a subject matter test. Prior to the enactment of the *No Child Left Behind Act*, the American Mathematical Society issued a report that called for teachers having a "solid understanding of the mathematics they teach" (CBMS, 2000, p. 3). The research to support this injunction is found in part in the qualitative work of Ma (1999) and Ball (1991) and the quantitative studies of Monk (1994) and Monk & King (1994). These studies and others support the claim that knowledge of subject matter is an important variable in accounting for variance between more effective and less effective elementary school teachers.

In 1998, Delaware initiated a statewide assessment of student learning in reading, writing, and mathematics (the Delaware Student Testing Program, DSTP), as a response to the Delaware standards movement that began in 1991 and to the adoption of content standards for all major school subjects in 1995. Each year since 1998, Delaware's public school students in grades 3, 5, 8, and 10 are tested in reading, writing, and mathematics. Five waves of data have been collected (1998–2002), which include both student test scores and key demographic information about the students. The release of the year 2000 data provided the first chance to study a specific longitudinal cohort, namely, the 3rd graders tested in 1998 who were tested again in 2000 as fifth graders.

There were 8,061 third grade students from 66 schools in Delaware who took the test in 1998, and there were 8,066 fifth grade students from 43 schools who took the test in 2000. Of these, nested in 43 schools, 6872 students took both the 5th grade test in 2000 and the 3rd grade test in 1998.

Our study primarily addressed the following research question: What is the relationship between the strength of teachers' mathematical backgrounds and the improvement from third to fifth grade in mathematics performance of their school's to students?

Method

SAMPLING SCHOOLS

Of all the measures collected by the state, we found that the Grade 3 scores were the most significant predictor of the Grade 5 scores ($r = .79$, $p < .001$) and alone accounted for up to 63% of the variance of the latter. Since the differences in student characteristics were already reflected in the variation in Grade 3 scores, we used the residuals of the Grade 5 mathematics scores regressed on the Grade 3 scores to stand for estimates of improvement in mathematics achievement from Grade 3 to Grade 5.

Because the database available to us did not provide information on the specific classrooms the students came from within a school, we used schools as the unit of analysis. For each of the 43 schools that had fifth graders who also took the test as third graders, we calculated the percentage of students whose change scores, or improvements, were two standard deviations or more above or below the state mean change score. In only sixteen schools did more than 5% of the students gain more than two standard deviations or lose more than two standard deviations in terms of the change scores. These 16 schools were distributed in 10 out of the16 school districts in Delaware.

Most of the schools did not have both grades three and five, the Delaware pattern being schools with grades K–3 or schools with grades 4–6. We found three schools in the Lenape School District (a fictitious name) that had both grade three and five in the same school and also had more than 5% of their students above or below two standard deviations of the State mean. Two were high performing schools (School A and School B) in this regard, and one was a low performing school (School C). Because these schools have students at all three grades (3, 4, and 5), it is possible to estimate the accumulative teacher effect on the school level gains (or losses) experienced by these schools. By focusing on schools from a single school district, we eliminated the small but real between-district variance we also found in students' mathematics scores. Also, these three schools did not suffer unduly from the shifts in school attendance and mobility patterns that plague research into gains in student achievement from one grade to another. On average, 90% of the Grade 3 students in the schools remained through Grade 5 (See Table 1).

SAMPLING PERFORMANCE

Among the three schools, 15.6% of School A's students performed two standard deviations above the mean of residual gains and had an average gain score of 32.46 on a test with scores that ranged from 150–800. School B had 6.9% of its students with residual gain scores two standard deviations above the State mean, and its average residual gain score was 15.30. In contrast, 5.5% of School C's students had residual scores two standard deviations below the state mean, and the school residual average loss was –13.89. The demographic information about the three schools can be found in Table 1.

In 2001 Delaware established four math performance levels: below standard (424), meets standard (449), exceeds (503), and distinguished (525). Between grades 3 and 5 slightly more than half the district's students showed no change in performance level from 1998 to 2000, while about 34%

TABLE 1

Numbers or Percentages of Students from Schools A, B, and C in Each Category and Other Characteristics of Each School

Category	School A	School B	School C
Number of Grade 5 Students	32	87	55
African-American Students	40.6%	8.0%	47.3%
Low Income Students	42.9%	17.2%	58.4%
Special Education Students	21.9%	16.1%	36.2%
Male Students	62.5%	55.2%	58.2%
Students per Teacher	16.2	14.7	12.3
Number of Grade 3–5 Teachers	7	15	7
Mean Teachers' Age	38.43	41.07	46.57
Grade 5 Students Who Were Also Grade 3 Students	90.0%	94.3%	87.3%

gained in performance level and 13% lost ground in the same period. While the mean performance of Schools A, B, and C differed, with B outperforming A and C, the mean scores of the three schools fell within the state "meets standard" level of performance for the fifth grade.

Teacher Background

The analysis of teacher background effects on the residual gain scores from Grade 3 to Grade 5 included the teachers of all three grades (3, 4, & 5) as presumably they all contributed to gains or losses in mathematics achievement from grades 3 to 5. There were 29 teachers, all female (15 from School B, 7 from School A, and 7 from School C), who taught in grades 3, 4, and 5. Their undergraduate and graduate (when applicable) transcripts were coded and compared to search for possible differences in teachers' academic backgrounds, averaged within schools, and their relationships to the school level performances of students, on average, in terms of residual gain scores on the DSTP from Grade 3 to 5.

To learn about the strengths of the mathematics backgrounds of the teachers in the three schools selected for study, a research team visited the Delaware Department of Education to carry out a documents analysis for the 29 teachers. The teachers' files were made available to us, after our procedures had been approved by the University of Delaware Human Subjects Review Committee and the appropriate administrators at the Delaware Department of Education. The 29 teachers represented a wide variety of ages, and the data included in their Department of Education files differed substantially from the older teachers to the younger teachers. For example, almost all of the younger teachers had records of having taken the PRAXIS 1 or PPST tests. None of the older teachers was required to take any license examination when they were hired. In summary, our data collection effort provided us with interesting evidence bearing on the strengths of the mathematical backgrounds of teachers, but for the older teachers the records were incomplete. Our analysis of the records yielded evidence for the following variables related to the strength of their mathematical backgrounds (See Table 2).

Table 2
Variables Related to Strength of Mathematical Backgrounds

Variable	Abbreviation	Elaboration
Praxis or PPST Mathematics Score	PPST Mathematics	A standardized test score of high school mathematics ability
Mathematics credits earned in UG Program	UG Math Credits	The count of all mathematics credits reported on college transcripts at the UG program.
GPA in Mathematics earned in UG Program	MATH GPA-UG	Grade point average on a 4-point scale

Results

The evidence on three variables, the teachers' PRAXIS Mathematics scores, number of mathematics credits, and undergraduate mathematics grade point index, are described in Table 2. The means and standard deviation for each variable are presented in Table 3 for each school. The null hypothesis for each variable was that the means of Schools A, B, and C were not different from each other. The findings are reported in Table 3.

The only significant difference ($p < .05$) among the three schools was the average number of college mathematics credits earned by the teachers. Post hoc comparisons showed that the School B teachers had significantly more mathematics credits ($p < .05$) than those of the School C teachers. The difference in the number of mathematics credits was not significant between School A and School B, or between School A and School C. When the two high performing schools (School A and School B) were combined, however, the difference in the number of math credits taken by the teachers between them and School C was significant ($t = 2.06$, $p < .05$) (See Table 3).

In terms of student background (Table 1), School B had significantly lower proportions of students who were African-American, low-income, or in special education than the other two schools (Chi-square, $p < .05$). The differences in the proportions of minority, low income, and special education students between School A and School C were not significant. Collectively the differences in the variables in Table 1 between School A and School C were also insignificant (Sign test, $p > .05$), although five of the seven variables associated with greater school math achievement favored School A (viz., proportions of minority, low SES, and special education students, males, and proportions of fifth graders who were third graders in the same school).

We extended our analysis of the teachers' backgrounds in School A and C by examining evidence not directly related to the strength of their mathematics backgrounds. We examined such variables as holding masters' degrees, years since masters' degrees, number of graduate credits, and others. This evidence of professional development and experience was taken from teachers' files as part of the document analysis process described above.

The equivalence in student background between schools A and C justified the direct comparison of these non-math teacher preparation measures of the two faculties (Table 4). None of these differences, however, was individually significant at the .05 level. Taken as a whole, the differences in Table 4 between the schools are also insignificant by the Sign test ($p > .05$) in that School C exceeded School A on only seven of the 12 variables from the transcript analysis (See Table 4).

		UG Math	**UG MATH**
Schools	**PPST Math**	**Credits**	**GPA**
School A			
Mean	174.7	5.0	2.8
Standard Dev	.6	3.2	.8
N	3 out of 7	7 out of 7	6 out of 7
School B			
Mean	181.3	8.1	2.7
Standard Dev	4.1	3.8	.8
N	8 out of 15	13 out of 15	13 out of 15
School C			
Mean	177.3	3.4	3.2
Standard Dev	4.9	4.2	1.0
N	3 out of 7	7 out of 7	4 out of 7
F statistic with df's	3.43 with 2,11 df	8.53 with 2,24 df	.43 with 2,20 df
p-value	$p < .07$	$p < .002$	$p < .658$

TABLE 3

Mean PPST Score, Math GPA, and Math Credits of Grade 3–5 Teachers in Schools A, B, and C

Discussion

TRANSCRIPT VARIABLES

The transcript analyses did not support any clear and simple feature of the teachers' academic preparation that would account for the significant and striking differences in the academic performance of the students among the three schools. Two of the three variables bearing on the strength of

TABLE 4

Means and (Standard Deviations) in Teacher Background Characteristics for Schools A, B, and C

Teacher Characteristics	School A	School B	School C
PPST Math	174.67 (0.58)	181.25 (4.13)	177.33 (4.93)
Math Credits*	5.00 (3.16)	8.08 (3.77)	3.43 (4.19)
Math GPA	2.77 (0.78)	2.74 (.77)	3.16 (.99)
Number of U/G Credits	117.8 (5.12)	128.15 (13.94)	132.43 (10.53)
U/G GPA	3.11 (0.59)	3.07 (.51)	2.92 (.48)
Number of Graduate Credits	37.00 (2.83)	33.60 (6.29)	29.75 (8.02)
Graduate GPA	3.88 (.12)	3.85 (.12)	3.91 (.12)
Master's Degree Holders	28.6%	73.3%	71.4%
Rank of U/G Institution	3.00 (.82)	3.00 (1.04)	3.00 (1.29)
Rank of Graduate Institution	3.50 (.71)	3.09 (.70)	2.50 (1.00)
Years since Bachelor's Degree	15.00(11.63)	19.64 (8.96)	22.00 (5.61)
Years since Master's Degree	2.50 (3.53)	6.30 (4.44)	12.50 (10.84)

*F = 3.78 Significant at .05 level

mathematical background identified in the teacher transcripts failed to show significant differences among the three schools. The only exception was the number of mathematics credits the teachers took in their colleges or universities. The higher performing schools had teachers who, on average, took more mathematics course credits in college than teachers on average took in the lower performing school (See Tables 3 & 4). When the data are inspected school by school, the overall link of mathematics credits in college with higher proportion of high-gain students is not perfect, because the teachers in School B, which had relatively lower gains than School A, had taken more mathematics credits than the teachers in School A. The relationship is perfect, however, among the three schools between the number of math credits taken by the teachers in each school and the mean fifth grade math score in each school (viz., A>B>C).

The faculty of the school with the greatest gains (School A), however, showed no significantly greater mathematics preparation than the faculty of the school with large losses (School C). There were also no significant differences between Schools A and C in the underlying demographic factors (poverty and special education) that are often associated with low academic performance. It is striking that these two schools, with their equivalent demographic characteristics, should show such a large difference in the academic performance of their students.

The profiles of the faculties in Schools A and C reveal a complex picture. The faculty members in School A were younger teachers without much teaching experience and had earned fewer masters degrees, but from more highly ranked institutions. They had slightly lower PPST scores in mathematics and took more math credits in college, but earned lower grades in them. They also took fewer undergraduate credits overall, but earned higher grades in them than the faculty in School C (Table 4). Given that the students in School A showed higher regressed gain scores than most in the state and the students in School C lost more than most from grades 3 to 5, and given equivalent social demographics of the two schools, these uneven differences in faculty profiles only indicate that the factors that operated in each school are complex and merit further study.

OTHER FACTORS

It was not the case that the Lenape District did not emphasize elementary mathematics. At the outset of DSTP the district initiated a math curriculum and math club program that subsequently earned national recognition, and in 2002 Schools A and B posted scores about 20 points above the state mean, while School C posted scores just below the state mean of 477. Why School C did not benefit as much from the pioneering district math initiative as School A is unclear. There is some support from interviews with school leaders for the proposition that the faculty of School A, being younger and less experienced, were more open to new ways of teaching mathematics, and that the faculty of School C, being more experienced and having completed their masters degrees, were more settled in their instructional approaches and less enthusiastic about the accommodations that are required in an *all kids can learn*, or a *leave no child behind*, teaching regime.

Our analysis of the state database showed that significant achievement differences existed between schools that could not be explained simply by characteristics of the students in the schools. Our study of the three schools revealed that one index of the strength of the teacher's mathematics background, the number of mathematics credits earned, was sufficiently robust to show itself years later in the academic gains and losses of the teachers' students. Our method of identifying high and low achievement schools through the computation of residual gain scores, rather than by mean scores, also showed that schools that otherwise performed at the same state performance level overall exhibited academic strengths that were masked in the traditional approach to identifying academic accomplishment at the school level.

REFERENCES

Ball, D. L. (1991). Research on teaching mathematics: Making subject matter knowledge part of the equation. In J. Brophy (Ed.), *Advances in research on teaching* (pp. 1–48). Greenwich, CT: JAI Press.

Conference Board of the Mathematical Sciences. (2000). The mathematical education of teachers. *Issues in mathematics education, Vol 11.* Washington, D.C.: American Mathematical Society.

Ma, L. (1999). *Knowing and teaching elementary mathematics: Teachers' understanding of mathematics in China and the United States.* Mahwah, NJ: Lawrence Erlbaum Associates.

Monk, D. H. (1994). Subject area preparation of secondary mathematics teachers and science teachers and student achievement. *Economics of Education Review, 13,* 125–145.

Monk, D. H., & King, J. A. (1994). Multilevel teacher resource effects on pupil performance in secondary mathematics and science. In R. G. Ehrenberg (Ed.), *Choices and consequence* (pp. 29–58). Ithaca, NY: ILR Press.

What About the Children? Studying the Professional Development School's Impact on Students' School Experience

6.

Nancy Fichtman Dana, Diane Yendol-Silva

Nancy Fichtman Dana is currently Professor of Education at the University of Florida. Prior to her appointment at the University of Florida, she served as the Co-Director of the State College Area School District - Pennsylvania State University Elementary Professional Development School program, which was named as a Distinguished Program in Teacher Education by ATE in 2002. Her research interests include: teacher inquiry, teacher leadership, school-university collaboration, and professional development schools.

Diane Yendol-Silva is currently an Assistant Professor of Education at the University of Florida and partner in the Diversity, Democracy, and Literacy Communities (DDL). Her research interests include: creating communities of inquiry, teacher leadership, mentoring, and school-university collaboration.

ABSTRACT

The purpose of this paper is to recognize the relative absence of systematic study of children in our professional development school literature. The authors raise questions about why children have been largely missing from PDS research to date by synthesizing existing PDS literature into three waves of studies, and calling for the fourth wave of study focused on turning the gaze of study to children. Finally, the authors share their initial effort at documenting the impact of their local PDS on children, while simultaneously analyzing why this attempt was insufficient, yet instrumental, to their continued local PDS work. Conclusions are drawn for local PDS work, as well as the collective PDS work of researchers across the nation.

In an effort to simultaneously renew public school education and teacher education to better meet the unique needs of children today; many educators have advocated the creation of professional development schools (Darling-Hammond, 1994; Levine, 1997; Trubowitz, & Longo, 1997). In fact, almost every commission and report on teacher education (Goodlad, 1994; Holmes, 1986, 1990; Levine, 1992) advocates the professional development school as a powerful vehicle for provoking educational change. Darling-Hammond (1994) characterizes PDSs as special cases of school restructuring that simultaneously restructure schools and teacher education programs by redefining teaching and learning for all members of the learning community. To date, conspicuously missing from the professional development school conversations are the experiences of the largest group of PDS constituents—children.

Children are rarely mentioned or even discussed in the literature. In an extensive literature review on PDSs, Silva (1999) named only one study completed by Hall (1996) that discussed the impact of the professional development school initiatives on public school students. In this study, Hall described an increase in small group work and individual student attention due to the participation of pre-service teachers in classroom instruction. Few additional studies have surfaced that focus on PDS children. For example, Knight, Wiseman, and Cooner (2000) investigated the impact of PDS activities on student achievement through the use of collaborative action research. Additionally, Pine (2000) conducted a longitudinal comparative analysis of the Michigan Educational Assessment Program test scores achieved by students of the Longfellow Professional Development Schools in Pontiac, Michigan. As studies focused on children are few in number, documenting the impact of PDS work on children is a critical component that is clearly missing from the current literature.

For over a decade, our work as teacher educators interested in school-university collaboration has taken us to numerous conferences across the nation focused on professional development school research. These conferences include such meetings as the American Association of Colleges for Teacher Education, the Association of Teacher Educators, The American Educational Research Association, and The Holmes Partnership. Yet, throughout our travels, we have been disturbed by a recurring absence of systematic study about the most important participant in the PDS—the children. Most conference presentations proceed something like this:

The participants present a model for their PDS, discuss the changing roles of various participants, highlight the importance of building relationships between universities and schools, share PDS deals made with teacher unions, and proudly display new teacher education programs and curricula for pre-service teachers. When it is time for questions from the audience, we query, "How is life in your PDS different for the children?" There is often a silence, a puzzled stare, and then one of the following answers: (a) Life for the PDS children is pretty much the same as before the school became a PDS", (b) "We have not yet been able to study the lives and achievement of PDS children", or (c), "We never thought of looking at the children."

The purpose of this paper is to raise awareness of the lack of systematic study of PDS children, raise questions about why children have been largely missing from PDS discourse to date, and share our initial attempts at documenting the impact of our local PDS on children.

The Omission of Children from PDS Discussion

There are several good reasons children have not been featured in the literature and research on PDSs to date. Perhaps the most apparent reason is the relative youth of the PDS movement in general. The youth of the movement has not lent itself to study and understanding of the impact of the PDS on children for two reasons. First, PDSs have multiple goals including long-term systemic change in the education of prospective teachers, the growth of practicing teachers, and the educational experiences for PDS children. Long-term systemic change takes time. Sirotnik & Goodlad (1998) believed that "For a school-university partnership to effect major educational reconstructions in a relatively short time frame, say five years, would be miraculous" (p. 188). Thus, one could argue that many PDSs have not been in existence long enough to assess the impact on children. The second problem associated with studying change for children was that PDSs are changing and growing so rapidly that Teitel (1998) characterized them as "moving targets." He further stated that PDSs are "changing and evolving so fast that no evaluation could capture what they are doing" (p.1). There is surely a danger in studying the impact of PDSs on children and children's learning prematurely. Clearly, when studying long-term systemic changes it is important not to attempt measurement before the changes are in place. Additionally, PDS relationships take time to build and grow and have been characterized frequently in the literature as fragile (see, for example, Levine, 1997; Teitel, 1996; Trubowitz & Longo, 1997). Premature evaluation might place additional stress on these already delicate relationships (Teitel, 1998).

Due to the relative youth of the PDS movement, the natural evolution of the PDS may not have leant itself to the immediate study of children. Rather, the PDS evolution has resulted in three waves of study: (a) School-university relationship building, (b) Impact on prospective teachers, and (c) Impact on practicing teachers. Since PDS relationships require a tremendous time investment and are so fragile, the first wave of studies focused on the time and energy spent developing relationships (Dana, Dana & Hernandez, 1997). Once relationships were established, prospective teachers were introduced into the PDS setting. Since prospective teachers were an obvious change, student teacher studies emerged (see, for example, Hoffman, Rosenbluth & McCrory, 1997; Schneider, Seidman & Cannone, 1996; Silva & Dana, 2001). Next, with relationships in place and some initial understanding of prospective teachers in a PDS, the third wave of study focused on practicing teachers in a PDS. For example, studies by Bullough, Kauchak, Crow, Hobbs, & Stokes, (1997). Walters (1998), Stanalis (1995), and Silva (1999) shed insights into the lives and professional development of veteran teachers. Just as a study of prospective and practicing teachers provides a picture of their PDS work, in the logical next wave of study we will turn our gaze toward examining the impact of the PDS on the children. This turning of the gaze is not meant to imply that the first three waves are less worthy. Rather, the turning of the gaze to the children is meant to remind us that understanding the ways PDSs impact children is indeed worthy of our attention.

As we approach the time to launch this fourth wave of study, we offer two methodological approaches to capturing the children's experiences: studies that shift the gaze or research questions toward the experiences of children and studies that shift the data source to include the voices of children. In the first case, research is designed to capture the children's experiences by collecting data from the adults with whom they live and work, as well as ethnographic data targeted at identifying changes for children within the classroom. In the second case, research focuses on collecting and sharing the voices of children who attend a PDS.

Focusing on children in the PDS is difficult for many reasons. First, PDS evaluation work that discloses the varying experiences of children is political. For example, the political nature of PDS evaluation work emerges as school districts become reluctant to collect or report data that compares non-PDS schools within the district to the PDSs. If it were demonstrated that PDSs have a positive impact on the children, the district fears a political nightmare of parents demanding special placement of their children in PDSs, and teacher morale plummeting as test scores of children in PDS schools and non-PDS schools are compared and contrasted. Patton (1990) discusses the complexity of evaluation work:

> Beauty is in the eye of the beholder, and the evaluation beholders include a variety of stakeholders: decision makers, policymakers, funders, program

managers, staff, program participants, and the general public. Any given design is necessarily an interplay of resources, possibilities, creativity, and personal judgment by the people involved. (p. 13)

The political nature of evaluation work provides an extra challenge to those interested in understanding how PDS work impacts children.

Perhaps another reason children have been so rarely mentioned in studies of professional development schools is that across the nation elementary PDSs are far more numerous than middle school or secondary PDSs. Capturing young children's first hand impressions and experiences in an elementary school can be challenging. For example, interviewing elementary age children presents readiness challenges. Children of this age have difficulty assessing their own growth and development, as well as articulating their experiences as members of a PDS community. Questionnaires are also limiting, since very young children have limited reading ability and limited understanding of assessed concepts. Additionally, gaining permission to study children from Human Research Review Boards is often a complex and time-consuming process.

While the study of children in PDSs presents a host of challenges, we believe the PDS researchers, teachers, and administrators can address these challenges. In the remainder of this paper, we share our initial attempt at documenting impact on children in our local PDS by shifting the gaze and research questions that guided our study to understanding the experiences of and impact on the children. We acknowledge that our look at the children in our PDS is only partial, as we have not included the voices of children and we were plagued by many of the same issues discussed in this paper. These issues include the relative youth of our program, the vulnerability of our school-university relationships, our fast-paced PDS evolution, on-going changes during the pilot year, district's political fears of comparing schools, and the struggle of capturing young children's experiences. While we acknowledge our attempt to document impact on children is incomplete, we offer our methods and results to call attention to the ways the PDS community can begin addressing the question of how PDS work impacts children using three perspectives: teachers, prospective teachers, and parents.

Description of Our PDS

Drawing on the goals of the PDS movement nationwide, this university and school district located in the northeastern part of the United States partnered in creating two professional development schools. The first PDS was a small, six classroom kindergarten through second grade early childhood school where each of the six teachers worked with a yearlong intern. The second school was a kindergarten through fifth grade elementary school, where eight interns worked along side classroom teachers throughout the school year.

The teachers, administrators, and university faculty in these two PDSs met continuously during the 1997–98 school year to plan for the pilot year. As a part of its collaborative work the partnership committed to achieve three goals. The first and foremost goal emphasized a commitment to enhance the educational experiences of all children. The second goal focused on ensuring high quality field experiences for prospective teachers. The third and final goal called for furthering the professional growth of school and university based teachers and teacher educators (Dana, Silva, and Colangelo, 1999).

To these ends, the professional development schools became the "living classrooms" for prospective undergraduate teachers to learn the art and science of teaching through the completion of a full-year internship. The yearlong internship was an intensive field based program, where learning to teach was accomplished as an intern planned, taught, and inquired about teaching alongside their mentor and university supervisor on a daily basis for an entire school year. Please note that a detailed description of our program is beyond the scope of this paper. For more information on the structure of our PDSs, please see Dana, et al.; Silva & Dana, 2001; and Dana, 1999.

From the onset, the members of our partnership believed that documenting the impact of the PDS work on children was of central importance. Yet, faced with the challenges described previously, we needed to find ways to document children's experiences that were reasonable and doable during our pilot year. Hence, we entered the world of the PDS child through the gaze of those individuals closest to the children—their parents and teachers. Our first year of studying the child explored the ways in which parents and teachers believe the PDS work impacted the lives of their children.

Data Collection

In order to document and further understand the impact of the pilot year of the professional development school on children, three types of data were collected and analyzed: (a) parent questionnaires, (b) mentor questionnaires, and (c) inquiry projects.

PARENT QUESTIONNAIRE

The parent questionnaire was developed and sent to all parents of children in PDS classrooms with yearlong university interns at the close of the school year. Three hundred and six questionnaires were sent home, along with a stamped self-addressed return envelope. One hundred and thirty-five questionnaires were returned, marking the return rate at 44%. The core component of the parent questionnaire contained eight statements, followed by a likert scale of 1 through 5, with the number 1 representing "Strongly Disagree," 3 representing "Neutral," and 5 representing "Strongly Agree." Parents were asked to circle the number 1 through 5 that best described their feelings in response to each statement. The statements read:

1. My child benefited from having an intern in the classroom.
2. I established a positive relationship with my child's intern.
3. I believe my child having an intern in the classroom enhanced communication.
4. I believe my child having an intern in the classroom enhanced instruction.
5. My child developed a positive relationship with his/her intern.
6. My child received more individual attention this year as a result of having an intern in his/her classroom.
7. My child received more attention during small group instruction time this year as a result of having an intern in his/her classroom.
8. I believe the classroom teacher had more time to get to know my child this year as a result of having an intern in the classroom.

In addition, parents were asked to indicate the name of their child's school, the ways in which they got to know their child's intern, and any comments they had about their experiences and their child's experiences with the intern during the school year. Finally, parents were asked to provide their names and telephone numbers in case the researchers would want to pursue telephone interviews. Sixty parents volunteered to be interviewed by telephone about their child's experiences with a university intern. As the response to the 8 core items were consistently positive across the returned surveys and 97 parents included narrative comments with their surveys, it was decided that parent interviews were not necessary at this point in time. However, names of parent volunteers were retained for later in-depth interviews focused on gaining longitudinal data about the impact of a PDS on a child over time (multiple years in classrooms with full year interns).

The narrative data drawn from the comment section on each individual questionnaire were reviewed and compiled together into one word processing file. Each questionnaire was assigned a number (P1–P135), in order to allow the analyst to match narrative data to questionnaire responses during analysis. Next, the data were read and categorically analyzed across responses. Any unique or outlying responses were also noted and reported, along with a description of each category, in the results section of this paper.

Teacher Questionnaire

In addition to the parent questionnaire, a mentor teacher questionnaire was developed and sent, with a return stamped self-addressed envelope, to each of the 14 mentor teachers during the last week of school. The work of Berry & Catoe (1994) provided the foundation for the development of the mentor teacher questionnaire, as some of the same questions were taken from the survey they developed to assess policy and practice in South Carolina's PDS initiatives. The mentor teacher questionnaire contained forty-one statements followed by a likert scale of 1 through 5, with the number 1 representing "Strongly Disagree," 3 representing "Neutral," and 5 representing "Strongly Agree." Mentors were asked to circle the number 1 through 5 that best described their feelings in response to each statement. The forty-one statements on the survey were grouped into five sections: (a) My Participation in the PDS; (b) Impact of the PDS on my Own Classroom and Teaching Practice, (c) Inquiry, (d) Where We Are in Building and Creating PDSs, and (e) Where We Are in Changing Teaching and Learning in PDSs. Space was provided for narrative comments at the end of each section of the questionnaire, as well as at the end of the entire questionnaire. Eight out of 14 surveys were returned, marking the return rate at 57%.

Additionally, five of the eight teachers included some type of narrative comment on various sections of the questionnaire. The narrative data from each individual questionnaire were compiled together into one word processing file. Each questionnaire was assigned a number (M1–M8) in order to match narrative data to questionnaire responses during analysis. This paper only reports an analysis of the survey section entitled, "Impact of the PDS on my Own Classroom Teaching and Teaching Practice," as this section was directly linked to understanding mentor teachers' perceptions of the PDS's impact on children.

INQUIRY PROJECTS

The final form of data included a document analysis of the intern and mentor inquiry projects and presentations. Since a large component of the PDS experience was the interns' and mentors' engagement in conducting teacher inquiry in their own classrooms, we believed that examining the content of these inquiries might illuminate specific ways in which children were impacted during the course of the year. As a result, the researchers' gaze turned to fourteen inquiry projects that were analyzed to identify how the content, focus, and conclusions drawn from inquiry related to children in the PDS.

Results

How Did Our Parents Feel About the Impact of the PDS on their Children?

Parents' responses to the core component of the questionnaire were based on their own knowledge of their child's experiences with the intern assigned to the respective classroom. In order to capture how parents developed familiarity with the intern, parents were asked to indicate any interactions they had with the intern. Parents reported that their knowledge of their child's experiences was most frequently based on conversations with their child at home (82%). Additionally, parents reported getting to know their child's intern through interaction at the goal setting (parent-teacher) conferences (76%), as well as through the intern sharing observations during informal interactions with the parent (57%). Less frequent ways parents reported gaining knowledge about their child's intern included after school activities (25%), written communications (23%) and phone conversations (4%).

Parents' responses to the core items in the parent questionnaire are summarized in Table 1.

Based on this analysis, parents had strong feelings that their children benefited as a member of a PDS classroom. Responses to items 5 and 8 indicate that according to parents, children develop stronger relationships with the classroom teacher, as well as a positive relationship with the classroom intern in the Professional Development School. Many educators discuss the critical nature of building caring relationships between children and teachers as foundations for a child's academic, social, and psychological development (Gilligan 1982; Noddings, 1984, 1992). Similarly, parents believe that strong relationships are in place in these PDS classrooms.

TABLE 1
Parent Responses to Core Items

		Response Mean/Median/Mode
1.	My child benefited from having an intern in the classroom.	4.612 / 5.0 / 5.0
2.	I established a positive relationship with my child's intern.	3.9 / 5.0 / 4.0
3.	I believe communication was enhanced by my child having an intern in the classroom.	4.2 / 5.0 / 4.3
4.	I believe instruction was enhanced by my child having an intern in the classroom.	4.5 / 5.0 / 5.0
5.	My child developed a positive relationship with his/her intern.	4.7 / 5.0 / 5.0
6.	My child received more individual attention this year as a result of having an intern in his/her classroom.	4.6 / 5.0 / 5.0
7.	My child received more attention during small group instruction time this year as a result of having an intern in his/her classroom.	4.5 / 5.0 / 5.0
8.	I believe the classroom teacher had more time to get to know my child this year as a result of having an intern in the classroom.	4.5 / 5.0 / 5.0

Note: Each item was measured on a scale ranging from 1 to 5 with 1 representing strongly disagree to 5 representing strongly agree.

Also of interest was the congruence with Hall's (1996) finding regarding an increase in small group work and individual attention. Responses to items 4, 6, and 7 indicate that, according to parents, children in these PDSs are receiving more attention as individuals, as well as during small group instruction time, and that instruction is enhanced in the PDS classroom.

Finally, responses to items 2 and 3 indicate that, according to parents, they are building positive relationships with interns and communication is enhanced when interns are present in their child's classroom. As the majority of home-school communication occurs between the classroom teacher and the parent, we viewed the response rate to items 2 and 3 as positive. Parents are afforded opportunities to know their child's intern, as well as the classroom teacher. As a result, home-school communication may be expanded.

Five categories emerged from an analysis of the narrative data provided in the parent comment section. We labeled these categories: "Naming and commendation of individual interns," "Benefit of one-on-one instruction with individual children," "Benefits of children having two teachers for the entire school year," "Continuity provided by full year internship," and "General benefits of the PDS for all."

The first striking category was the "Naming and commendation of individual interns." Of the ninety-seven narrative comments analyzed, forty-two contained the name of a particular intern, praising and thanking the intern for her work. One of many examples follows:

> Ms. W- is a fantastic teacher! After being in the classroom to help, I was very impressed with her classroom management, instruction, and especially her caring and love for the children. My daughter was very comfortable with her. I am also a teacher and Ms. W- is a student that Penn State should be proud of. She is top notch! (P53)

As evidenced in this representative excerpt, parents clearly acknowledged and appreciated the work of individual interns.

A second category of comments that emerged was the "Benefit of one-on-one instruction with individual children." Comments noted individual children's general progress, as well as specific progress in social skill development, reading and math:

> I was extremely pleased when Miss A- chose my daughter to do part of her work with individually. She was so good with C- and really tried and, I believe, succeeded at finding ways to help C- learn and helping C- gain more self control in classroom settings. (P22)

> The intern particularly helped and encouraged my child with reading. It sounds like they worked one-on-one quite a bit and she challenged him to go further than he might have. (P26)

A third category of comments that emerged focused on the "Benefits of children having two teachers for the entire school year":

The relationship that our child had with her intern was extremely positive. When discussing the events of the school day, the intern's involvement with the classroom activities received "equal time" with that of the full-time teacher. According to our child, it was almost as if she had the benefit of two teachers throughout the school year. As a parent, I can appreciate the preferred ratio of teachers to students (2:22 vs. 1:22). I could only hope that Hillside Elementary School would consider incorporating the usage of teaching interns to assist with the various individual developmental needs of each student. Our child has become a stronger student this year, and we are thankful for this extended relationship between the university and the school district. (P43)

My child enjoyed his school year and I believe that the intern was a big factor. The intern is absolutely necessary for the large classroom size. The teacher couldn't do without the intern. (P131)

One outlying comment that was grouped within the "Having Two Teachers" category focused on what one parent believed to be a drawback, rather than a benefit of having two teachers:

Although I wholeheartedly agree that these programs are beneficial to both child and student—I believe the classroom teachers tend to take advantage and use this type of programming to do "other" things (i.e. meetings, seminars and such) that leaves the intern to be the primary teacher for much of the day. (P16)

This sentiment was evident in only one of the ninety-seven narrative comments. While this comment is clearly not indicative of the majority of parents who responded to the survey, it called our attention to the necessity of keeping communication about PDS activities open with parents, continually educating parents about PDS work, and engaging teachers in recognizing the power of team teaching throughout the entire school year.

A fourth category of comments focused on the "continuity a full year intern provided for children":

I believe the yearlong program (vs. semester only) was structured to meet the needs of the university student *AND* the elementary students. It really allowed for continuity and minimized disruption. (P33)

One unique comment that was grouped within this category noted continuity the intern was able to provide for children when a substitute teacher was working in the classroom:

The one thing I found important is that when there was a substitute teacher for the main teacher, the children were less apt to take advantage of the substitute because the intern was there. Classroom instruction could go on as normal. I believe this helped particularly in the kindergarten classroom, since children of this age tend to need more individual attention. (P99)

A final category of comments focused on the "general benefit of the PDS for all!" Many parents utilized the phrase "everyone wins" or "everyone benefits."

I think the intern program is much more valuable than just student teaching the traditional time. They spend a whole school year together – just like real life; the children learn from the intern and vice versa all the time. In traditional student teaching, the student teacher often observes most of the time and teaches very little. In this relationship more co-teaching goes on. Everyone benefits! (P17)

I feel that each of the children, and the classroom teacher as well, benefited from our intern's presence in the classroom. This is truly a situation where everyone involved is a winner! (P35)

How Did Our Mentors Feel About the Impact of the PDS on their Children?

Mentor responses to individual survey items that dealt with children are presented in Table 2.

Most striking in this section of the questionnaire is a response mean of 5 (Strongly Agree) to three items (9, 12, and 13). Every mentor who responded to this questionnaire strongly agrees that the children in their classrooms benefit from having an intern, and that their children received a greater amount of individual attention, as well as a greater amount of attention during small group instruction time. This finding is consistent with the findings reported on the parent questionnaire. In our PDS, parents and teachers agree that children are afforded a greater amount of attention. This finding is consistent with the literature on PDSs as reported by Hall (1996). Hall described an increase in small group work and individual attention for PDS students, due to the participation of pre-service teachers in the classrooms.

While not receiving a response mean of 5 as in the 3 items reported above, each of the remaining 5 items in this section received extremely high responses (a mean range of 4.36–4.75). Concurring with responses received from parents, teachers agree that they get to know their children better, and that both communication and instruction are enhanced as a result of having an intern in the classroom. In addition, teachers tried new instructional

TABLE 2

**Mentor Response to Survey Section Entitled:
"Impact of the PDS on My Own Classroom
and Teaching Practice:**

		Response Mean/Median/Mode
9.	My children benefited from having an intern in the classroom.	5.0 / 5.0 / 5.0
10.	I believe having an intern in the classroom enhanced communication.	4.71 / 5.0 / 5.0
11.	I believe having an intern in my classroom enhanced instruction.	4.75 / 5.0 / 5.0
12.	My children received more individual attention this year as a result of having an intern in the classroom.	5.0 / 5.0 / 5.0
13.	My children received more attention during small group instruction time this year as a result of having an intern in the classroom.	5.0 / 5.0 / 5.0
14.	I had more time to get to know my children this year as a result of having an intern in the classroom.	4.36 / 5.0 / 5.0
15.	I tried things in my classroom this year that I would not have tried alone.	4.38 / 4.5 / 5.0
16.	I grew professionally this year as a result of having an intern in my classroom.	4.5 / 5.0 / 5.0

approaches or activities in their classroom that they would not have tried alone and grew professionally as a result of having an intern in their classrooms.

Interestingly, a narrative comment from Mentor 4 offers an outlying perspective on getting to know children better, despite the strongly agree rating on item 14 by mentors and strongly agree rating on item 8 on the parent questionnaire. Mentor 4 believed having to direct additional adults in the room-required time that she would normally use to get to know her children:

> "It was more difficult to get to know my children this year. I believe part was due to helping other adults in the classroom and part was due to a quieter, more reserved group of children." (M4)

This comment by Mentor 4 underscores the importance of acknowledging that the inclusion of extra adults may have an impact on the classroom teacher. We now realize that mentors may need support to be able to manage the extra adults in the classroom, and in some contexts, the inclusion of an intern in a classroom may detract, rather than add to a teacher's ability to know her children. While in general, teachers believed they knew their children better, each situation should be individually considered.

Mentor Seven commented that responses to this section of the questionnaire might vary based on the strength of an intern:

> My intern was a natural—many others may not have been. I felt so strongly about her influence in our children's lives because she was so effective and talented. I'm afraid my answers would have been much different if my intern was weaker. (M7)

Two other mentors offered comments in this section of the questionnaire, highlighting their strong feelings about the impact the PDS has had on their own classrooms and teaching practice:

> I feel this area is the most important aspect to the program. It would be very difficult to return to the traditional student teaching model. (M5)

> It was like having two teachers in the room. The needs of my/our students were met in a more timely and efficient manner. (M8)

WHAT DID CLASSROOM INQUIRY MEAN FOR OUR PDS CHILDREN?

Interns and mentors conducted a total of fourteen classroom inquiries during our pilot year. As we read each inquiry, they were sorted into one of four categories: (a) inquiry into a particular child/children in the classroom, (b) inquiry into a pedagogical technique, (c) inquiry into a teacher's own professional practice (exploring one's own skills, attitudes, and beliefs about teaching), and (d) inquiry into curriculum. Through this sort, we discovered that 8 of the 14 inquiries (57%) conducted during our pilot year focused on individual children. Since the pilot year, we have continued to categorize and analyze the inquires that have been conducted in the PDS context, and inquiry into a particular child/children in the classroom continues to be a popular focus for intern and mentor inquiry (Dana & Yendol-Silva, 2003). Table 3 describes and summarizes the eight inquiries into particular learners that were conducted during the pilot year.

Even at a glance, Table 3 demonstrates that the lives of eight individual children were impacted during our pilot year through intense systematic investigations into their learning. We believe this data is important to offer within this discussion of impact on PDS children in that inquiry, deemed by the Holmes Group (1986) as a central feature of any PDS, has the potential to impact the lives of children on a very individual basis. These inquiries were used in our district to develop new insights into ways to enhance the learning for these students and develop action plans for their learning and school experience. Although all eight projects contributed to the teacher's and the intern's understanding of the children involved, the results of the inquiry into one child's emotional needs ultimately provided the evidence needed to build the case for the district to hire a paraprofessional for this child as she entered her next academic year of schooling.

Discussion and Conclusions

While we acknowledge that this study of our pilot PDS year's impact on children was rudimentary and basic, the data we collected was important to the development of our PDS for a number of reasons. First, we established initial methods of exploring the uncharted waters of the impact of PDSs on children and we did so during our hectic pilot year, where Teitel notes that PDS participants are "too busy making the partnership happen to document their work" (p. 2). By beginning an initial documentation of the lives of our children, we renew our commitment to PDS work making a difference in the lives of PDS children, as well as our commitment to continue to research children's learning in the PDS context. With a precedence established for studying PDS children, we continue to collect and analyze data as our PDSs become better established and we have been "in the PDS business" long enough to study long-term systemic change (see, for example, Snow & Lehman, 2000; Snow-Gerono, 2002; Snow-Gerono, Dana, & Nolan, 2001; Nolan,). Correspondingly, we did establish baseline data and a research protocol during our pilot year to track the continued impact of the PDS on chil-

TABLE 3

Summary of Inquiries Conducted During the PDS Pilot Year

Subject of Inquiry	Inquiry Question	Conclusions
Child's needs and the IST Process	What happened to this 1st grader as he proceeded through the IST process?	☐ Student began to see himself as a learner. ☐ Student became more socially involved in the class. ☐ Student began to transfer skills practiced in isolation to his class-room work.
Emotional Needs of an Individual Child	How does this 2nd graders' emotional needs influence her success in a regular education classroom setting? What strategies are effective in redirect-ing this child when her day becomes a challenge? What did I learn about my own practice?	☐ Served as a living document to describe the experience of this included child in both a learning support classroom and a regular education classroom setting.
Behavioral Struggles of a High Achieving Student	What are the relationships of this high achieving student with his peers and teachers? How can I help this high achieving student participate	☐ Child's behavior was consistent across contexts. ☐ Teacher expectations/reactions differed; were less consistent across contexts. ☐ Child needed support

(continues on next page)

TABLE 4 (continued)		
Subject of Inquiry	**Inquiry Question**	**Conclusions**
	appropriately in the classroom and support his unique needs?	to identify the need to to identify the need to according to different contexts.
Teacher/Parent Interaction	How does a child become disengaged? How can I make changes in my own teaching or in my way of interacting with students so that I could engage them during each day? In what ways can I connect with parents on behalf of student learning?	☐ Dialogue journals are useful tools for parent/teacher communication. ☐ Involving parents of children at-risk in the classroom is key to building relationships with parents and building knowledge of school curriculum and daily life.
Student Achievement	How can I help a child to become more skilled in reading, writing, math, and staying on task?	◆ Improved achievement in math and reading. ◆ Heightened time on task.
Meeting a Child's Emotional and Academic Needs	How can I help a child with attention difficulties be more successful in school?	◆ Served to document the specific needs of this child. ◆ Identified the high degree of adult/child interaction needed to help this child be successful in school.

(continues on next page)

TABLE 4 (continued)		
Subject of Inquiry	Inquiry Question	Conclusions
ESL Student's Oral and Written Language Development	How does peer interaction facilitate an ESL child's writing at the kindergarten-writing table?	◆ ESL Child relates writing to speaking out loud. ◆ As ESL Child's language developed, so has his drawings and interactions with peers. ◆ The writing table facilitates an ESL child's written and oral language.
Using Music as a Tool for Learning to Read	In what ways can music help this child become a better reader? What happens when music is used as a pedagogical technique to enhance reading instruction?	◆ Music became a motivator. ◆ Music became a confidence builder. ◆ Music provided a context for making meaningful connections.

dren longitudinally. For example, we plan to contact parents who agreed to be interviewed after their children "graduate" from the PDS.

The results of our study were also important to the development and the future of our PDS, in that it calmed a number of initial PDS worries. For example, one of our district's initial hesitations concerning beginning PDS work was the past inundation of student teachers in their schools, as they serviced not only our university, but also other universities in our state. Historically, district parents had voiced strong feelings about their children not being placed in a classroom with a student teacher. Their concern was often for the student teacher's short stay in the classroom (16 weeks) and the student teacher "taking over" so that their child was not being taught by a "real teacher." In general, the data collected from parents in this study was highly positive. This data served to allay this parental concern. We have been able to point to this data as we present the PDS work at School Board and Parent Teacher Organization meetings. We have found that this data, as well as the data reported in the mentor questionnaire, has served to replace much skepticism and trepidation that existed about our PDS work during the pilot year with overwhelming support for the continuation, expansion, and future study of our PDS work.

A third way our study was important is that it provided documentation and evidence that parents and teachers believed that the PDS work had positive outcomes for the children during our pilot year. As all that worked within our PDS during the pilot year were physically and mentally exhausted from meeting the challenges PDS work presents, the report of positive outcomes served to renew and reinvigorate our mission. While boosting PDS morale was an incidental and unintended outcome of our study, we believe that the importance of renewing enthusiasm for PDS work will continue to escalate, as Bullough and his colleagues (1997) reported that desire to engage in PDS work wanes after time. If study of the impact of PDS work on children proves positive, such studies may fuel the stamina needed to engage in and sustain the study of PDS work long enough for us to truly understand the impact of PDSs on children and other members of the PDS community.

A final way our study was important was in heightening the visibility of classroom-based inquiry in the PDS and the role classroom-based inquiry may play in impacting children. The Holmes Group (1986) deemed teacher inquiry as a central feature of any PDS. Yet, it appears that in many PDSs across the nation, teacher inquiry remains within the four walls of the classroom. When contained within the PDS classroom walls, PDS researchers and scholars miss an important opportunity to document the ways in which PDSs may be making a difference for individual children. As teacher inquiry is systematic study, it can be included as a valuable source of data in our quest to understand its impact on PDS children. By collectively analyzing classroom based inquiry, it is possible to gain insights into the ways individual children are impacted as part of a PDS community that is committed to teacher inquiry. In the absence of a collective analysis of PDS classroom inquiries, research documenting PDS impact on individual children may be lost.

While our study was important to us in a number of ways, it clearly is lacking. First and foremost, the methodology we share in this paper did not include the voices of children. We believe it is imperative that children's experiences in PDSs be captured through talking directly with children themselves. While we noted in an earlier section of this paper some of the difficulties of studying young children (i.e., developmental readiness of children for interviewing; limited reading proficiency for questionnaires; tendency to report only positive features), all of these obstacles and hurdles can be overcome. For example, future studies of children's experiences in the PDS may borrow from the recently emerging methodological traditions utilized by sociologists. Montandon (1998) offers insight into these traditions in her discussion of the theoretical and methodological issues involved in the study of children. Her work presents a conceptual framework for soliciting and organizing children's points of view on their own education.

A second obvious way our study is lacking is in it's inability to answer what is perhaps the most nagging question across the nation: "What is the relationship between student academic achievement and their participation in a PDS classroom?" While it is possible to make inferences from some of our data points about the academic achievement of our children, to date, we have no direct data linking participation in the PDS with enhanced student achievement. While our PDSs, as many across the nation, are too young to track changes in student achievement based on PDS participation, we believe that establishing a plan to understand student achievement in the future is of paramount importance. We are currently embarking on a study of the academic achievement of our first class of PDS children who just graduated from the early childhood K–2 PDS. Rather than comparing school to school, we will track the graduates from this PDS in the new school environment they enter in Grade 3. Measures that might be used include a Grade 3 California Achievement Test and grade level district created assessments. We plan to compare our PDS graduates achievement on these tests with the whole Grade 3 population of our district. In this way, we respect our district wishes to avoid school against school comparison, and hope to gain valuable insights into the academic achievement of PDS children. While the academic achievement question is important, we believe there are many additional ways the PDS may impact children that need further discussion and exploration. For example, "What is the relationship between children's social and emotional growth and participation in the PDS?" This initial study of children in our PDS has also raised our awareness of social and emotional impacts on children. In a journal entry, one of our teachers wrote:

Having an intern is beneficial because I have . . .

An extra pair of hands . . .

  —to help with projects

  —to tie shoes

  —to wipe noses

—to hug children

An extra pair of ears . . .

   —to hear correct answers and give positive reinforcement

   —to hear incorrect answers and provide assistance

   —to hear disputes and help with conflict-resolution

An extra pair of eyes . . .

   —to see learning in progress

   —to see when a child is struggling and provide teaching

   —to see positive behaviors

   —to see behaviors that may need to be addressed

An extra voice . . .

   —to communicate with children and make them feel special

   —to teach

An extra mind . . .

   —to bring energy and enthusiasm to my classroom and to my teaching

   —to remind me that I am a life-long learner

   —to provide ideas and a new perspective to a lesson

An extra heart . . .

   —to love the art of teaching

   —to care for and love children!

(Kim Bryan, 12/99)

As we continue our PDS quest to understand the ways children are being impacted in our local PDSs, we raise questions such as: (a) What counts as valuable impact on children in a PDS? (b) What counts as worthy evidence to document that impact? and (c) Who decides what impact is valuable and which evidence should count? We believe that these are worthy questions for the members of the PDS community to discuss across the nation. The purpose of this article was to initiate such discussion by calling attention to the absence of talk about children in PDS dialogue, as well as share and analyze our initial attempts at researching impact on PDS children. We end this article by calling for members of local PDS communities across the nation to begin this discussion by posing the rhetorical question that opened this paper, "How is life in our PDS different for the children? If the answer to this question is "Life for the PDS children is pretty much the same as before the school became a PDS," then let us ask why and in what ways we would like schooling to be different. If the answer to this question is "We have not yet been able to study the lives and achievement of PDS children" or "We never thought of looking at the children," then let us begin.

REFERENCES

Berry, B., & Catoe, S. (1994). Creating professional development schools: Policy and practice in South Carolina's PDS initiatives. In L. Darling-Hammond (Ed.), *Professional development schools: Schools for developing a profession* (pp. 176–202). New York: Teachers College Press.

Bullough, R.V., Kauchak, D. Crow, N.A., Hobbs, S., & Stokes, D. (1997). Professional development schools: Catalysts for teacher and school change. *Teaching and Teacher Education, 13*(2), 153–169.

Dana, N. F. (1999). *The professional development school story: Assessing the impact of year one (1998–1999) of the State College Area School District—Pennsylvania State University Elementary Professional School Program.* Evaluation report submitted to the name of school district board of directors.

Dana, N. F., Dana, T. M., & Hernandez, D. (1997). Stages in the evolution of a school-university collaboration—The Matternville Elementary School experience. *Pennsylvania Educational Leadership, 17*(1), 30–37.

Dana, N. F., Silva, D. Y., & Colongelo, L. (1999). *The mentor teacher research guide.* Program documentation submitted to State College Area School District—Pennsylvania State University Elementary Professional Development School.

Dana, N. F., Silva, D. Y., Gimbert, B., Nolan, J., Zembal-Saul, C., Tzur, R., Sanders, L., & Mule, L. (2001). Developing new understandings of PDS work: Better questions, better problems. *Action in Teacher Education, 26*(4) 15–27.

Dana, N. F., & Yendol-Silva, D. (2003). *The reflective educator's guide to classroom research: Learning to teach and teaching to learn through practitioner inquiry.* Thousand Oaks, CA: Corwin Press.

Darling-Hammond, L. (Ed.) (1994). *Professional developments schools: Schools for developing a profession.* New York: Teachers College Press.

Gilligan, C. (1982). *In a different voice: Psychological theory and women's development.* Cambridge: Harvard University Press.

Goodlad, J. I. (1994). *Educational renewal: Better teachers, better schools.* San Francisco: Jossey-Bass.

Hall, J. (1996). A Qualitative look at the Indiana State University Professional Development School Program. *Contemporary Education, 67*(4), 249–254.

Hoffman, N. E., Rosenbluth, G. S., & McCrory, K. (1997). The story of changing school-university relationships. In Hoffman, N.E., Reed, W.M., & Rosenbluth, G.S., (Eds.), *Lessons from restructuring experiences: Stories of change in professional development schools.* (Pp 24–36) State University of New York Press.

The Holmes Group (1986). *Tomorrow's teachers: A report of the Holmes Group.* East Lansing, MI: Author.

The Holmes Group (1990). *Tomorrow's schools: Principles for the design of professional development schools.* East Lansing MI: Author.

Knight, S. L., Wiseman, D. L., & Cooner, D. (2000). Using collaborative teacher research to determine the impact of professional development school activities on elementary students' math and writing outcomes. *Journal of Teacher Education, 51*(1), 26–38.

Levine, M. (1992). A conceptual framework for professional practice schools. In M. Levine (Ed.). Professional practice schools: *Linking teacher education and school reform.* New York: Teachers College Press.

Levine, M. (1997). Can professional development schools help us achieve what matters most? *Action in Teacher Education, 21*(2), 63–73.

Montandon, C. (1998). Children's perspectives on their education. *Childhood: A Global Journal of Child Research,* (3), 247–63.

Noddings, N. (1984). *Caring: A feminine approach to ethics and moral education.* Los Angeles: University of California Press.

Noddings, N. (1992). *The challenge to care in schools: An alternative approach to education.* New York: Teachers College Press.

Nolan, J., Snow, J., & Lehman, H. (2000). *Year two evaluation report of the State College-Penn State Elementary Professional Development School Collaborative.* Submitted to the State College Area School District Board of School Directors.

Patton, M.Q. (1990). *Qualitative evaluation and research methods.* Newbury Park: Sage Publications.

Pine, G. J. (2000, April). *Making a difference: A professional development school's impact on student learning.* Paper presented at the annual meeting of the American Educational Research Association, New Orleans, LA.

Schneider, H., Seidman, I., & Cannone, P. (1996). Ten steps to collaboration: The story of a professional development school. *Teaching and Teacher Education, 12*(3), 260–287.

Silva, D. Y. (1999). *Telling their stories: Mentor teachers' ways of being and knowing in a professional development school.* Unpublished doctoral dissertation, The Pennsylvania State University.

Silva, D. Y., & Dana, N. F. (2001). Collaborative supervision in the professional development school. *Journal of Curriculum and Supervision, 16*(4), 305–321.

Sirotnik, K. A., & Goodlad, J. I. (1998). *School-university partnerships in action: Concepts, cases, and concerns.* New York: Teachers College Press, Columbia University.

Snow-Gerono, J. L. (2002). *The professional development school story continued: Assessing the impact of year four (2001–2002) of the State College Area School District-Pennsylvania State University Elementary Professional Development Schools.* Submitted to the State College Area School District Board of School Directors.

Snow-Gerono, J. L., Dana, N. F., & Nolan, J. F. (2001). The Professional development school story continued: Assessing the impact of year three (2000–2001) of the State College Area School District-Pennsylvania State University Elementary Professional Development Schools. *Submitted to the State College Area School District Board of School Directors.*

Stanalis, R. N. (1995). Classroom teachers as mentors: Possibilities for participation in a professional development school context. *Teaching and Teacher Education. 11*(4), 331–334.

Trubowitz, S., & Longo, P. (1997). *How it works—Inside a school-college collaboration.* New York: Teachers College Press.

Teitel, L. (1996). *Professional development schools: A literature review.* Professional development school standards project. National Council for Accreditation of Teacher Education.

Teitel, L. (1998, April). *Going beyond a leap of faith: Developing an assessment framework for professional development schools.* Paper presented at the annual meeting of the American Educational Research Association, San Diego, CA.

Walters, S.A. (1998). *Professional learning in a professional development school: The impact of a pre-service educational program on experienced teachers.* Unpublished doctoral dissertation, University of Maine, Orono.

7.

Linking Teacher Preparation and Student Performance through Practitioner Research

Carole G. Basile and Stephanie S. Townsend

Carole Basile, Ed.D. is Division Coordinator for the Initial Professional Teacher Education program at the University of Colorado at Denver. Her research focus is on the use of pluralistic contexts and the role it plays in student learning.

Stephanie Townsend, Ph.D. is a senior instructor at the University of Colorado at Denver. Her teaching and research focus is in the area of practitioner research. Stephanie has chaired the University of Colorado at Denver's Action Research conference for the past six years.

ABSTRACT

Teacher preparation programs are constantly bombarded by questions from schools, school districts, and accrediting agencies regarding the link between teacher preparation and student performance, especially those that utilize professional development schools (PDS). This paper provides an example of a project designed to use practitioner research as a method for linking teacher preparation and student learning. These professional development schools created practitioner research projects that not only informed the school's practice linking teacher preparation to student learning, but also the results have given this teacher education program direction for more comprehensive, future research. Presented here is a brief description of practitioner research, a description of our teacher education program, and exemplars from schools that describe their focus, goals, and results.

T eacher preparation programs are currently bombarded by questions from schools, school districts, and accrediting agencies regarding the link between teacher preparation and student performance, especially those that utilize professional development schools (PDS). In 1988, Marsha Levine called for the institution of professional practice schools that would support student learning, improve teaching practice, and educate future teachers. Linda Darling-Hammond (1994) discussed the need for professional development schools to provide new models of teacher education and development by serving as exemplars of practice, builders of knowledge, and vehicles for communicating professional under-standings among teacher educators, novices, and veteran teachers. Essentially, professional development schools provide teacher candidates with pluralistic contexts (i.e. social, cultural, and physical) for learning to teach.

Goodlad (1994) states "there is much to overcome in seeking to get beyond unimaginable conventional practice in schooling and teacher educa-tion" (p. 123). Today, with schools and teacher education programs held to high accountability measures, work in professional development schools must be intentional and well planned. The work of teacher candidates and others who may be working in the school must be carefully delineated so these programs have the potential to positively impact student learning. When we make the assumption that we as teacher educators are working in schools because we want to do more than just educate pre-service teachers, then we need to be able to make a case that the work we do also has an impact on ultimate outcome of schools-student learning. We believe that one place to begin is with practitioner research.

We provide a brief description and background on practitioner research. The paper focuses primarily on a project developed through Eisenhower Professional Development funds that led participating schools to create research projects that have not only informed practices linking teacher preparation to student learning, but have given the teacher preparation pro-gram direction for more comprehensive, future research.

Practitioner Research and the Practice of School

Whether you call this work teacher inquiry, action research, or practitioner research, it is a form of research designed by practitioners who seek improvement and a solution to daily classroom or school dilemmas (Stringer, 1999). For the purposes of this paper, the authors use practitioner research because we feel it is broader and encompasses work and collaboration by more than just classroom teachers. Practitioner research, helps practitioners in the field of education investigate their own practice systematically and intentionally (Ayers, 1993; Cochran-Smith & Lytle, 1999; Schon, 1983).

Teacher research is connected to the early work of Dewey (1916/1997) and Lewin (1948), who both argued that the primary aim of practitioner research was to enhance understanding and to improve learning and teaching. Some perceive that practitioner research is beneath the scholarship of academics in universities. Others view practitioner research as a form of "local knowledge" (Cochran-Smith, 1999) that may lead to change within particular classrooms and schools but is not claimed as being generalizable.

However, Zeichner, and Noffke (2001) claim that practitioner research should not be judged with the same criteria as outsider research. They note that trustworthiness is an alternative to the term validity. Anderson and Herr (1999) suggest that validity might be better accomplished in practitioner research with a variety of criteria, with each appropriate to the specificity of each inquiry. This helps us individualize the inquiry to meet the school's needs and provide initial insight into the complexities of specific problems in the school. The addition of elements (i.e. teacher candidates, additional resources, and impacts on clinical teachers' time) of a professional development school creates another dimension that must be taken into account.

Practitioner research may be a way to link teacher preparation and student learning. The work in a professional development school is complex; connections are complicated by instability of schools, the fidelity of the school to the philosophy of the partnership, the culture and climate of the school, and the personalities and biases of the people responsible for the partnership in a given school (National Commission on Teaching and America's Future, 2003). In other words, even though a program may be in multiple schools and may involve the same basic components and systems, significant differences can still exist in the way those components and systems are presented or carried out.

Practitioner research gives schools and university partners an individualistic way of looking at the partnership within a school context and provides them with information that informs their practice and their constituencies. The project described in this paper demonstrates how this can be done and how practitioner research can be used as a tool for creating a link between teacher preparation and student learning.

Initial Professional Teacher Education

The Initial Professional Teacher Education (IPTE) division at the University of Colorado at Denver (UCD) offers both graduate and undergraduate teacher licensure programs. The graduate program, in existence for ten years, is for individuals with a minimum of a bachelor's degree, typically in liberal arts, who seek initial licensure (elementary, secondary in mathematics, science, social studies, English, and foreign language, and/or K–12 special education) and a master's degree. Many are entering teaching as a second career, some with advanced degrees in their content area.

The graduate program admits approximately 250 K–12 candidates per year in two cohort groups of 125, all with content majors from liberal arts. Although a very small number of UCD's students earn a license while working as teachers, most are full-time students who are licensed following two semesters and a summer of full-time congruent university and field-based work in one of UCD's 25 professional development schools (PDSs). Elementary and secondary teacher candidates enroll in some courses together, a program plan which ensures that they consider how students develop as learners over the K–12 school span. In addition, general education and special education students are in many courses together, ensuring that all elementary and secondary classroom teachers are well-prepared to work with students with special needs and that all special educators have a solid foundation in general education in curriculum and instruction. Students in the graduate program may choose dual licensure as both general and special education teachers, and many of the courses serve as requirements for both fields. A group of lead instructors (the professors responsible for each course and its multiple sections) ensures the consistency and congruence of coursework with partner school internships and across courses.

The entire teacher education program was designed with the end in mind—a series of assessments in content knowledge, literacy, math, democratic schooling, differentiated instruction, instruction, assessment, classroom management, and technology. Course instructors are responsible for teaching and assessing the knowledge base of teacher candidates in each of these areas while partner school personnel, including site professors, are responsible for ensuring performance in each of these areas and conducting a final assessment of the implementation of each of these areas in the classroom and school.

During the licensure portion of their program, teacher candidates work in professional development schools two to four days per week, depending on the internship. University courses are closely interrelated with four internship experiences in which teacher candidates gradually assume responsibility for teaching. Elementary teacher candidates generally spend an entire academic year in a single elementary PDS school, while secondary teacher candidates spend their four internships in one of the middle or high school PDSs. The PDSs are in six Denver metropolitan districts with most serving large populations of low-income and/or minority students, a sizeable number of students for whom English is a second language, or who have special needs. Each partner school is supported by a site professor from the university one day per week and by a full-time master teacher, or site coordinator.

Once licensed, teacher candidates complete a master's degree in Special Education or Curriculum and Instruction in their first or second year of teaching in one of several emphasis areas, including special education, literacy, ESL, or content areas, including math and science, assessment, and technology. This ensures that UCD's new teachers are provided with continued support from the university in their first few years of teaching.

In the spring of 2002, the Colorado Commission of Higher Education and the Colorado Department of Education approved an undergraduate program at UCD in the areas of elementary education and secondary English. The undergraduate program has similar admissions requirements and professional coursework, internships, and performance based assessments as the graduate program.

Modeling the teacher education program components after what Goodlad (1990) has described in *Teachers for Our Nation's Schools,* UCD faculty and their partner school colleagues prepare teachers who know how to teach and who have strong content knowledge. In addition, each stakeholder (university faculty, school faculty, administrators, and teacher candidates) has roles and responsibilities related to four partner functions: teacher preparation, professional development, student learning, and inquiry. Simultaneous renewal of both schools and the university is key to this partnership.

Vital to the congruence of the teacher candidates' experience across university courses and school internships is the IPTE Council, a body made up of all the school site coordinators (master teachers released full time to work with the 10–15 teacher candidates in each school and on other partner school functions) and all the site professors (who earn 3/5 courses of their teaching load to work in the PDS one day per week for the year), chaired by the Division Coordinator of the program. The IPTE Council meets monthly for two hours, makes all admission decisions through a combination of application review and group interviews, places internships, and serves an advisory role to the IPTE Executive Council. The Executive Council is made up of an equal number of school and university representatives from IPTE Council and is the decision-making body of the program.

2001–2002 Eisenhower
Professional Development Grant

Inquiry has always been a part of our culture. Students have taken inquiry classes and have conducted projects in professional development schools since the beginning of the program nine years ago. They also are responsible for "legacy projects" many of which are inquiries that inform practice related to student learning. We have held leadership academies to guide professional development schools through processes of practitioner research, and in May 2003, we will hold our 7th Annual Action Research Conference. We believe that when teachers participate with other practitioners and university faculty to investigate important dilemmas, they increase the possibility of developing a richer understanding of their students and themselves, as well as having the potential to improve students' learning and to inform their own teaching practice.

In 2001–2002, we embarked on a project, funded by an Eisenhower Professional Development Grant, to address some of the questions we were getting about connecting the partnership with student achievement. Our main goal was to become more articulate about what was going on in schools so that we could address questions clearly and coherently. As we thought about the framework of the grant project, we focused on each individual school, recognizing that each school was experiencing some things in common but many things that were not. Schools needed time to look at their own school goals, the partnership as it played out in their school, and their own dilemmas related to both. Schools needed time, trust, talk, and tasks to accomplish inquiry as a systemic part of the organization (M. Cochran-Smith, personal communication, December 9, 1999). They needed time to think about obstacles that were standing in the way of change, and finally, they needed to have a method for discovering whether the changes they implemented actually made a difference for the school and students.

The project began with a one-day "train the trainer" session related to critical friends and how critical friends' protocols (Annenberg Institute for School Reform, 1998) could be used to stimulate a thoughtful dialogue among partnership participants. This "train the trainer" day occurred so that site professors and site coordinators could facilitate dialogs for other schools, as well as be knowledgeable of the process for their own school. After this initial training, individual PDSs determined the logistics for the dialogues. The agenda for each PDS was determined by the principle investigators of the grant.

Once the facilitators were trained, site coordinators and site professors invited at least 10–12 clinical teachers (general education and special education), school administrators, and teacher candidates to participate in a day of dialogue. Each school chose its own date, location, and timeframe (typically a 7–8 hour block with lunch). Fourteen of the sixteen partner schools volunteered to be involved in the project. In attendance were teachers, teacher candidates, site professor, site coordinator, and in most cases, the principal and/or assistant principal.

Briefly, the agenda for each dialogue day included a review of the current state of the partnership and set forth the guiding question, "How do we become articulate and intentional about how the partnership can have an effect on student learning?" After a review of the "big picture," small groups (4–6 participants) reviewed the school's improvement plan or student learning goals.

At the completion of this review, groups brainstormed dilemmas about the partnership relevant to their student learning goals. For example, an appropriate dilemma might be: "How can teacher candidates help with student writing achievement?" or "How can we use the teacher candidates' performance-based assessment on literacy as professional development?" Both dilemmas have a school and university component. A non-example would be, "How can I get more parents to volunteer in my classroom?" because it doesn't have a university component.

Across all the schools the most prevalent dilemmas were (a) professional development through university resources; (b) alignment of performance based assessment and school curriculum; (c) communication and collaboration between teacher candidates and clinical teachers; (d) integration of the teacher candidate to the professional development school; (e) communication about the partnership within the greater school community; and (f) balancing workload of clinical teachers. Other categories were also represented, but in much smaller numbers (five or less occurrences), such as the role of part-time teacher candidates, professional development of site technicians (university provided school technology assistance as a result of a PT3 grant), partnership stability, the quality of clinical teachers, expectations of teacher candidates, the quality of teacher candidates, communication between the school and university, and the role of the site coordinator as a professional developer.

After each group brainstormed dilemmas, they chose two that they believed, if solved, could have the most impact on student learning at your school. At the conclusion of this session, groups selected one dilemma that they believed they could act upon and use to stimulate a practitioner research project in the school. Each of these was posted, and the whole group selected one strategy for implementation. Guidelines for selection included reasonableness, control, and high probability for a measurable increase in student learning.

Once the dilemma was selected, the group was guided through steps to create a practitioner research project for their school (Caro-Bruce, 2000). We believed that moving the dialog to action was critical to the project. The dialog was only beneficial if it had some element of accountability for implementation. Each selection was deemed a practitioner research project, and the facilitators helped the group walk through an additional protocol for thinking about the inquiry. These steps included: (a) generating ideas, questions, or area of concern ("the dilemma"), (b) providing background, (c) creating an action plan, (d) gathering data, (e) identifying resources, (f) negotiating and considering ethical issues, (g) developing a rough time line, (h) identifying audiences, (i) planning for sharing and reporting (The Action Research Center, 1994) Examples of practitioner research questions included the following issues:

- How can we better utilize co-teaching strategies between clinical teachers and teacher candidates?
- How can we teach coaching skills to clinical teachers?
- How can a site professor and site coordinator communicate and coach clinical teachers more effectively?
- How can teacher candidates provide literacy intervention to low-performing students?

Schools were provided with additional grant funds, up to $1000, to support this work after the initial dialogue day. Schools used money to fund substitutes, videotapes, books, gift certificates to book stores, release time to analyze data, release time to prepare for presentation of the inquiries, and food at meetings. Schools submitted their plans for expenditure with an explanation of their action plan. Many school/university teams presented these practitioner research projects at our annual action research conference and other conferences and submitted papers for publication in a variety of professional journals.

Practitioner Research and Results

The following represents a brief synopsis of projects that school and university faculty embarked on as a result of the partner school dialogues. Space does not allow for an in-depth explanation of each of the projects, but by providing a sample of projects, an overview, and conclusions, the value of each project should be evident. Represented in this sample are four elementary school inquiry projects (one project was conducted jointly between two schools) and a middle school inquiry project. They represent the variety of projects utilizing a variety of methodologies and each helps to answer the larger question, "How does the partnership impact student learning?"

The first inquiry focused on their stakeholders and their perceptions of the partnership. The second inquiry looked at professional development related to co-teaching and the impact co-teaching could have on student achievement. The third inquiry took a more direct and qualitative approach, using teacher candidates' direct teaching of literacy and second language acquisition constructs to students as a way to impact student achievement, and the fourth project utilized teacher candidates indirectly to provide release time for clinical teachers to observe in each other's classrooms. Even though we, the investigators of the grant, used the phrase, "student learning" and thought about it in the broadest and most wholistic sense, you will notice that most schools narrowed the definition in their studies to student achievement in the academic sense. In any case, the work begins to define for each school the questions and wonderings they have related to the partnership and being a professional development school. The ability to individualize through practitioner research was valuable to each school and has helped each school increase its capacity for thinking intentionally about how the partnership can impact student learning.

Practitioner Research Project # 1: In What Ways Does the Partnership Influence Student Achievement at S. Elementary?

In this first investigation, the elementary school leadership team took on the broad question of student achievement, with a primary focus on classroom instruction and academics. This school has been part of the partnership for approximately six years and the leadership team wanted to hear from all stakeholders about their perceptions of the partnership and its impact on student achievement. During the investigation, sub-questions were developed collaboratively with school and university partners. Teachers, parents, students, and teacher candidates were all asked about their perceptions of how the partnership impacts student achievement. Teachers participated in both individual interviews and focus groups.

The majority of teachers who participated in the focus group reported that they felt that the teacher candidates helped them improve their instructional skills by bringing fresh perspectives and information to the school and classroom. Teachers said that they were more reflective of their own practice and more accountable for their practice knowing that teacher candidates were present and that site professors and site coordinators were visiting often. They also reported that there was more stability in the classroom, since they could use teacher candidates as substitutes and hire them as new teachers the following year. And finally, teachers suggested that there was more individualized instruction for students.

Individual interviews with teachers revealed both positive and negative impact on student achievement. Positive comments about teacher candidates in classrooms were that they allowed more one-on-one reading time, provided additional adults to work with students, gave students more opportunities to experience different teaching styles, and facilitated guided reading groups. Negative comments about the impact of teacher candidates in the classroom included difficulty in meeting different standards (i.e. student content standards and teacher education standards), differences among teacher candidates who may teach at various levels, and the time it took to work with teacher candidates.

Responses from parents were generally positive. Parents felt it was wonderful to have teacher candidates who were energetic, had new ideas, provided a talent pool for the school, gave students individual help, and brought new points of view to teachers and administrators. A group of fifth grade students reported that it was easier to get through school because they felt safer with more teachers, they liked the extra help when they needed it, they were glad the teacher candidates were there to learn from and help their teachers, they liked being able to work in smaller groups more often, and they enjoyed consistency when their teacher was away.

As a result of the interviews and focus groups, teachers reviewed the data and were asked about issues and concerns they had and what they would like to continue or change with regards to the partnership. These responses were compiled also, and this year, the faculty will use these questions as an impetus for further research. Overall, it is easy to see the overlapping responses made across the groups, such as a decrease in student/teacher ratios, a greater sense of differentiated instruction, and teacher candidates as future teachers in the school. Some gaps arose, however. Site professors and site coordinators did not mention professional development or the value of inquiry. As these are foci for the partnership, the school leadership team views these issues as contributions that need to be emphasized in the future.

Practitioner Research Project #2: An Investigation of the Effect of Co-Teaching on Student Learning

This second study looked at the strategy of co-teaching and how co-teaching could impact student achievement. The leadership team felt that if they could increase awareness, knowledge, and performance related to co-teaching models, there would be a benefit to clinical teachers, teacher candidates, and especially, students.

Clinical teachers and teacher candidates were initially surveyed about co-teaching methods used and the impact they had in classrooms. Observations of co-teaching were also completed in the classrooms of peers. This group found a lack of awareness of different co-teaching formats. Some formats were easier to implement, and therefore, used more frequently. Some formats required a closer relationship between teacher and teacher candidate. However, the group teachers did believe co-teaching would benefit classroom instruction by increasing student engagement, providing more individual instruction time, enabling students were to see varied approaches and modeling, increasing clinical teacher awareness and accountability, and providing an impetus for stronger planning and reflection.

As a result, a half-day focus group comprised of volunteer clinical teachers, former teacher candidates, and an administrator discussed co-teaching issues and classroom impacts. Suggestions and concerns related to co-teaching included more planning time, more training, and requiring the clinical teacher to give up some responsibility in the classroom. In another focus group with clinical teachers and teacher candidates, facilitators asked about ways in which they could provide more support for co-teaching. Their responses included training, release time, communicating the value/purpose of co-teaching, modeling co-teaching, and offering ideas to the university as to how co-teaching can be incorporated into assignments.

Practitioner Research Project #3: In What Ways Do Teacher Candidates Increase Student Achievement in Primary Grades?

The focus of this project was to evaluate whether teacher candidates impact student literacy at the primary level. Inquiry focused on spelling for seven third graders, comprehension strategies for second language learners, alphabet recognition for early childhood children, and Developmental Reading Assessment (DRA) or Evaluación del Desarrollo de la Lectura (EDL) improvement for a group of first graders and second graders. Throughout the school year, teacher candidates wrote about the activities, techniques, and reflections of their teaching in an on-line journal, and pre- and post-assessments were completed with students using DRA, Brigance, Qualitative Reading Inventory (QRI), and wordless picture book assessments, depending on their age and ability. The findings showed that all students improved academically. The value of the collaboration with clinical teachers mirrored the responsibilities teachers encounter daily in their classrooms, and teacher candidates brought different ideas from the latest research in literacy and in second language acquisition.

The teacher candidates saw improvement in each area on which they were working. Each teacher candidate presented their data to the school faculty. The teacher candidate who was working on spelling with third graders met her goal for the children to spell correctly the high frequency words. The teacher candidates who were working to develop oral language revealed that the children showed improvement in the Language Assessment Scale (LAS) test. And the students of the teacher candidate who was working with second language learners in comprehension improved one to two levels in the non-fiction reading assessments.

Practitioner Research Project #4: To What Extent Do Teachers Observations of Peers Impact Their Own Practice?

In this fourth inquiry project, a middle school leadership team wanted to determine if they could expand teachers' understanding of the curriculum and instructional environment outside the context of their own classroom. A strategy was developed to provide release time for structured observations of a variety of classrooms (i.e. grade levels and content areas). In order to facilitate this process, teacher candidates were used to provide "release time" for clinical teachers so that they could visit and observe others' classrooms. This process allowed teachers to gain insight into other teachers' practices, inform their own practice, and impact student achievement. The leadership team felt that without the partnership, this process would not have taken place.

Teachers discovered the continuum of curriculum, especially in mathematics. They witnessed differences in teaching styles and differences in relationships with students they didn't realize existed before. Teachers reported learning a variety of instructional strategies they hadn't tried before, seeing room arrangements and décor that they thought would also be effective for them, and identifying common threads among content areas for greater integration of content.

Beyond Practitioner Research

Practitioner research is a methodology that should be considered in the search for research methodologies to examine the link between teacher preparation programs and student learning. The projects above demonstrated how schools can begin to investigate their own questions about impact and formulate projects that reflect their own culture, students, and teachers. Each of these schools, as well as others in the partnership, have continued to work this year and are using what they learned to create environments of sharing and learning for their students. Many school teams have reported that this inquiry has led to more inquiry, and they are beginning to broaden the definition of student learning, even though in the current political climate, academics is the primary component of consideration for schools.

In the beginning of the paper, we mentioned the idea that the partnership was based on the philosophical underpinnings of simultaneous renewal, so we would be remiss not to talk about how these projects also have helped university faculty think about courses, performance based assessments, and work in schools that will also help us directly or indirectly impact student learning. First, there have been several suggestions by clinical teachers that were integrated into coursework. For example, one suggestion that came out of the co-teaching project was for university instructors to incorporate co-teaching into the performance-based assessments. A group of lead instructors is currently working on implementing this idea. In addition, the university has created a co-teaching module for clinical teachers and teacher candidates.

These projects and results have also given us a framework for a more formal research design in the coming years. They have caused us to wonder about whether the results cited here are generalizable to our entire group of professional development schools and how, as a partnership, we are affecting student learning. However, it's difficult to isolate the added value of any partnership in order to measure the direct impact on student achievement; especially when student achievement is associated primarily with high-stakes test scores.

Comparison or experimental studies with control groups are even more difficult to accomplish without a tremendous amount of funding. As evidenced in fugitive literature (Abdul-Haaq, 1998), many partnerships across the country have anecdotal stories about how their partnership has impacted students. As Cochran-Smith (1997) states, the development for effective work in urban sites "is about interpretation, ideologies, and practices" (p. 30) and the ways they are interdependent with and informed by each other.

Observation, anecdotal reflection, and other qualitative data sources are more compatible with these frameworks for partner school relationships. In addition, the work in professional development schools is defined differently in each school context, giving credence to the fact that it is difficult to collect similar data on the impacts on student learning across schools, and thereby compounding the difficulty of collecting data on children's growth and connecting it to teacher preparation.

Even so, a research design has been created to look at a number of different components (i.e. professional development, the work of the site coordinator and site professor, perceptions of students, teachers, administrators, hidden curriculum, school culture). We are trying to use both quantitative and qualitative data-gathering techniques so that we can address the multi-tude of audiences that see this as an important accountability of professional development schools. Most importantly, the research design has stemmed from university researchers and school practitioners thinking about schools and their individual complexities and issues, developing practitioner research projects specific to the schools population, and then using those results to inform the larger research agenda.

REFERENCES

Anderson, G., Herr, K., & Nihlen. (1999). The new paradigm wars: Is there room for rigorous practitioner knowledge in schools and universities? *Educational Researcher, 28*(5), 12–21.

Abdul-Haaq, I. (1998). *Professional development schools: Weighing the evidence.* Thousand Oaks, CA: Corwin.

Ayers, W. (1989). *The good preschool teacher: Six teachers reflect on their lives.* New York, NY: Teachers College Press.

Ayers, W. (1993). *To teach: The journey of a teacher.* New York, NY: Teachers College Press.

Bissex, G., & Bullock, R. (Eds.). (1987). *Seeing for ourselves: Case-study research by teachers of writing.* London: Heinemann.

Caro-Bruce, C. (2000). *Action research facilitator's handbook.* Wichita Falls, TX: National Staff Development Council.

Clark, R.W. (1994). *Partner schools and The National Network for Education Renewal: A compact for simultaneous renewal.* Seattle, WA: Center for Educational Renewal, University of Washington.

Cochran-Smith, M. (1997). Knowledge, skills, and experiences for teaching culturally diverse learners: A perspective for practicing teachers. In J.J. Irvine (Ed.), *Critical knowledge for diverse teachers and learners* (pp. 27–88). Washington, DC: American Association of Colleges for Teacher Education.

Cochran-Smith, M. & Lytle, S. L. (1992). Communities for teacher research: Fringe or forefront. *American Journal of Education, 5,* 299–324.

Cochran-Smith, M., & Lytle, S. L. (1993). *Inside outside. Teacher research and knowledge.* New York, NY: Teachers College Press.

Cochran-Smith, M., & Lytle, S.L. (1999). The teacher research movement: A decade later. *Educational Researcher 28*(7), 15–25.

Darling-Hammond, L. (1994). *Professional development schools: Schools for developing a profession.* New York, NY: Teachers College Press.

Dewey, J. [1916] (1997). *Democracy and education: An introduction to the philosophy of education.* New York, NY: Free Press.

Dewey, J. [1935] (1985). *How we think; a restatement of the relation of reflective thinking to the educative process.* Boston: Heath.

Goodlad, J. I. (1994). *Educational renewal: Better teachers, better schools.* San Francisco, CA: Jossey-Bass.

National Commission of Teaching and America's Future. (2003). *No dream denied: A pledge to America's children.* Washington, DC: NCTAF.

Levine, M. (1988). Introduction. In M. Levine (Ed.), *Professional practice schools: Building a model* (Monograph No. 1). Washington, DC: AFT.

Lewin, K. (1948). *Resolving social conflict: Selected papers on group dynamics.* New York: Harper.

Paley, B. G. (1986). *Molly is three.* Chicago: University of Chicago Press.

Schön, D. (1983). *The reflective practitioner.* New York: Basic Books.

Stringer, E.T. (1999). *Action research.* 2nd ed. Thousand Oaks, CA: Sage.

Walsh, D.J., Baturka, H. L., Smith, M. E., & Colter, N. (1991). Changing one's mind-maintaining one's identity: A first grade teacher's story. *Teachers College Record 93,* 73–86.

Zeichner, K.M., & Noffke, S. E. (2001). Practitioner research. In V. Richardson (Ed.), *Handbook of research on teaching,* 4th ed. (pp. 298–330). Washington, DC: American Educational Research Association.

—

Summary and Implications

Gwendolyn T. Benson

Methods of Making Connections Between Teacher Education and Student Learning

The four chapters in this section encompass four distinct methods of connecting teacher education and student learning. These methods cut across teacher education program models, teacher quality, professional development schools, and practitioner research.

Chapter 1 describes how three teacher preparation programs are changing in order to have a more positive impact on student learning. The three programs include a pre-service undergraduate program, a pre-service graduate program and an in-service continuing certification program. The major impetus for changing the programs includes both state and national standards (INTACS, 1992; NCATE, 2002; NBPTS, 1996). The requirement to demonstrate positive impact on K–12 cuts across all standards and requires demonstration and documentation that teacher education graduates can produce positive K–12 student outcomes.

Various methods of documenting impact are presented including performance based assessment, Teacher Work Sample Methodology, and action research. The NCATE document, "Assessing Education Candidate Performance: A Look at Changing Practices," supports the use of varied, innovative, and authentic forms of assessment such as portfolios, reflections, surveys, and vignettes (Elliott, 2003).

Each of the programs described in this chapter developed a different model designed to determine positive impact on student learning. The pre-service undergraduate program developed three *Positive Impact Products*. These include a Comprehensive Instructional Plan, a Positive Impact Plan and a Professional Growth Plan. The graduate program used *action research*.

Chapter 2 addresses the strength of teacher preparation programs in mathematics. Various studies are cited that support the claim that knowledge of subject matter is an important variable in determining the variance accounted for in predicting teacher effectiveness. (Ball 1991; Ma, 1999;

Monk, 1994; Monk & King, 1994). The central question was: What is the relationship between the strength of teachers' mathematical backgrounds and the improvement from third to fifth grade in mathematics performance of their school's students? Three schools with grades three and five in the same school were selected. There was a difference in the test scores across the three schools; however, the reported transcript analyses in this study did not support any clear and simple feature of the teachers' academic preparation that would account for the significant and striking differences in the academic performance of the students among the three schools. Results were mixed, as is frequently the case in teacher quality studies (Goldhaber, 2002; Sanders & Horn, 1998).

Additional findings suggest that the higher performing schools had teachers who, on average, took more mathematics course credits in college than teachers on average took in the lower performing school. They also reported a perfect relationship among the three schools between the number of math credits taken by the teachers in each school and the mean fifth grade math score in each school.

In Chapter 3, a strong emphasis is placed on K–12 students in professional development schools. The question is raised regarding the relative absence of students from the PDS research to date followed by a discussion on why student have been omitted. Reasons offered include the relative youth of the movement, other goals that have been the main focus such as long-term systemic change in the education of perspective teachers, the growth of practicing teachers, and the educational experiences for the students. Political reasons for the lack of focus on students are also discussed, such as, comparing non-PDSs within the district to PDSs.

Three types of data were collected to determine the impact on students. These include parent questionnaires, mentor questionnaires, and inquiry projects. Most of the discussion related to the value of the process as opposed to the data from the questionnaires and the inquiry projects. Specifically these processes are, establishing initial method of exploring student impact, the importance of the results to the development and future of the PDS, documentation that parents and teachers believe PDSs work had positive outcomes for students, increasing the visibility of classroom based inquiry in the PDSs and the role classroom based inquiry may play in impacting children.

The authors were clear on two weaknesses. First, the methodology did not include the voice of children and the study is lacking in its inability to answer what is a nagging question across the nation: What is the relationship between student academic achievement and their participation in a PDS classroom?

Chapter 4 offers a model that may be used to select research projects that link teacher preparation and student learning. Though action research is the term used more frequently, the authors choose to use the term practitioner research because they feel it is broader and encompasses work and collaboration by more that just the classroom teachers.

This project had participating schools create research projects that have not only informed practices linking teacher preparation to student learning, but also given the teacher preparation programs direction for more comprehensive, future research. A group process arrived at consensus on one dilemma that, if resolved, could have the most impact on student learning. The process included guidelines for selection of dilemma and specific steps to create a practitioner research project.

More importantly, the projects demonstrated how schools can begin to investigate their own questions about impact and formulate projects that reflect their own culture, students, and teachers. Additionally, the authors indicate that the project helped university faculty think about courses, performance based assessment, and work in school that will also help teacher education directly and indirectly impact student learning.

Implications

A recurring theme throughout the four chapters is the value and necessity of school-university partnerships in making the linkage between teacher education and K–12 student learning. The most powerful commonality among the studies was the increased opportunities for future teachers to be involved in school settings and particularly conducting research relevant to their schools. These studies are an indication of the importance of documenting and reporting on the work occurring in partner schools and teacher education programs throughout the country. It is also an answer to critical reports from within and outside the profession (Wilson, Floden, & Ferrini-Mundy, 2001; Zeichner & Schulte, 2001).

There is little guidance and few models for systematic research and inquiry about how partnership relationships affect student learning, behavior, and attitudes and fewer that address the problems underlying the paucity of research (Wiseman & Knight, 2003). The four chapters offer valuable lessons learned in regard to teacher preparation models, teacher quality, professional development schools and action research. They also point out the difficulty in conducting the type of research that will answer the questions regarding student outcomes. Of major importance are the recommendations and insights on how we should proceed in developing partnerships that will ultimately bring K–12 educators and teacher education faculty to consensus on how to make the linkage between teacher education and student learning.

REFERENCES

Ball, D. L. (1991). Research on teaching mathematics: Making subject matter knowledge part of the equation. In J. Brophy (Ed.), *Advances in research on teaching* (pp. 1–48). Greenwich, CT: JAI Press.

Elliott, E. (2003). *Assessing education candidate performance: A look at changing practices.* National Council for Accreditation of Teacher Education. Washington, D.C..

Goldhaber, D. (2002). The mystery of good teaching. *Education Next, 2*(1), 50–55.

Interstate New Teacher Assessment and Support Consortium (INTASC). (1992). *Model standards for beginning teacher licensing and development: A resource for state dialogue.* Washington, D.C.: Council of Chief State School Officers. ED 369767.

Ma, L. (1999). *Knowing and teaching elementary mathematics: Teachers' understanding of mathematics in China and the United States.* Mahwah, NJ: Lawrence Erlbaum Associates.

Monk, D. H. (1994). Subject area preparation of secondary mathematics teachers and science teachers and student achievement. *Economics of Education Review, 12,* 125–145.

Monk, D. H., & King, J. A. (1994). Multilevel teacher resource effects on pupil performance in secondary mathematics and science. In R.G. Ehrenberg (Ed.), *Choices and consequences* (pp. 29–58). Ithaca, NY: ILR Press.

National Board for Professional Teaching Standards (NBPTS). (n.d.). *What teachers should know and be able to do.* Detroit, MI: Author.

National Council for Accreditation of Teacher Education. (2002). *Professional standards for the accreditation of schools, colleges, and departments of education: 2002 edition.* Washington, D.C.: Author.

Sanders, W., & Horn, S. (1998). Research findings from the Tennessee Value-Added Assessment System (TVAAS) database: Implications for educational evaluation and research. *Journal of Personnel Evaluation in Education, 12*(3), 247–256.

Wilson, S., Floden, R., & Ferrini-Mundy, J. (2001). *Teacher preparation research: Current knowledge, gaps, and recommendations.* A research report prepared by the Center of the Study of Teaching and Policy: University of Washington.

Wisemen, D., & Knight, S. (2002, January). *Rethinking teacher education research structures and approaches: Making linkages between school-university partnerships and PK–12 student outcomes.* Paper presented at the American Colleges of Teacher Education, New Orleans, LA.

Zeichner, K. M., & Schulte, A. K. (2001). What we know and don't know from peer-reviewed research about alternative teacher certification programs. *Journal of Teacher Education, 52*(4), 266-282.

Division

3

Models for Assessing Teacher Impact on Student Learning

Overview and Framework

Linda F. Quinn

Linda F. Quinn is Professor and Associate Dean at the University of Nevada, Las Vegas College of Education. Her research interests span the continuum of teachers' lives from preparation, through induction, to fulfillment as master teachers in the U.S and in international settings. She is currently revisiting the use of video to increase teacher candidate effectiveness in field placements.

New emphasis on student and teacher performance is profoundly influencing the ways that teachers are selected, prepared, licensed, and recognized. Policymakers now expect teachers and teacher candidates to show evidence of knowledge and skill and the ability to apply them to teach effectively (Galluzzo, 1999, i).

At the beginning of the 20th Century, Herbert Spencer (1910) asked, "What knowledge is of most worth?" of a society experiencing similar developments to the ones we currently face (Payne, 2003). Answers to Spencer's question over the past 96 years have been numerous and varied resulting in lively and fruitful debate. At the moment, however, it seems the professional community is close to agreement regarding what teachers need to know and be able to do. Professionals in the field and in colleges of education are working together to leave no doubt as to what the correct response to Spencer's question should be. Identifying the link between teacher education and student achievement may be one of the most complex tasks undertaken by the education community. Nowhere else are the lines that separate inputs from outputs more difficult to define, are the variables more numerous and changeable, or are the participants more influenced by myth, history, and policy.

The preface to Galluzzo's (1999) NCATE monograph, *Aligning Standards to Improve Teacher Preparation and Practice*, states succinctly the present climate surrounding teacher preparation and performance. A teacher's influence has been shown to be a powerful variable on student learning (Rivkin, Hanushyek, and Kain, 1998), and Sanders and Rivers (1996) have data to support ways the effectiveness of teachers can have a dramatic effect on the performance of students over time. At long last there is affirmation in the form of evidence that teachers do make a difference and those teachers who incorporate specific teaching interventions appear to have a greater likelihood of making a positive difference in the achievement of their students. Not a big surprise, but encouraging in the attention that is being focused on all levels of the profession to initiate and maintain teacher quality. The transformation of schooling relies heavily on the professional development of teachers (Guskey, 1997, 1).

There are over 1,100 colleges and schools of education in the nation, and I would venture to guess that all but a few, perhaps all, in response to the current call for accountability, have given considerable attention to teacher education "interventions" that will result in student learning. As teacher preparation programs are aligned with expectations of the No Child Left Behind Act (2001), and anticipate passage of the Title II, Ready to Teach Act, educators are well aware of the requirement to provide documentation to support their claims of preparing quality teachers. It is a tremendous undertaking, highly public, and politically charged.

The chapters in this section of the Teacher Education Yearbook XII describe interventions that extend or augment traditional teacher education course work, interventions that emphasized new teaching methods and learner orientation. The research describes interrelated approaches to preparing quality teachers and for strengthening the link between teacher education and student performance. The interventions presented here are dependent for success on the existence of dedicated professionals working in collaborative environments to change the learning landscape for teachers and students. They include

1) Creating and redesigning programs to promote interventions,
2) Forming partnerships and implementing professional development that support and encourage the implementation of such interventions, and
3) Conducting research that supports teacher educators' collection and analysis of evidence to help determine the effect of such interventions.

Redesign of Teacher Education Programs

The Title II Ready to Teach Act authorizes State grant monies to be used to reform teacher preparation requirements at the state level. It can be anticipated that one of the primary requirements of the bill "flexibility in program structure" will promote charter colleges of education and other alternative preparation routes. One example of conflict between differing routes to certification (Turley & Nakai, 2000), illustrates the dilemma of accommodating students in traditional programs who are already teaching under alternative licensure. Regardless of which side of the debate one supports on alternative or nontraditional routes to licensure (Chapella & Eubanks, 2001; Holmes, 2001), traditional teacher education programs can expect an increase in scrutiny from funding agencies and the American public. The emergence of The American Board for Certification of Teacher Excellence (ABCTE) as an alternative route to teacher certification for "individuals who would be turned off by traditional teacher preparation and certification programs" (Brassell, 2003, 1), requires that teacher educators defend, with reliable data, the importance of pedagogical knowledge, and devise meaningful ways such knowledge can be readily acquired through authentic learning opportunities. Redesign of approved programs may be necessary to meet the challenge of "not keeping pace" (Herrera & Murry, 2003, 5), or to define the role of teacher education to reverse what is viewed as a negative trend.

Professional Development Partnerships to Facilitate Interventions

The emphasis on standardized test results of students has generated a heightened interest in the effect of professional development of teachers on student learning (Kelleher, 2003). When teachers engage in professional development that enables them to make connections with teaching they are more likely to sustain the development over an extended period of time (Garet, et.al., 2001; Wenglinsky, 2000). Smylie (1996) tells us that ". . . teachers' opportunities to learn should be problem-oriented and grounded in inquiry, experimentation, and reflection" (p. 10). The mission of professional development, as defined by WestEd (2000) is to prepare and support all educators to help all students achieve high standards of learning and development.

The National Foundation for the Improvement of Education (1996) defines high-quality professional development as that which is "designed and directed by teachers, incorporates the best principles of adult learning, and involves shared decisions" (xv), and suggests that in order for teachers to grow professionally, they need:

- partners who can help them enhance their knowledge & skills,
- time & opportunity to plan collaboratively,
- sustained, in-depth teacher learning, and
- opportunities to take on new roles within the school.

These needs can be satisfied through sustained efforts in designing and implementing collaborative partnership programs that are directed toward the professional growth of classroom teachers and interventions that result in student achievement.

Partnerships should establish a structure of exemplary practices in education and these practices should be capable of "transforming both teacher preparation and the schooling of children" (Millian & Vare, 1997, p. 711). When schools and colleges of education form partnerships, both partners do so with a hope that the partnership will establish richer learning environments than either partner is capable of providing on their own. "There is virtually no limit to what teachers can do, once given authority and support—and time" (Checkley, 1997, 7).

Teachers need a working environment "where the discourse of teachers is shaped by the experiential realities of the classroom" (Proefriedt, 1994, p. 33), "where they can actively work with ideas, have choices, and work individually and collectively and share and demonstrate their learning with others through increased self-responsibility" (Glickman, 1997). Each chapter in this Division of the Yearbook demonstrates the power of the combined effort of teachers and teacher education faculty working together to identify the effects of interventions on student learning. A greater understanding of the balance between academic theories and classroom realities is achieved through focused interactions with peers. Talking about teaching and listening to others talk about teaching provides access to the events of teaching that build teacher knowledge (Carter, 1993). And teacher knowledge to improve student learning is at the heart of teacher education interventions.

Research on Teacher Education Interventions

Current research on teacher education provides the profession with reliable data on which to base future investigations. Making sense of the complex world of teaching and learning requires close examination of what teachers do. The challenge of "capturing the complexity of teaching" (Galluzzo, 1999) is one all teacher educators must respond to by engaging in the collection and aggregation of reliable evidence. The professional problem-solving ethos described by Joyce (1991) should be promoted in teacher education interventions and prepare teacher candidates to approach their own teaching with a researchers eye for design, treatment and outcomes. The authors of the following four chapters have been participants in learning about teaching through intimate involvement in the research process. Their experiences provide valuable data about teacher education interventions and establish a backdrop for future research in this area.

REFERENCES

Bolich, A. M. (2003). Reduce your losses: Help new teachers become veteran teachers. Atlanta: Southern Regional Education Board.

Carter, K. (1993). The place of story in research on teaching and teacher education. *Educational Researcher, 22*(1), 5–12.

Chappelle, N., & Eubanks, S. (2001). Defining alternative certification and nontraditional routes to teaching: Similarities, differences, and standards of quality. *Teaching and Change, 8*(4), 307–316.

Checkley, K. (1997). Linking teacher learning with student learning. *Professional Development Newsletter,* Spring. Alexandria, VA: ASCD.

Dewey, J. (1939). *Intelligence in the modern world: John Dewey's philosophy.* New York: Random House, Inc.

Dewey, J. (1964). John Dewey on education: Selected writings (R. D. Archambault, Ed.). Chicago: University of Chicago Press.

Doyle, W. (1986). Classroom organization and management. In M. Wittrock (Ed.), *Handbook of Research on Teaching* (3rd ed., pp. 392–431). New York: Macmillan.

Fullan, M. G., Bennet, B., & Rolheiser-Bennet, C. (1989). *Linking classroom and school improvement.* Paper presented at the annual meeting of the American Educational Research Association, San Francisco, CA.

Galluzzo, G. (1999). *Aligning standards to improve teacher preparation and practice.* Washington: The National Council for Accreditation of Teacher Education.

Garet, M. S., Porter, A. C., Desimone, L., Birman, B., & Yoon, K. S. (2001). What makes professional development effective? Results from a national sample of teachers. *American Educational Research Journal, 38*(4), 915–945.

Glickman, D. (1997). Keynote address at the annual meeting of the Association of Teacher Educators, Washington, D.C.

Guskey, T. R. (1997). Results-oriented professional development: In search of an optimal mix of effective practices. *http://www.ncrel.org/sdrs/areas/rpl_esys/pdlitrev.htm.*

Holmes, B. J. (2001). Understanding the Pros and Cons of Alternative Routes to Teacher Certification. *Teaching and Change, 8*(4), 317–330.

Joyce, B. R. (1991). Doors to school improvement. *Educational Leadership, 48*(8), 59–62.

Kelleher, J. (2003). A model for assessment-driven professional development. *Phi Delta Kappan, 84*(10) (pp. 751–763).

Knowles, J. G., Cole, A. L., & Presswood, C. S. (1994). *Through preservice teachers' eyes: Exploring field experiences through narrative and inquiry.* New York: Macmillan.

Little, J. W. (1982). Norms of collegiality and experimentation: Workplace conditions of school success. *American Educational Research Journal, 19,* 325–340.

Little, J. W. (1988). Assessing the prospects for teacher leadership. In A. Liberman (Ed.). *Building a professional culture in schools,* 78–106, New York: Teachers College Press.

Payne, R. (2003). What's Really Behind it All? Part I. *Texas Elementary Principals and Supervisors Association,* March.

Proefriedt, W. A. (1994). *How teachers learn: Toward a more liberal teacher education.* New York: Teachers College Press.

Rivkin, S.G., Hanushek, E.A., & Kain, J. F. (1998). *Teachers, schools and academic achievement.* National Bureau of Economic Research. Working Paper No. 6691.

Sanders, W.L., & Rivers, J.C. (1996). *Cumulative and residual effects of teachers on future academic achievement.* University of Tennessee Value-Added Research and Assessment Center.

Schon, D.A. (1987). *Educating the reflective practitioner.* San Francisco, CA: Jossey-Bass.

Smylie, M. A. (1996). From bureaucratic control to building human capital: The importance of teacher learning in education reform. *Educational Researcher, 25*(9), 9–11.

Sparks, D., & Hirsh, S. (1997). *A new vision for staff development.* Alexandria, VA: Association for Supervision and Curriculum Development.

Spencer, H. (1910). *Education: Intellectual, moral and physical.* New York: Appleton.

Turley, S., & Nakai, K. (2000). Two routes to certification: What do student teachers think? *Journal of Teacher Education, 51*(2), 122–134.

Wenglinsky, H. (2000). *How teaching matters: Bringing the classroom back into discussions of teacher quality.* Princeton: Educational Testing Service.

West, Ed. (2000). *Teachers who learn, kids who achieve: A look at schools with model professional development.* San Francisco: WestEd.

8.

Empowering Beginning Teachers to Analyze Their Students' Learning

Wendy Burke

Wendy M. Burke, Ph.D. is an assistant professor at Eastern Michigan University in the Department of Teacher Education. Her research interests are teacher education, building and sustaining teacher communities, professional development, and novice teacher induction and mentoring.

ABSTRACT

At EMU, five student teachers created teacher work samples during the winter 2001 term as a part of the student teaching experience. This study follows two of these student teachers into their first year of teaching and examines the degree to which they have incorporated some of the strategies involved in producing the teacher work sample, in addition to exploring the specific needs and concerns they have as beginning teachers. It examines the degree to which participation in the pilot program that brought together a diverse group of faculty and practitioners resulted in our student teachers being prepared to be effective as teachers for the teaching context in which they are employed. Within this context, being effective as teachers means that our teacher candidates learn to use information about the learning-teaching context and student individual differences to determine and assess learning goals, assess student learning, and modify instruction to facilitate learning for all students.

What do beginning teachers need to know and be able to do in order for their students to be successful learners in the classroom? This is a difficult question to answer for many reasons. A discussion about learning to teach should begin with a discussion about the learning process itself. The process of learning is a highly abstract, complex human endeavor that is reflective of components such as one's readiness, experiences, and interests, in addition to the learning context and environment, motivation, and challenges. Of course, the process of learning to teach is equally complex. As Davis and Sumara (1999) so beautifully argue, teaching should be understood as "complex" rather than "complicated."

> Complicated systems can be understood by breaking them down and analyzing their individual parts; complex systems, by contrast, cannot be discerned by deconstructing them, as these systems are often greater than the sum of their parts – they are more dynamic, more unpredictable, more alive. Teaching, therefore, cannot be looked at piecemeal; the web of relationships, experiences, outside influences, and unknown factors that play into the teaching and learning situation must be explored as the complex, whole system it is. (p. 237)

This longitudinal qualitative study emerged from a larger five-year research project funded by the Renaissance Teacher Quality Project currently underway at Eastern Michigan University. In the process of examining the complexity of teaching, it also explores some of the issues related to the complexity of learning to teach for two novice teachers, Mary and Heidi. These beginning teachers participated in this pilot project during their semester of student teaching. The larger project is grounded in the belief that student teachers skilled and knowledgeable about how to analyze their own students' learning are able to engage in making more relevant and meaningful pedagogical decisions than those who do not have these experiences.

My study begins with a discussion of the external and internal demands for greater accountability in teacher education and its impact on a specific teacher education program. It then includes a brief introduction to the use of Teacher Work Samples and their use at Eastern Michigan University. Narratives are provided to share some of Mary and Heidi's learning experiences during their semester of student teaching and first year of teaching. The larger research project involved a comparison between these two teachers and three other novices who did not participate in this project, but because of page limitations, this comparison will not be shared here.

Learning to Teach and Teacher Education

Teacher education programs have long endured many rounds of criticism from the public, researchers, and school personnel. But the public is not alone in how it characterizes teacher education programs and how to improve them. Many teachers also have characterized and condemned their teacher education preparation as inadequately preparing them for the realities of the classroom. That many student teachers repeat the phrase, "I learned to teach by teaching in my own classroom" unfortunately doesn't encourage other students of education and the public to view teacher education programs as relevant, necessary, or well-connected to what teachers do in the classroom as teachers. While this sentiment fails to recognize the continuum of experience that captures the process of learning to teach (Griffin, 1992), it accurately captures the limited ways many teacher educators candidly reveal and discuss the complexity of our roles and our mixed opinions about the outcomes of our programs with our teacher candidates. As a beginning teacher educator, I often feel compelled within my professional community to speak with too much confidence and authority as I discuss what I believe my students learn, know and are able to do, and how I assess their learning in my classroom. In this way, I am a poor role model with secondary student teachers for sharing the complexity of assessing student work.

Learning to teach is often viewed as the systematic learning of discrete skills and knowledge, a process that is characterized by learning to write lesson plans, curriculum units, and classroom management plans. In many instances, teacher education programs provide a range of teaching experiences for their candidates. In these instances, student teacher candidates are engaged in teaching lessons to K–12 students and reflecting on those lessons within the context of a university course. And while these practices do prepare candidates for some of the aspects of teaching, learning these skills alone cannot fully prepare beginning teachers for recognizing and responding to the multitude of possible events, responsibilities, and the unpredictability of students, classrooms, and schools. What can be learned during a teacher education program is largely dependent on such variables as the readiness of the student teacher, the relevance, content, and methodology in professional education courses and assignments, and the ability of the program and its instructors to communicate contextually relevant connections between theory and practice. All of these components of teaching, including the personal aptitude of the student teacher, represent complex dimensions of the process of learning to teach and are better understood as the teacher practices and reflects on his or her teaching repeatedly over time (Schön, 1987).

The notion that teacher candidates could be fully prepared to become master teachers during their teacher education program ignores the complexity of the process of learning to teach. Such thinking is more reflective of the lack of differentiated role status among all teachers than it is reflective of the realities of what is possible to learn prior to one's working for the first time with his or her own classroom. A teacher with five, ten, or twenty years experience is likely to have a range of experiences from which to draw and learn, and this includes life experiences related to one's life stages, in addition to those experiences in the classroom (Fessler & Christensen, 1992). That beginning teachers learn a great deal during their first years of teaching should not be used as an argument against the value of one's teacher education program. Instead, realizing that learning to teach is a developmental process necessitates that we as teacher educators be involved in the ongoing support and mentoring of our teacher candidates during their initial teaching years (Griffin, 1992).

Accountability and Teacher Education Reform

The National Council of Accreditation of Teacher Education (NCATE) and the Interstate New Teacher Assessment and Support Consortium (INTASC) have raised the expectations for the outcomes of teacher education programs. Teacher educators are now expected to take a more central role in the evaluation of our teacher education programs and to provide the public and various stakeholders with evidence of our concern for quality and accountability. At the same time, we must also consider how to work more collaboratively and thoughtfully to improve our programs so that they provide experiences that cultivate the skills and knowledge that beginning teachers need, to better analyze and reflect on their practice as it impacts student learning. Ideally, meeting the demands for greater accountability to various stakeholders should be a by-product of improving our teacher education programs. Yet, bringing together a group of individual teacher educators and Arts and Sciences professors with distinctive research and teaching agendas does not always lead to a more coherent and sustainable program. Like many teacher educators across the country, we at Eastern Michigan University are struggling to revise the content of our courses, the programs and sequence of the courses, and how we envision the qualified, competent graduate who is ready to meet the demands of the K–12 school setting as we also work to define our own interests in the process.

Most teacher candidates are currently required by their state certification boards to pass at least a basic skills test and a test in the content area in which they are seeking certification (Tom, 1996). But teacher candidates' performance on such tests tells us very little about candidates' ability to analyze what K–12 students understand, the contextual factors for teaching and learning, how to use such information to make more appropriate and effective pedagogical decisions, how to better incorporate technology to enhance student learning, and how to reflect on one's practice in making a positive impact on students' learning. "Licensing exams are designed to assess a narrow set of skills needed for basic competency as a beginning schoolteacher, and to separate unqualified people from those who have minimum qualifications," states a report released in March 2001 by the National Research Council. "Because a teacher's work is complex, state and federal policy makers who want to judge the quality of teacher-education programs should look at a variety of factors, including graduates' performance as schoolteachers" (Basinger, 2001, p. 4).

This project advocates the use of multiple data points as a means for gaining richer, more personalized, comprehensive and a more collaboratively constructed profile of student learning, of both preservice student teachers and K–12 student learning. It provides an example of one plausible alternative to the use of exit exams for teacher candidates. In order for teacher educators to become full participants in the accountability movement, we must be willing to share the multiplicity of our visions for what beginning teachers should know and be able to do as a result of completing a teacher education program. This vision must somehow recognize that every teacher candidate has skills, knowledge, and emerging teacher identities that should be understood as "works in progress". When working with preservice student teachers, I remain firmly committed to the process of making my own decision-making, thinking, and planning more visible to my students as I teach, supervise, and mentor them. I openly share the following questions with them as we collectively think about what effective teaching looks like: (a) What is it that effective teachers do when planning for and working with students in diverse classrooms? (b) How has the accountability movement affected this relationship? (c) How can we work with teachers and schools to create a more shared and collaborative vision of the necessary work involved for those who prepare teachers and those who teach? and (d) How can we best determine the impact of our teacher education program on our student teacher candidate's learning to teach? Not only do these questions guide discussions with student teachers about what they have learned, but they also provide the forum for discussing the complexity of learning to teach.

The Renaissance Teacher Quality Project

There is a commonly held belief that student teaching experiences often fall short in continuing the educational experiences and environment initiated during a teacher education program. Fieman-Nemser and Buchmann (1989) argue that student teachers often receive little feedback and engage in few conversations with their university professors during student teaching. As a result, the student teaching semester is regarded as a capstone experience that signifies the end of a student's university preparation and the introduction to one's initial attempts at trial and error. This stage often is experienced with the immediate guidance of a cooperating teacher, coupled with a limited amount of support from a university supervisor. In contrast, the Renaissance Teacher Quality Project relies on a collaborative model of support, mentoring, and instruction for teacher candidates. Arts and Sciences professors, teacher education professors from Reading, Assessment, and Methods divisions, cooperating teachers, and student teacher candidates have been working together for three years to think about and reflect on issues and practices relevant to learning to teach.

During semi-monthly workshops, all participants in the project learn about how to use methods of the Teacher Work Sample (TWS) to articulate the "web of relationships" embedded in learning to teach within the context of the classroom. The TWS methods require student teacher candidates to learn how to identify, analyze, and reflect on specific contextual information about the students, the classroom, and the school in which they are student teaching. After conducting an analysis of the contextual factors, student teachers determine their learning goals, assessment plans, and designs for instruction. As part of their assessment plans, they create and administer a pre-assessment instrument to assess their students' prior knowledge, skills, and experiences relevant to the specific learning goals for the unit. This information is analyzed to determine how to proceed with their designs for instruction. After teaching their units, student teachers administer a post-assessment of their students, using the same assessment instrument used in the pre-assessment step. They conduct an analysis of this post-assessment in terms of the whole classroom, the subgroups they chose to examine, and two individual students identified by the student teachers. Then they reflect on what they could learn about their students' learning from the process, which strategies were effective in improving student mastery from a chosen set of learning objectives, and which skills and knowledge they have acquired during the process, and which, they still need to address.

Analyzing one's context for teaching before designing learning goals, activities, and assessment plans is emphasized to establish a "habit of mind" about how one engages in learning to teach. Assessment plans and instruments are constructed as part of the lesson design and activities so that there is alignment and it is used as a formative component of thinking about what students are learning, reteaching, and skill/knowledge differentiation among students.

The notion that teachers are *trained* to teach misrepresents the sheer complexity of the process and variables involved in teaching. The word "training" connotes an agreed upon set of steps, procedures, or discrete skills that are easily transmitted, can be learned within a bounded time frame, can be transferred from one context to the next, and are easily assessed. And although the TWS outlines a set of learning tasks that must be completed by the student teacher, the workshops that these student teachers attend reflect the reiterative, ongoing process of learning to teach as a developmental process. As Schalock & Myton (2002) suggest, "Teacher Work Sampling can be thought of as an unusually complex applied performance assessment system that is embedded in a teacher's daily work" (p. 8).

Within this larger project, teacher educators focus on the teacher candidates' use of standards to make more informed decisions about what K–12 students know and are able to do. The literature informs us that it becomes increasingly important to provide teacher candidates with specific skills and knowledge of assessment within a spiraling teacher education course sequence (Carver & Krajewski, 1985; Shepard, 2000). Progression through professional education courses relies on the candidates' ability to assess their own performance, on their ability to conduct pre-assessment and post-assessment, to analyze the data, and to reflect on and improve their chosen instructional strategies in light of its impact on their own students' learning. This is the primary focus of our Renaissance Teacher Quality Project.

As Lorrie Shepard (2000) argues, "The transformation of assessment practices cannot be accomplished in separate tests and measurement courses, but rather should be a central concern in teaching methods courses" (p. 4). In order to assess our teacher candidates' knowledge of their conceptions and use of assessments within the K–12 classroom setting, we realize that we need to go a step further. We need to examine and reflect on our own assessment practices and to consider ways to incorporate learning opportunities that are embedded in school contexts throughout the entire sequence of professional education courses (Loughran, 2001). In this way, we meet the demands of NCATE, and also improve the quality of our program.

As discussed in the introduction, learning to teach is complex. In thinking about and sharing the goals and outcomes of our separate courses and phases, those of us working on this larger project are working towards a more collaborative model for teacher preparation. This model provides our students with well-connected assignments, course materials, and field experiences that each require a level of assessing K–12 student learning, to design, implement, and assess one's curriculum planning and teaching. Following two novice teachers into their first classrooms furthers this discussion about the complexities of learning to teach and how this specific project may transform our teacher education program in the age of increased accountability and assessment.

A Context for Study and Research Questions

Eastern Michigan University has a large teacher education program. On average, 600 teacher candidates are immersed in their student teaching practicum each semester. A significant number of our students explore another career prior to beginning a teacher education program. Many of our students work more than 20 hours a week, have family responsibilities, and are often first generation college students. As part of our recent efforts to redesign our teacher education program, students ideally complete their professional education courses in three sequenced phases. Such phases reflect our belief that learning to teach is a developmental process that requires the learning of skills and knowledge in a spiraling curriculum in which ideas and skills are continually revisited throughout the sequence of courses (Bruner, 1960; Shulman, 1986). The first phase is called a "pre-admission phase" as students are allowed to enroll in courses prior to being admitted into the College of Education. After admission students enroll in their curriculum methods, assessment, and early field experience courses as part of Phase I of their professional education courses. Phase II provides students a course in reading methods, educational technology, another early field experience, and a methods course in the teaching of their content area. Finally, during Phase III, students experience their student teaching placement.

The following represent the guiding research questions for this study:

1. Is there any evidence that these beginning teachers are using skills, knowledge, or experiences that could be linked to their involvement in the previously described pilot project? If so, in what ways and to what degree?
2. What are the concerns and needs of these novice teachers and how do they compare to the well-studied concerns and needs of most novices?
3. What evidence, if any, do these two first year teachers have that indicates that their students are learning more than others in a comparable classroom with a first or second year teacher in their school?
    4. As these teachers begin to work within their own classrooms, what suggestions do they have for improving the general teacher education program at EMU and specifically the use of K–12 student work samples in assessing the impact of their instructional decision making and practice?

Data Collection and Methodology

During the 2000–2001 academic year, five EMU student teachers participated in a pilot project. During the first semester, five secondary student
teachers were enrolled in Phase I, or the phase that requires students to take
their curriculum methods and assessment courses. Three of these five students were in a blocked course that integrated the coursework in these two
required courses. The other two students were also in Phase I, but were not
in the blocked course. This blocked course involved 25 students taking the
courses as a cohort with two professors who work closely together, thus
bridging the connections between the curriculum unit, lesson plans, objectives, and assessing student learning whenever possible. Incidentally, the
professors of these two courses were the co-directors for the five-year
Renaissance Teacher Quality Project and invested in and knowledgeable
about the process of using the teacher work sample.

A separate course in assessment provided our students multiple opportunities to think about how curriculum, instruction, and assessment are insep-
arable and essential components of one's teaching practice and
decision-making. The curriculum methods course used a textbook entitled,
Teaching as Decision Making (Sparks-Langer, Pasch, Starko, Moody, &
Gardner, 2000). The use of this text reflected a strongly held belief among
many in the teacher education department that learning to teach is a constructivist process that is personal and learned by being engaged in pedagogical decision making, teaching, and reflecting on one's teaching with
specific relevant prompts.

Three student teachers in the blocked course collected pre-assessment
and post-assessment data about the middle school students they were planning to teach in order to make informed modifications to the units they were
planning for their student teaching placements in Phase III of the program.
They met regularly with other teacher education professors, Arts and
Science professors, their cooperating teachers, and their university supervisor throughout the year. My role in this project was strictly as a researcher
and confidante. I conducted semi-structured, open-ended interviews 2–3
times during the 2000–2001 school year with these student teachers in order
to document their experiences as they participated in the pilot study during
Phase I of the program. I also attended and collected field notes during the
monthly workshop seminars during which they learned about and shared
their experiences using the TWS. It was during this time that these student
teachers also discussed their experiences as students of teaching. The workshops were designed to support the student teachers as they completed the
TWS and to provide a forum for all participants to learn how to use the
process to improve one's teaching.

I conducted semi-structured interviews with the professors and the cooperating teachers in order to capture their perspectives' of the strengths and weaknesses of the project. The participants were interviewed in order to establish a multidimensional view of the project and its impact on improving our teacher education program.

During the summer of 2001, I invited each of the student teachers to participate in a follow-up study during their first year of teaching. One of the teachers was not able to find a permanent teaching position; two others decided that being a first year teacher was more than enough to focus on, and two of the teachers agreed to participate in the 2001–2002 school year. During the 2001–2002 academic year, I had planned to observe the teaching of two of these five beginning teachers and conduct follow-up interviews and discussions with them. Following up on these two beginning teachers was more problematic than I had envisioned when I first proposed this project. One teacher moved to North Carolina and the other took a position 45 miles away from our campus. I decided that I would use a multi-method approach to data collection that involved frequent emails, several phone conversations, videotapes of the teacher in North Carolina, and observations of the teacher within driving distance. I also interviewed three beginning teachers who did not participate in the project in order to collect comparative data about how other novice teachers might discuss their experiences while learning to teach. Each participant was paid for her time.

DATA ANALYSIS

All data collected were reviewed several times to look for emerging themes as reflective of qualitative case study methods (Stake, 1995). Using the variables identified in Veenman's (1984) study of the needs and concerns of novice teachers, the following issues were specifically examined and discussed: classroom management, classroom procedures, teaching strategies, assessment, student motivation, lesson planning, students with special needs, linguistic diversity, time related concerns, financial concerns, learning standards, and standardized testing. Each novice teacher's needs and concerns were analyzed separately using the above-mentioned variables. Narratives were written to summarize the key issues of the two novices who participated in the project. Then these needs and concerns were compared among all five novices. This last step of the process resulted in a narrative summary of the themes, relying on supporting evidence from the entire data set. This summary is used to further discuss and analyze the impact participation in the Renaissance Teacher Quality Project on the novice teachers and their pedagogical decision making. In addition, this study is discussed in light of its providing direction for improving our teacher education program.

Two Novice Teachers and Their Use of TWS

This discussion focuses on the two novice teachers, Mary and Heidi, who participated in the follow-up study.

Mary's Experiences. Mary was an outstanding student teacher, in spite of the challenges of working with a cooperating teacher who was neither an inspiring middle school teacher nor much of a mentor to her. Even though she came into the project later than the other student teachers and was not a member of the blocked class that conducted a smaller TWS, Mary quickly progressed in her thinking about how the contextual factors that included the community, the school, and her student teaching classroom might influence her work as a teacher. Only a few weeks into the semester, it was clear to Mary that any support or guidance she needed as a beginning teacher would come from her peers or others attending the regular workshops, as her cooperating teacher had all but "checked out" of teaching.

In the TWS she prepared for this project, Mary highlighted diversity as the most outstanding feature of this community. Mary is a white woman in her late 20's. It was in this summary that her understanding of the complex relationship between students' cultural and socioeconomic backgrounds, as well as prior learning experiences and their collective impact on her own pedagogical decision making became evident. Mary clearly articulated the need to assess, appreciate, and become responsive to the differing learning styles, needs, and expectations in this particular classroom. Her ability to identify the challenges she would face as a student teacher and to weigh how to negotiate the difficult relationship with her cooperating teacher were noteworthy.

Mary hoped that her cooperating teacher would retire at the end of the year and had discussed with the principal the possibility of her taking his position. But her cooperating teacher did not retire, so Mary accepted a position as a 7th grade social studies teacher in a large middle school with 75 faculty members and 1,125 6–8th grade students. Mary, a single parent, now commutes 60 miles to and from school each day, dropping her two preschool age children off before 7:00 a.m. and returning to pick them up after 5:00 p.m. on most days. "Some days I feel like I've lost my mind," she told me one day. "There is so much to do and I'm just trying to do the best I can." When Mary and I spoke about her new position, she shared that, on average, 60% of the students graduate from this high school. "Five to ten percent may eventually graduate from an alternative program. The other 25–35% just do not care. Most of them hope to get jobs in the local factory and can't imagine doing anything else," she said.

During her first year of teaching, Mary learned many things about the school, community, students, and teachers. First she learned that teachers who could keep their classes quiet, orderly, and in line were deemed to be successful by the administration and a majority of the parents. That her classes typically were loud and students were involved in cooperative learning activities made other teachers express concern for her ability to teach and manage her classroom. Though Mary did not feel that classroom management was a challenge, she did recognize that her methods and ideology differed from the other teachers in the building and that this became a reoccurring issue that emerged during team meetings. Mary's classroom was brightly colored with student work, sign-up forms, and inspirational quotes selected and presented through student-made posters. Despite the fact that her classroom barely held the 32 desks required for her five classes, Mary relied a lot on cooperative learning and highly interactive activities.

Mary spent most of her first year thinking about the activities that would help her to reach her students. She worked hard to try to teach each group in ways that would help them to remember the most. Like many teachers, both novice and experienced, Mary said that she designed lessons that she thought were "brilliant," only to find that they did not work with a specific group of students. She believed that this first year provided her the learning opportunity for trying to determine what worked best with each individual class and with each student. Mary believed that some lessons did not work well with her students because a majority of students had previously only experienced traditional, didactic teaching methods. Taking a greater role in their own learning was a new expectation for Mary's students.

Mary believed that it was extremely challenging to set up and arrange her first classroom. "It was more complicated than I remembered when student teaching, because the structure of the class was set up by the cooperating teacher," she wrote to me one day. Her current classes also reflected a less culturally diverse community than the one in which she student taught. Designing pre-assessment instruments, as well as learning goals and activities, was challenging for Mary this year, she believed primarily, because she was working with a different age group. "I knew that I could use pre-assessment quizzes and worksheets in order to determine what my students knew, but I didn't know enough about them yet even to do this. I plan to use pre-assessment and post-assessment data much more systematically next year, since I now know the curriculum, the students, and the school." Mary had a clear, no-nonsense tone as she discussed the assessment of her students. "I know that they are learning when I see they are awake, looking at me, contributing answers in class, relating comments to things they had seen or heard, and providing evidence that they study at night." She spent a considerable amount of her day trying to use students' language to communicate ideas to them, while relating social studies to their lives. Mary believed that these students had not yet learned how to take responsibility for their own learning and therefore worked to instill good study habits as part of her curriculum.

The district in which Mary worked offered an induction program for beginning teachers. Once a month, novice teachers were required to participate in programs offered by the New Teacher Academy. Topics discussed included: methods to work with special education and at-risk students, ways to manage stress, brain-based research, and parent-teacher conferences. Mary commented, "They were okay in terms of the content and format, but generally everyone was just zoned out." Mary also was assigned a building mentor, another social studies teacher in the building, but whose different teaching style made it difficult for the two to connect on the same goals. In addition, she was assigned a district mentor who was a retired administrator. This person observed Mary once and, according to her, lectured to her about the importance of completing district paperwork. Most helpful to Mary was her building team. They provided ongoing support, feedback, and guidance about curriculum, content, and building procedures.

Monthly departmental meetings also provided helpful information about curriculum content. As far as Mary was concerned, the least helpful professional development concerned preparing students for the standardized tests. "They told me that I needed to spend many weeks preparing my students for standardized tests. I told them that not only was this a waste of the students' and my time, but that I would not do it. I haven't experienced any repercussions yet about this issue," Mary told me. "If you believe that standardized tests are the only valid measurement of student learning, then you have to ignore other variables in students' lives." She was confident in her own abilities to create assessment instruments that were aligned with her learning goals and activities and helped her to gather information about what her students knew and were able to do on a regular basis. "I feel really confident about my knowledge of assessment, but the teachers I worked with did not have the same kinds of experiences in their teacher preparation programs," she said.

In Mary's classroom, the middle level students lived up to their reputations for being highly social. Mary relied on activities and assessment strategies that encouraged students to see social studies as a series of stories about people, countries, cultures, and ideology. "I wrote out parts of history like a story and asked students to fill in the omitted parts, names, and explanations." She also worked to create a culturally diverse perspective of history.

She first tried using this strategy as a student teacher and improved her approach to introducing it to students during this first year of teaching. When she realized that the textbook included no information about American Indians being pushed off their land, she supplemented the content without teaching from a "war perspective." As Mary said, "War is a physical manifestation of political ideas." To teach history or social studies as a series of wars, dates, and names neglected the necessary learning about cultural difference and complexity. Students in Mary's class habitually created timelines in order to see the broader connections among events, ideas, and people. Students learned about Afghanistan while learning about the presence and power of propaganda. The emphasis of her curriculum was to help her students develop higher order thinking and organizational skills.

Mary believed that she was well prepared for this current teaching position. "I think that the greatest insight that I gained from teaching this unit is that teaching is an art. That with every day of teaching I learned to modify my behavior and I believe the students did the same," wrote Mary in her TWS during student teaching. "Because I participated in this project, I'm confident that I can see student learning from beginning to end." As Mary discussed how she now assesses her students, it became clear to both of us that she relied on regular, formative assessment strategies. She worked to closely monitor her students' learning on a regular basis and incorporated activities that are interactive and social. Her attention to and ongoing assessment of the contextual factors and their affect on student learning was a skill Mary learned well during her student teaching practicum and one that she transferred and applied to her own classroom on a daily basis.

Heidi's Experiences. Heidi, also a white woman in her 20's, was an equally strong student teacher candidate and experienced some different challenges than Mary. Heidi and the teacher first assigned as her cooperating teacher mutually agreed that they were not as compatible as they should be in terms of their personalities. She was able to switch cooperating teachers at the last minute with another student in the project. Heidi's ability to negotiate this change was reflective of her confidence and ability to approach situations that many might otherwise avoid.

For her Teacher Work Sample, Heidi created a language arts unit that centered on improving students' reading comprehension, written and oral communication skills, cooperative learning skills, and literary terms and concepts. In her contextual analysis, Heidi discussed the challenges of dealing with a high rate of student absenteeism and the need to modify her lesson plans to meet the diverse needs and abilities of her students. Heidi said that she benefited tremendously from having the support of her peers and faculty members from both her content area and teacher education as she completed her student teaching practicum. She believed that what was most valuable about using the Teacher Work Sample was having a document that helped her to see all of the ways she grew as a teacher over the course of the semester and those areas that she still needed to address as a beginning teacher. Heidi wrote in her TWS reflection,

"Looking back on my pre-assessment, I came to one conclusion. My pre-assessment reflects the insecurities I felt at the beginning of the semester. I walked into the classroom very shy and unsure of myself. My pre-assessment shows that I was very insecure with the novel and insecure with my skills to teach. It also reflects the importance of pre-assessment and post-assessment coordination. With my pre- and post-assessment not coordinating, it made aligning goals and questions extremely difficult".

Heidi accepted a position teaching high school English in North Carolina. This highly diverse school enrolled 1,200 6–8th grade students and employed approximately 60 full time faculty members. The student and teacher communities were similar to those Heidi experienced while student teaching. She was one of eight beginning teachers at this school. She would love to move back home, but has heard that jobs are in scarce supply and is now afraid to move before securing a position. She said that she spent most of her time thinking about and handling the paperwork. "A lot of the times, I filled out the same information but on different forms," she said. "But as for my classroom, in my social studies classes I spent a lot of time thinking about how I was going to get the lesson across so the students would do well on the end-of-grade test. I worried about making sure my lessons reflected my assessments. In literature class, I spent time thinking about how I could get those students motivated." During her first year at this school, Heidi experienced tremendous pressure to prepare her students for the test that every student must successfully pass at the end of each grade level. This test drives most of the curriculum being taught—and in many ways, its presence caused Heidi to feel that she didn't have the luxury of using some of the strategies that she was taught in her teacher education program, such as the inquiry approach.

As she reflected on what she learned as a novice teacher, as compared to her experiences as a student teacher, Heidi often felt overwhelmed. "During student teaching, I graded papers and put together lessons, but now I have three times the papers to grade and I'm responsible for EVERYTHING! During student teaching, I somewhat depended on my cooperating teacher being in the room or at least nearby. Now when I get into a jam, I have to be quick-minded. The entire experience is, for me, really different from student teaching," she told me.

Early in the year, Heidi shared that she did not feel she had the same support network at this school that she experienced while working in the project. She often felt that she could not share her stress, concerns, or frustrations with anyone. Specifically, she would have liked to discuss her lessons with a knowledgeable colleague. She frequently felt different from others in her building about how she thought about and planned for instruction. "I have yet to meet anybody here who has any background in using pre-assessment and post-assessment data to analyze student learning, so I feel that I don't have any support for continuing to use it at this school," Heidi said.

This district provided Heidi four workshops to discuss new teacher issues and concerns as part of a novice teacher program. She was assigned a mentor. "My mentor and the other mentors were a great asset to me. They went above and beyond their duties to help me. My mentor observed me three times. He wasn't supposed to tell me what I was doing wrong; he was there as a sounding board during my lessons if I needed him. He usually gave me advice, though, on how to handle difficult situations I would run into," she told me later in the year.

She reflected that she plans much more in advance now in her own classroom. "I used to be able to plan a week ahead, but now I find that I need to think two or three weeks in advance," she shared. During her student teaching, Heidi often thought about and made modifications in her lesson plans for advanced students. But in her own classroom, she no longer felt she had the time for such modifications. She spent most of her time in a state of worry and anxiety about her students' learning and performance. She worried that she wouldn't be able to get all of the work graded. She worried that her students wouldn't be able to pass the end-of-grade test. "Basically, it was a checking system that was not enforced in terms of determining whether students moved on to the next grade level. But if teachers were not doing their job, this was supposed to catch them," she explained. Heidi worried that her students' writing scores would be low. It was very stressful to her and she did not want to fail her students.

Heidi incorporated a variety of strategies to assess her students' learning. One of Heidi's professional goals for this year was to actively involve students in doing research and using authentic forms of assessment, but she often quizzed her students over the specific content and discussions each day. During a telephone interview, Heidi said

'There were times when I thought we needed to move on and after taking a quiz, I realized we needed some review and perhaps another class discussion or another assignment. I gave tests after each chapter. My tests were usually matching (vocabulary words), multiple choice, and 2–4 essay questions. I have done one authentic assessment project with students doing research in a specific topic relating to Africa.

Heidi believed that the most valuable lesson she learned while participating in the pilot project was in aligning her curriculum with her assessment. When she made a test, she stewed over whether or not she had taught that material in class. "I am very aware of how my assessments are created. I think the Project made me a stronger test giver and helped me to reflect on their meaning. After each test I looked at how the students did as a group and then I tried to go back and look at the questions to see if any were unfair. Also, I really thought about how my particular group of students learned." Heidi compared how her different classes performed on any given test and tried to modify her instruction, pace, and content to adapt it to the group's abilities, readiness, and interests. She consciously worked to help her students move from more traditional strategies that were more teacher-centered to ones that engaged her students in the learning process as independent researchers and thinkers. Overall, Heidi faced many challenges as a beginning teacher. In one email, Heidi shared,

'Teaching is rough! It's been a constant learning experience. Everyday I reflect on what I've learned. And every day it's something new. I've learned to juggle grading papers, making lesson plans, attending meetings, helping students after school, among other things. I've also discovered how to better accommodate my different students. I still need to work on this, but I practice the different techniques to use, such as taking things slower, giving more advanced students further assignments, and using review games'.

She felt that learning to teach placed her in a very different place professionally than her peers who entered other professions. "It doesn't feel like they are as isolated, alone, or struggling to learn how to be successful in their careers as I am," she explained.

Analysis and Discussion

Several themes related to the issues of the complexity of learning to teach emerged during data analysis. First, assessing student learning was a daily challenge that required an ongoing formative view of the learning process itself and a close relationship with each student. Second, designing assessment instruments for a curriculum that they were still learning was especially challenging. As both Mary and Heidi shared, it was difficult to know what students were capable of learning and what the outcomes for the unit should be when the curriculum was new to the teacher. Third, the project provided additional support to the novice teachers that helped them to think about the process of analyzing students' work and learning more systematically than the other novice teachers interviewed, but learning to manage, organize, and lead one's classroom is difficult for any new teacher.

Using pre-assessment and post-assessment data in one's classroom to drive pedagogical decision-making was a difficult and complex process, with or without the support of a collaborative group. Both Heidi and Mary were uncomfortable when they were creating the assessment instruments prior to teaching the lessons. "Sometimes, I felt like I was 'dumbing-down' my objectives in order to create an assessment instrument that could easily measure them as a pre-assessment and post-assessment," said Heidi. Mary, on the other hand, faced difficulties when her post-assessment instrument reflected the actual lesson and activities that she taught more than the pre-assessment. It was difficult for her to then determine what students had learned through a comparative analysis of the two. These difficulties were just a few that the teachers faced as they were learning to use the TWS and they were still present as the teachers tried to incorporate them into their own classroom.

The multiple choice, true–false, and fill-in-the-blank test items often used on standardized tests reflect the ease at which one can then assess whether or not students have learned any given discrete bits of information. But these tests often fail to assess what students already knew prior to their instruction. Providing students the opportunity to tell or show you what they have learned using more authentic assessment strategies makes using the same pre-assessment instrument all the more difficult. In our discussions, the novice teachers and I realized the value of thinking about all of the components of the TWS as a methodology for assessing student learning, but we also realized that this methodology should be looked upon as open-ended and multidimensional. Understanding the importance of a teacher assessing her own students' work as a means for reflecting on how and what she is teaching was a lesson Mary and Heidi learned as part of participating in the pilot study. Each of these teachers believed that this assessment strategy provided much richer, useful data than a standardized test. Teaching and reflecting on one's teaching is a dynamic, complex process; using the teacher work sample is one part of these novices' repertoire for reflecting on and planning to teach.

Overall, each of these novice teachers experienced a generalized level of anxiety about teaching and learning to teach. Each has been concerned about classroom management, time management, standardized testing, and assessment issues. If these novices represent a majority of beginning teachers, some aspects of learning to teach remain universal, with or without the additional support, knowledge, and skills learned by participating in this TWS project (Huling-Austin, Odell, Ishler, Kay, & Edelfelt, 1989; Veenman, 1984). Neither Heidi nor Mary ever conducted a formal analysis of the contextual factors as prescribed by the Teacher Work Sample. But Mary and Heidi freely spoke about conducting informal analysis of their classes by small subgroup categories and also of individual students who did not perform as well as they believed they could. Mary and Heidi placed a noticeable emphasis on using formative assessment on a daily basis with their students, instead of relying solely on summative quizzes and tests. These teachers did not use the formal structure or tasks required when creating the TWS, but they did incorporate the concepts as they planned, taught, and assessed each lesson.

Mary and Heidi spoke much more extensively about their attempts to differentiate their instruction and adapt their assessment strategies for their students than I had anticipated. They also gave a fair amount of attention to thinking about what students were learning and what they could do better to adapt their instruction to meet students' needs and learning styles. It seemed as if a "habit of mind" was carried over from their student teaching experiences. In addition to Mary and Heidi providing a rich discussion of the need to do this, these teachers felt they possessed the necessary skills and confidence.

Using pre-assessment data during their student teaching encouraged Mary and Heidi to think through what they wanted their students to learn and be able to do and, equally important, how they might know what they have learned. That they were unable to fully incorporate the TWS methodology into their first year of teaching does not negate the value of using it as a means for either assessing student teacher candidates or as a means for making informed pedagogical decisions. That these teachers plan to incorporate some of the concepts next year as they gain more knowledge and confidence with their curriculum is important and serves as a testimony to its relevancy and value in the classroom.

Evidence of Student Achievement

At the time of this study, it was too soon to empirically assess the degree to which the use of TWS methodology resulted in K–12 students learning more than when teachers do not use it. Yet Heidi and Mary provided some anecdotal information about how this approach worked with their students. Mary frequently engaged her students in metacognitive exercises when thinking about what they were learning in her classes, how they might know what they were learning, and what they still needed to learn. Using this interactive approach involved students in the assessment process and provided Mary specific information about how her students saw themselves as learners. It also provided her information about what students felt they still needed to learn. Mary believed that this approach allowed her to focus her attention on those students who saw themselves as struggling learners. She had been told by the students and other teachers that this approach was particularly helpful in engaging students who typically do not take ownership of their own learning.

Other teachers have told Heidi that she has been much more successful in preparing her students for the end-of-grade test than the teacher she replaced. She had specific results about her students' performance on this test that she could use to evaluate and reflect on her own teaching. Several groups of her students performed very well on this important test. However, one did not. Specifically, some of her students did not perform well on the writing portion of this test. In discussing how her students did on this test as compared to students of other teachers, Heidi discovered that, overall, her students performed comparably to students of other teachers in her grade level. She was somewhat in awe of the one teacher whose students all had passed the writing portion of the test, as compared to the 76% pass rate of her own students. She discussed how she would use this information to change her instructional choices next year.

Just as Mary and Heidi were able to discuss their strategies for assessing what students know and are able to do, other teachers who had participated in the project also had the language for analyzing their students' learning based on whole group, subgroup, and individual student analysis. They had a better understanding of how to work with the students and how to create relevant learning activities that would help them achieve their learning goals. When Mary and Heidi reflected on what their students' had learned, they were also able and inclined to discuss the ways in which they might further incorporate assessment practices.

Implications for Teacher Preparation

What can this project tell us about how to improve our teacher education program? In addition to giving us the means for authentic performance assessment of our teacher candidates, the Renaissance Teacher Quality Project also provided us invaluable data about the coherency of our program in helping beginning teachers to prepare for their first years of teaching. Both Mary and Heidi experienced difficulties when trying to incorporate the process prescribed by the TWS during both their student teaching and first year of teaching. Their explanations included not having enough time, not having knowledgeable or experienced cooperating teachers, not knowing the curriculum, and being overwhelmed by the demands of their first classroom of students.

While Mary and Heidi believed that the TWS was a useful way to learn about their students' knowledge and skills, each confided that she approached the TWS as an additional assignment to be completed, in order to successfully finish her student teaching experience. Certainly, from the student teachers' perspective, there is just too much to consider when one is experiencing student teaching to add the TWS. The issue of how to incorporate the Teacher Work Sample methodology as an integral dimension of learning to teach within our comprehensive teacher education program is still being examined at EMU. What could have been reduced or changed in order to accommodate the added requirement for these student teachers? If these student teachers had been given a reduced teaching load, would they have more fully incorporated the TWS as a way of thinking about and planning for their instruction? As the literature on school reform reminds us to ask, when we add a new requirement, what are we eliminating (Fullan, 1992)? Perhaps if these novices had a reduced teaching load as they tried to incorporate this methodology into their first year of teaching, they could have been more successful in implementing its strategies.

It is also the case that beginning teachers need support. It is impossible to prepare teachers for all of the situations that a teacher may encounter, but helping teacher candidates to assess the contexts of their teaching and their individual students provides them important insight into the specific needs of their students. This project encourages us to think about assessing our students as they work through the decision-making and assessment of their own students' learning. Rather than assessing our student teachers and their work as fixed and static and created outside of the context of actual classrooms, this project models the practice of using authentic performance of students to better assess what knowledge and skills are transferable, usable, or still "in the rough". In addition to focusing on how to complete the TWS, this project also provides a model for how various members of the education community can collaborate and reflect on their roles as they help to support the professional development of beginning teachers.

Using the Teacher Work Sample represents an analytical approach to learning to teach. While it provides strategies, it does not necessarily address some of the other important issues in learning to teach, such as how to negotiate the necessary freedom and support from one's colleagues, how to learn how to work with an administration, how to find and secure the materials needed in one's first years of teaching, how to manage a classroom, and how to manage one's time. Many beginning teachers also are learning how to engage with an adult community as an adult. As a teacher educator, I believe my next task is to assess how I can better provide the necessary ongoing support for our teacher candidates, as they become beginning teachers struggling with a new role, new responsibilities, and new questions about learning and teaching.

REFERENCES

Basinger, J. (2001, April). *Report bashes reliance on teaching exams.* The Chronicle of Higher Education, 47,4.

Bruner, J. (1960). *The process of education.* Cambridge, MA: Harvard University Press.

Carver, F., & Krajewski, R. J. (1985, February). *Organization and operation in teacher education programs: Implications for change in professional education preparation.* A paper presented at the annual meeting of the American Association of Colleges for Teacher Education. Denver, Co.

Davis, B., & Sumara, D. J. (1999). Cognition, complexity, and teacher education. In E. Mintz & J. T. Yun (Eds.) *The Complex world of teaching: Perspectives from theory and practice* (p. 237–254). Cambridge, MA: Harvard Educational Review.

Feiman-Nemser, S., & Buchmann, M. (1989). Describing teacher education: A framework and illustrative findings from a longitudinal study of six students. *Elementary School Journal, 89,* 365–77.

Fessler, R., & Christensen, J. C. (1992). *The teacher career cycle: Understanding and guiding the professional development of teachers.* Boston: Allyn & Bacon.

Fullan, M. G. (1992). *Successful school improvement: The implementation perspective and beyond.* Buckingham, UK: Open Press University.

Griffin, G. (1992). Learning from the "New" schools: Lessons for teacher education. In R. M. McClure (Ed.) *Excellence in teacher education: Helping teachers develop learner-centered schools* (pp. 29–42). Washington, DC: National Education Association.

Huling-Austin, L., Odell, S., Ishler, P., Kay, R., & Edelfelt, R. (1989). *Assisting the beginning teacher.* Reston, VA: The Association of Teacher Educators.

Interstate New Teacher Assessment and Support Consortium. (1992). Draft standards for teacher licensing. Washington, D.C.: Council of Chief State School Officers.

Loughran, J. (2001, April). *Learning to teach by embedding learning in experience.* Paper presented at the American Educational Researchers Association, Seattle, WA.

National Council for Accreditation of Teacher Education. (1997). *Standards, procedures, and policies for the accreditation of professional education units.* Washington, D.C.: Author.

Schalock, H.d., & Myton, D. (2002). Connecting teaching and learning: An introduction to teacher work sample methodology. In G. R. Girod (Eds.). *Connecting teaching and learning: A Handbook for teacher educators on teacher work sample methodology.* (Pp. 1–19). Washington, D.C.: AACTE publications.

Schön, D. A. (1987). *Educating the reflective practitioner.* San Francisco, CA: Jossey-Bass.

Shepard, L. (2000). The role of assessment in a learning culture. *Educational Researcher, 29*(70), 4–14.

Shulman, L. (1986). Those who understand: Knowledge growth in teaching. *Educational Researcher, 15*(2), 4–14.

Sparks-Langer, G., M. Pasch, A. Starko, C. Moody, & T. Gardner. (2000). *Teaching as decision making: Successful practices for a secondary teacher.* Upper Saddle River, New Jersey: Merrill Prentice Hall.

Stake, R. E. (1995). *The art of case study research.* Thousand Oaks, CA: Sage Publications.

Tom, A. (1996). External influences on teacher education programs: National accreditation and state certification. In K. Zeichner, S. Melnick, & M. L. Gomez (Eds.). *Currents of reform in preservice teacher education.* New York: Teachers College Press.

Veenman, S. (1984). Perceived problems of beginning teachers. *Review of Educational Research, 54*(2), 143–178.

Complex Teaching and Learning
Connecting Teacher Education to Student Performance

9.

Christy Folsom

Christy Folsom is an Assistant Professor in the Masters Program in Childhood Education at Lehman College, City University of New York, Bronx, New York. Her research focuses on the intellectual and emotional infrastructure of teaching and learning, self-organized learning, and change in teacher thinking and practice evidenced in student performance.

ABSTRACT

Student performance depends on teacher knowledge and skills. This study investigated the effect of a teacher education intervention carried out by the researcher with four teachers who learned to facilitate the self-organization processes of decision making, planning, and self-evaluation with their students in the context of project method curriculum. The curriculum development intervention and data gathering, carried out over a one-year period, included classroom involvement, group, and individual meetings with the teachers. Baseline, midpoint, and final assessments included teacher interview, student interview, classroom observations, teacher-made materials analysis, and student project analysis. Baseline assessment revealed teachers' lack of knowledge and preparation in the area of teaching thinking skills. Qualitative analysis of the data resulted in four case studies that reveal connections between the teacher education intervention, change in teacher thinking and practice, and effect on student performance. Implications for teacher education programs are included.

D espite what are often the best efforts of teacher education programs to prepare teacher candidates for progressive education practices that involve complex teaching, student performance that reveals complex learning and thinking is often missing. It is well documented that teacher education programs have not adequately prepared teacher candidates with the knowledge and skills required for students to show complex learning (Darling-Hammond, 1997; Good, 1990; Goodlad, 1990, 1994; Hollingsworth, 1989; National Commission on Teaching and America's Future, 1996; Tom, 1997).

Darling-Hammond (1997) describes several characteristics of the kind of teaching that leads to complex learning:

> Work that is both rigorous and relevant, teach[ing] for high levels of disciplined understanding in content areas, student-based strategies, maintain[ing] a dialectic between students and subjects, [learning] experiences that allow [diverse] students to access ideas in a variety of ways, learner . . . breakthroughs in understanding. (p. 12)

Ogle (1997) offers more insight into what constitutes complex learning and complex teaching. In her description of appropriate education for "at-risk students," Ogle describes learning that involves "skills in critical and conceptual thinking," a "thinking curriculum," curriculum in which students "plan, organize, and evaluate their progress," and curriculum that supports the development of "metacognition or the ability to think about their own thinking and learning" (p. 2).

Metacognitive discussion, or the discussion of thinking and learning, is an important characteristic of complex teaching and learning. Sarason (1982), however, noticed in his many visits to classrooms that "there was something missing" and that was the "discussion of thinking and learning in the classroom" (p. 220). When Sarason asked the teachers about this missing discussion they replied that nothing in their teacher preparation had prepared them to discuss thinking.

Based on "cross-disciplinary" (Holland, 1995, p. 6) observations and teaching experience in various branches of education, I also recognized the absence. Similar to Sarason's study (1982), my observations also reveal that something important was missing in the interactions between teachers and students in most classrooms. Even in schools with exceptional facilities where student projects covered expanses of hallways and classroom walls, the explicit discussion of thinking and learning was missing.

My research addresses this gap within the context of student project work. Project work is can be an important strategy of complex teaching that supports the teaching of thinking and discussion of learning. Project work or "the project method," a major component of progressive education (Kilpatrick, 1921) is defined by Kilpatrick as "any unit of purposeful experience, any instance of purposeful activity where the dominating purpose, as an inner urge, (a) fixes the aim of the action, (b) guides its process, and (c) furnishes its drive, its inner motivation" (p. 283).

Yet, often project work entails little more than good intentions and vague directions. An example is one teacher's description of an immigration project he carried out with his third-grade students. He explained, "It [the project] had to have something to do with immigration. It had to depict some scene about immigration . . . they could construct what they wanted from cardboard" (Folsom, 2000, p. 293).

Potentially, project work that includes the explicit teaching of the processes of self-organization and infused with metacognitive discussion embodies the characteristics described by Darling-Hammond (1997) and Ogle (1997). Self-organization processes allow students to experience the opportunity to "develop and bring to execution their own ideas" (Dewey, as cited in Kliebard, 1995, p. 69). When teachers explicitly teach self-organization processes they give students the tools to "take an active role in the learning process" (Ogle, p. 2). Such teaching helps students develop the skills needed to take more responsibility for their own learning. Yet, in teacher education a glaring gap in the preparation of teachers for the complexities of project method teaching and metacognitive discussion exists.

Metacognitive discussions emerge from an understanding of intellectual processes. In order to benefit fully from the complexities of learning inherent in project work, students and teachers alike require a deep understanding of the intellectual processes that comprise the infrastructure of such teaching. Dewey (1964) notes:

> Only a teacher thoroughly trained in the higher levels of intellectual method and who thus has constantly in his own mind a sense of what adequate and genuine intellectual activity mean, will be likely, in deed, not in mere word, to respect the mental integrity and force of children. (p. 329)

Yet, the pedagogy of project work, specifically the intellectual operations and social-emotional or character traits that can be developed and discussed through project work, has not been adequately taught in teacher education. To extract consciously the full potential of project work as a complex teaching method, teachers must know how to teach students the skills required of the "new problem solver" (Devaney & Sykes, 1988, p. 19).

One of these skills, "successful organization and monitoring of one's own learning" (Devaney & Sykes, 1988, p. 19), involves the skills of decision-making, planning, and self-evaluation. Marzano (1993), in his discussion of mental dispositions, states that the processes of decision making, planning, and self-evaluation "render any activity more thoughtful and more effective" (p. 158) and are necessary for higher-order thinking to take place. The intellectual skills involved in self-organization result in transformational learning, defined by Clark (1993) as "learning that produces change. . . . [It] produces more far-reaching changes in the learners than does learning in general, and these changes have a significant impact on the learner's subsequent experiences" (p. 47).

Dewey (as cited in Kliebard, 1995) includes self-organizational skills in his description of project work at the Chicago Laboratory School. "Children . . . were called upon to evaluate their own handiwork on occasion as an apparent culmination of the effort to involve children, not only in the planning stages of their activities, but at their conclusion as well" (p. 63).

The question of when the strategies of complex teaching and learning can be taught effectively was a consideration in my research plan. In a study of teacher concerns, Fuller (1969) outlines three phases of teacher development: preteaching, early teaching phase, and late teaching phase. In a later study, Feiman-Nemser (1983) expands teacher development to include four phases. The first phase, *pretraining*, includes learning from parents and the years of schooling where impressions and attitudes about teaching and learning are formed. The second phase is *preservice,* or formal teacher preparation, where often little is accomplished in changing the attitudes and beliefs about teaching formed in the first stage (Feimen-Nemser; Fuller; Goodlad, 1990; Hollingsworth, 1989). Third is the "intense and stressful" (Feiman-Nemser, p. 158) first year of teaching or *induction phase.* The final phase, *inservice,* consists of three stages leading toward a sense of mastery in teaching. Practicing teachers with their own classrooms were chosen as research participants, because assessments involved student performance. First year teachers were not included, because the "feelings of uncertainty, confusion, and insecurity" common to the induction phase and the year-long commitment required would most likely result in an "unwillingness to try new teaching methods" (Burden, as cited in Feiman-Nemser, p. 162).

Purpose

This research was designed to investigate the effect of teaching teachers to incorporate the teaching of self-organization skills into project-based curriculum design. How will teacher thinking and practice change as they teach their students the self-organization skills of decision-making, planning, and self-evaluation in the context of project work? How will students reflect the learning of their teachers? How will my work as a teacher educator be reflected in student performance?

Method

This qualitative research study included a professional-development inter-vention involving four teachers teaching at the elementary school level in self-contained classroom settings. The intervention involved teaching strate-gies, hereafter called the *professional learning process or teacher education process,* designed to help the teachers learn to facilitate the self-organization processes of decision-making, planning, and self-evaluation with their stu-dents. The overall research procedure included teacher selection, baseline assessment, ongoing professional learning process (intervention) with mid-point assessment, and final assessment. I patterned my overall research pro-cedure after the research on student underachievement by Baum, Renzulli, and Hébert (1995). They defined four phases of the intervention procedure: (a) teacher selection, (b) familiarization, (c) treatment, and (d) assessment. Their model of providing an intervention or treatment to help students increase achievement was similar to my goal of helping teachers increase achievement in the complex learning and teaching involved in project work.

I *selected* four teachers from varied backgrounds to participate in the study based on their interest in progressive education, their ability to articu-lately evaluate the professional-development intervention, and their poten-tial as leaders in their schools willing to take risks. I saw that both Erica and Ted shared these characteristics, when I was her student teaching supervisor and Ted was her cooperating teacher. Stacy, the third teacher, demonstrated these characteristics in graduate courses we shared. Brian, who taught in Ted's school, was selected through a type of "snowball sampling technique" (Bogdan & Biklen, 1992, p. 70) after discussing possible choices with Ted. The four teachers, whose experience ranged from two to eight years, were paired in two Manhattan public schools with diverse student populations. Two of the teachers taught fourth and fifth grades in School #1; the other two taught second and third grades in School #2 (see Figure 1).

In addition, each of the participating teachers selected three students to take part in the assessment phases of the study. These students were selected based on three criteria. The students reflected a range of academic and organizational abilities; they had various amounts of skill in articulating feelings and thoughts about their learning; and they included those who had success with project work and those who had difficulty. Assessing student performance through interviews and analyzing their projects helped me

Research Participant	Grade Level	School	Years Teaching Prior to Research	Previous Experience
Erica	5th	School #1	2	Left law school to go into teaching Public school, 2 years
Stacy	4th	School #1	3	Preschool, 1 year Middle school, 1 year 3rd grade, 1 year
Ted	3rd	School #2	8	Private educational materials firm Preschool summer program Private school, asst. teacher Public Schools, 8 years
Brian	2nd	School #2	5	Musician Stock exchange trader Public school, 5 years

Figure 1. Characteristics of Research Participants

assess the effectiveness of each teacher's implementation of self-organization strategies in the classroom and my effectiveness as a teacher educator.

During the *familiarization* phase, I immersed myself in each of the four classrooms, becoming acquainted with the students, learning the culture of the class, and assessing each teacher's practice in relation to teaching self-organization skills. During this time, I conducted a formal baseline assessment with each teacher and the students. This information helped me decide how best to begin the professional learning process.

The research included three *assessments*. The baseline and final assessments provided information about how each teacher changed their thinking and practice over time. The baseline and final assessments included five data gathering instruments: classroom observations (see Table 1), interviews with individual teachers (see Table 2), group interviews with the students from each classroom (see Table 3), analysis of teacher prepared materials to

TABLE 1

Sample Criteria for Classroom Observations

Evidence of decision making, planning, self-evaluation in classroom work.

- Is there more extensive use of decision making, planning, self-evaluation evident in the teacher's curriculum planning?
- Is there evidence of formal student decision making, planning, and self-evaluation through use of decision-making grids, planning worksheets, and self-evaluation worksheets made by teachers?
- Are there charts with criteria for projects displayed in the room?
- Is there an increase in time spent on pre- and post-project discussions?

Evidence of a language of thinking and learning in the classroom.

- Are terms such as criteria, self-evaluation, planning, deciding, decisions, choice being used in the classroom by students and teacher?

Evidence of using a theoretical framework (TIEL) to contextualize, discuss, and plan self-organization processes.

- Is the vocabulary of TIEL framework (or an adaptation) used in teacher's conversations and teaching when teaching about decision making, planning, self-evaluation?
- Is the vocabulary of TIEL (or an adaptation) used by students in classroom discussions and interviews?
- Are charts or posters referring to the framework in the classroom?

Evidence of structural and contextual factors to support self-organization processes.

- Is there evidence of research going on?
- Is group work evident and used [more often]?
- Is there an [increased] atmosphere of creativity in the classroom?
- Does the teacher have classroom management routines in place to support autonomy needed for project work?
- Is the physical space and materials supply sufficient to accommodate project work?

teach self-organization skills (see Table 4), and analysis of student projects (see Table 5). Whereas the baseline and final assessments involved tape-recorded interviews, the midpoint assessment required written responses to questions developed to elicit personal reflections of the participants and assess the effectiveness of the professional learning process (see Table 6). The midpoint assessment helped in continually tailoring the treatment or professional learning process to the individual teacher's requirements.

The *treatment phase, professional learning* or *teacher education process,* involved half-day visits each week to each class over two 16-week semesters. Individually tailored to meet each teacher's needs, the professional learning process involved classroom participation and observations, individual meetings with each teacher, and monthly group meetings. All curriculum projects and discussions occurred within the context of the standard curriculum for each class.

A significant part of the professional learning process was the theoretical framework, Teaching for Intellectual and Emotional Learning (TIEL®). A theoretical framework was needed for the research that would connect the intellectual and emotional aspects of complex teaching and learning and help the teachers understand and teach the components involved in project work. The intellectual processes of critical thinking, setting criteria, decision making, planning, and self-evaluation are central in designing and developing projects. Yet, these self-organization processes do not stand alone. There are other intellectual processes involved, as well as social-emotional characteristics that can be developed when students are taught self-organization skills in the context of project work.

Drawing from psychologist J. P.Guilford's Structure of Intellect Theory (1977) and philosopher John Dewey's description of qualities of character (1964), I formulated a conceptual framework, the TIEL Design Wheel (see Figure 2; Folsom, 2000), that connects both intellectual and emotional aspects of learning. The upper half of the TIEL Design Wheel consists of five intellectual operations found in Guilford's theory, while the lower half consists of five qualities of character described by Dewey. Placing these components together provides a visible structure for teaching the complex processes embedded in project work. Color coding the components of the TIEL Design Wheel further assists the teacher and students in identifying and differentiating the thinking processes involved in complex teaching and learning.

Carefully planned and explicitly taught project work can help students develop the intellectual skills and social emotional characteristics described

TIEL® is a registered trademark of Christy Folsom.

TABLE 2

Sample Questions for Teacher Interview

- Describe for me how you facilitate students' decision making, planning, and self-evaluation in project work. What have you tried? What has worked? What has helped you be able to do this?
- As a result of the Professional Learning Process (PLP), what changes do you see in yourself as a teacher as you learn to use tools to explicitly facilitate student decision making, planning, and self-evaluation and incorporate these strategies into your teaching?
- Following the PLP, what changes do you see in the students or in their products?
- Reflect on any differences in your thinking as a result of the changes you see in the students.
- How do you see your approach to curriculum development now? Describe how you incorporate the strategies of self-organization into your curriculum planning.
- What parts of the professional learning intervention have most changed your thinking?
- How has the use of a theoretical framework changed your thinking about students, curriculum, or yourself as a teacher?
- What structural or contextual factors (e.g. teacher education, school system, school, classroom, students, parents, community) [have] prevent[ed] you from being able to facilitate decision making, planning, and self-evaluation as much as you would like?
- What do you think would help you facilitate the processes of self-organization better?
- How has the discussion of thinking theory helped you learn how to facilitate decision making, planning, and self-evaluation with the students?
- Do the theoretical framework (TIEL) visuals help you better understand the processes used in curriculum planning? Why? Or Why not?
- Do the theoretical framework (TIEL) visuals help the students understand and discuss their thinking?
- Why would being able to explain the processes of decision making, planning, and self-evaluation to others be important?

TABLE 3

Sample Questions for Student Interviews

- Tell me about your project.
- Tell me about project work you have done before in this class.
- Tell me about project work you have done before in other classes.
- How was the earlier project the same as or different from this project?
- Were you pleased with how this project turned out?
- What do you think helped make it successful? Or not so successful?
- Tell me about how you made the decisions about how to do the project. How did your teacher help you decide?
- How did you evaluate your project at the end?
- How did you know it was "good" or "not so good"?
- Do you think having a criteria for evaluation helped you succeed with your project?
- Did you like evaluating your own project/ Why?
- Have you ever evaluated your classmates' projects?
- Did you like evaluating your classmates' projects? Why?
- Did you plan your project?
- How did planning help you with your project?
- Do you think making decisions, planning, and evaluating your project helped you learn? How? or Why not?
- When you do a project in the future what might you do differently?
- Would you use decision making and planning?
- What decisions, plans, and evaluations have you made in activities outside of school?
- What suggestions do you have for your teacher as she/he helps other students learn to use these processes you used in creating your project?
- Do the thinking (theoretical framework [TIEL]) charts help you understand decision making, planning, and self-evaluation better?

TABLE 4

Sample Criteria from Teacher Materials Analysis

Do decision-making process worksheets meet the following criteria? Includes a place to:
- Describe the decision or problem; list group members or individual
- List alternatives for the decision or solution
- List and rate criteria by which to judge the alternatives

Do planning process worksheets meet the following criteria? Includes a place to:
- Record the due date and audience
- List the materials/resources to be used in creating the project
- List the student-developed criteria by which the project and presentation will be evaluated when the project is finished
- List the steps to take in development of the project and presentation
- State the possible problems that you can anticipate as you are working on the project

Do reflection worksheets used for students' narrative self-evaluations of project meet the following criteria? Includes a place to:
- Describe the challenges encountered in researching and developing the project, or to explain what might be done in future projects to assure that there is a challenge involved
- Describe the most difficult and easiest part of the project
- Evaluate the overall project including what you learned that would be useful in development of another project and presentation, and what you would do differently the next time

Are teachers and students effectively using teacher-made decision making, planning, and evaluation process worksheets?
- The teacher is comfortable using the language that refers to thinking processes on the worksheets and TIEL visuals with the students
- The teacher is able to manage the time and amount of work on process that is appropriate for his/her students
- The process worksheets are at the appropriate level for students' abilities.

TABLE 5

Sample Criteria from Student Project Analysis

Did the overall project and presentation meet the following criteria?
- Included written, speaking, and visual components to be presented to an audience
- Presentation and project were well organized
- Students had rehearsed and prepared
- Students had chosen ways to do the project and presentation that took advantage of the talents and abilities of the group members (or individual)
- Students had chosen ways to do the project and presentation that were appropriate to the subject matter as well as the audience
- Students were willing to take risks

Did the written part of the project meet the following criteria?
- The content contained the specified information and was accurate
- The content contained new information for the audience —
- The writing was well-organized and clearly written

Did the visual part of the project meet the following criteria?
- It was neat, clear, sturdy, and easily understood (i.e, chart, poster, pictures, diagram, 3-dimensional project)
- Lines were memorized, costumes and props were creative; it was well rehearsed (if a play or skit)
- Students had needed materials ready and organized

Did the speaking part of the presentation meet the following criteria?
- Speaking was clear and understandable
- Audience questions were evidence that the presentation made the audience think
- The students were knowledgeable about their subject by competently answering questions from the audience

Were the necessary processes included in the project and presentation by the students?
- Made decisions about their project and presentation using a decision-making rating guide

TABLE 5 (continued)
• Made plans for their project and presentation using a plan sheet. • Set criteria for evaluation during the initial part of the planning stage. • Evaluated their project using the criteria set for evaluation. • Reflected on their project by writing a narrative designed by the teacher • Evaluated their classmates through peer evaluation set by the group.

TABLE 6 **Sample Questions from Midpoint Assessment**

1. How do you learn? Describe your learning style and processes.
 	
2. What have you learned so far this semester?
 	
   What has helped you learn it?
 	
3. How do you feel about yourself as a student and what you are learning?
 	
4. Describe how you understand the Professional Learning Process.
 	
   What elements of the PLP have prevented you from learning as much as you'd like?
 	
   What changes in the PLP would help you learn better?
 	
5. Where do you need to go next for your own development?
 	
6. What do we need to do to help each of us make progress?
 	
   What do I need to do?
 	
   What do you need to do?
 	
7. Why are we doing research on this topic (decision making, planning, and self-evaluation in the context of student projects)?
 	
8. Why is the thinking and emotional context of TIEL important?

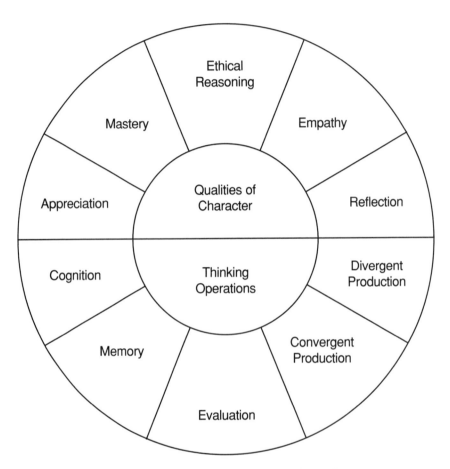

Figure 2. The TIEL Design Wheel

in the TIEL framework. While this research focuses on decision making, planning, and self-evaluation found within the intellectual operation of *evaluation*, other thinking operations involved in project work are cognition, gathering information; *memory*, connecting new information to previously learned knowledge; *convergent production*, logical, organizational thinking; and *divergent production*, creative, flexible thinking (Guilford, 1977). Qualities of character include *reflection*, learning about oneself; *empathy*, learning to care for oneself and others; *ethical reasoning*, acquiring the ethics of fairness, responsibility, and honest effort; *mastery* of basic skills and established knowledge; and *appreciation* for the arts, cultures, and nature (Dewey, 1964).

Results

At the end of the year-long professional learning process or teacher education intervention, there was evidence linking teacher education to teacher learning to student performance. All four teachers were developing project-based curriculum that explicitly included the teaching of decision making, planning, and self-evaluation (see Figure 3). The students reflected the learning of their teachers through articulate discussions of their thinking and learning about self-organization skills in the context of their projects. And finally, the teacher and student interviews gave evidence that my work as a teacher educator was clearly connected to student performance. In the following sections, I discuss how teachers changed their thinking and practice, how students reflected the learning of their teachers, and how my work as a teacher educator was reflected in student performance.

CHANGE IN TEACHER THINKING AND PRACTICE

Awareness of self-organization opportunities. Becoming conscious of self-organization processes was an important part of the professional learning process. One group meeting was devoted to a discussion of personal decision-making processes. The teachers described their personal projects such as buying a car, finding an apartment, or creating a curriculum unit. This activity helped the teachers develop an awareness of the opportunities for teaching self-organization processes to their students through classroom project work.

Ted, a third-grade teacher and veteran of the group with eight years of experience, was unaware of the potential power embedded in his teaching. While Ted's classroom management and curriculum were laced with choice and process, he was not explicit in teaching the students about their thinking. Ted had a great deal of expertise in the reading and writing process and included projects in his social studies units. While self-organization skills were embedded in the writing process, Ted had no vocabulary for recognizing and bridging those processes to the project work. As a result of the professional learning process, Ted became aware of those processes and how to make them explicit with his students. At the final assessment Ted reported,

> We *do* decision making. I just don't think I made enough of the connections. We've been doing decision making all year, like in choosing their jobs.

	Teaching Practice Baseline Assessment	Professional Learning Process	Teacher Practice Final Assessment	Student Performance Final Assessment
Erica 5th grade	Did not teach decision making, planning, and self-evaluation in context of project work Students not aware of s-o processes	Planning social studies units Development of tools: • decision making • planning • self-evaluation • daily monitoring of project work TIEL vocabulary	Planned 3 social studies projects that included teaching s-o skills Developed tools for teaching s-o processes Able to explicitly articulate planning	Enthusiastically discuss planning calendar Discuss how calendar helps them with due dates Discuss decision-making in context of *how* to make Mexico presentation Discuss criteria involved in evaluating Mexico projects
Stacy 4th grade	Did not teach s-o skills in context of project work Students not aware of s-o processes	Planning social studies units Development of tools: • decision making • planning • self-evaluation • daily monitoring of project work	Planned four project method social studies units to teach s-o skills Verbally and visually articulated s-o skills Gives responsibility to students	Discuss self-organization skills using metaphor Recognize patterns of s-o skills across projects Discuss using criteria to evaluate

Figure 3. Summary of Change in Teacher Practice
and Student Performance

	Teaching Practice Baseline Assessment	Professional Learning Process	Teacher Practice Final Assessment	Student Performance Final Assessment
Ted 3rd grade	Project work was ongoing Did not consciously teach s-o skills in context of project work Students not aware of s-o processes	Planning social studies and literature units Development of self-organization tools Ted's planning	Knew he needed to make decision-making opportunities explicit Understands his own need to plan more explicitly Planned 3 projects to teach s-o skills	Identify and describe problems in globe project
Brian 2nd grade	Did not teach in context of project work Students not aware of s-o processes	Planning three projects: 2 art, 1 literature Development of s-o tools	Learns to observe students' more deeply Ability to explicitly talk about thinking Understands importance of naming thinking process Planned 3 projects to teach s-o skills	Discuss choices Transfer use of s-o skills to activities out of school

Figure 3. (continued)

Choosing their desks. Choosing their homework partners. Choosing their rug spots. Choosing reading spots. It's all decision making. But I wasn't explicit. I didn't make enough connections from one to the other. I didn't highlight it enough.

Increased number of curriculum units. Each teacher increased the number of curriculum units that included project work. Teaching self-organization skills required something to organize, therefore, it was necessary for the teachers to institute project-work where few projects had existed before.

Erica had participated in the three-month pilot phase of the research a year and a half earlier. Although it was her first year of teaching, Erica did not hesitate to participate, since the pilot occurred during the last months of school and involved a relatively short time period. At that time Erica learned to teach decision making, planning, and self-evaluation within the context of one social studies project in her class. Before the pilot, Erica did not consciously teach the skills of self-organization to her students, nor did she use the words decision making, criteria, planning, or self-evaluation. Any discussion of self-organization skills was inexplicit and unplanned. Furthermore, since Erica did not feel prepared to manage student projects, she had not taught a project-based social studies or science unit prior to the pilot.

Erica changed her practice. During the professional learning process, she planned and carried out four major social studies units which all included student projects: School Study (a study of their own school), The United States, Mexico, and South America. For each project, she designed tools to help the students make decisions, plan, and self-evaluate at the conclusion of the project. Throughout the year, as Erica became more sophisticated in designing worksheets and discussing strategies to help the students manage their work, her students became more self-directed and empowered in the classroom. They were taking control of their work. Erica noted that even though both she and the students were at times disappointed when they had difficulties carrying out the processes of self-organization, the students were proud of their increasing self-efficacy. Erica said,

> They also felt really proud of what they'd done and powerful in doing it, no matter what happened in all the stuff. They completed something and they went through all these problems and they changed a lot because of it . . . a lot.

Purposeful planning. The teachers became more purposeful and explicit curriculum planners. Common planning strategies at the beginning of the intervention included a loose consideration of the time to be spent on a particular study and thinking about possible activities the students could do that connected to the topic. As the teachers became conscious of self-organization skills, they became more deliberate in their planning. Teaching self-organization skills required that the teachers needed to look ahead in their own planning in order to guide the students in their planning.

When it came to planning, Ted was a self-proclaimed meanderer. At baseline, Ted's curriculum planning at the beginning of the year involved making "an outline or skeletal sketch of certain topics that I plan to study with them." The curriculum components that he would emphasize in the studies of immigration and communities around the world would depend on "who [the children] are" and "what I feel they need."

While these were important considerations, Ted changed his planning practices. By the end of the professional learning process, Ted's projects were better structured, while still allowing students freedom in their learning. Expressing how his thinking and practice changed, he said, "[Learning about] planning helped me the most." The non-specific approach to curriculum development he described in the baseline interview gave way to conscious, purposeful methods of curriculum design. In the written midpoint assessment Ted described an important learning moment as when he discovered:

> That the final project must emerge first and foremost, which will shape the process and the learning outcomes. What helped me learn it was the drawn-out, meandering quality to my class's immigration study [the previous year].

Articulation. The teachers became more articulate in discussing thinking and learning with their students. Stacy, a fourth-grade teacher, came from a traditional Catholic school education and was the most traditional teacher of the four. In many ways, she appeared on the surface to fit the description of a teacher whose traditional ideas were affected little by her teacher preparation program (Hollingsworth, 1989). Yet, Stacy quickly expanded her teaching methodologies to include specific decision making, planning, and self-evaluation and developed fluency in discussing the full range of thinking processes with her students. At the final assessment Stacy reported that she had significantly changed her thinking about the strategies of decision making, planning, and self-evaluation. She explained, "I think that I'm seeing it as a more integral part of learning than I did at the outset."

Making a conscious effort to transfer responsibility to the students, Stacy gave a homework assignment requiring students to set criteria to decide how they would choose a time period to study for their final project. After giving them their assignment, the students replied, "What you're saying is, "*Why* are you choosing it?" Reinforcing the integration of self-management skills into her assignment she replied, "Exactly. If you're going to make an important decision about what you're going to study, then you should have some reasons."

Stacy was not only verbally articulate, but she provided visual clarity as well. Prior to the professional learning process, Stacy simply *gave* her students instructions for hands-on projects. During the professional learning process, Stacy learned to plan *with* the students. Stacy outlined the plan, the criteria for evaluation, and the research skills with the students on large chart paper. These written references remained attached to the chalkboard throughout the project.

Student observation. The professional learning process helped the teachers observe their students more deeply. As Brian, a second-grade teacher, became conscious of his own thinking, he became aware of the presence or absence of thinking and learning schema in his students. He wondered, "Do they have a 'way' of doing thinking—or is it just random?" Using TIEL as a lens for observing his students, Brian developed an understanding of why it is important to explicitly teach self-organization processes. He explained that he was concerned about the gap "between children who unconsciously have a way to plan, evaluate, and do [gather information, etc.], and those who don't, and the environmental factors that contribute to this."

Brian's empathy grew for "those who have not, for whatever reason, developed an internal way to think or make decisions." He found that students who lacked these internal self-organization skills seemed to lag behind in academic areas. Brian understood that teaching students explicitly about their thinking would allow them more control over their thinking, decrease their confusion, and help them make sense of the world. He said,

> You can tell kids who sort of have it [ways to make decisions, plan, self-evaluate], do it without thinking about it. And kids who don't have it, face everything again for the first time. You're not looking back to memories and you don't have any schema of thinking. You don't have any way to think [about thinking]. If you have it without realizing you have it, well fine, but if you know about it and you can talk about it, to me that always engenders being able to do it better.

Using the TIEL framework. While the research focused on self-organization skills, the TIEL framework helped the teachers see those skills in a larger perspective. Erica was uniquely qualified to comment on the effect of the TIEL framework as part of the professional learning process. When Erica participated in the research pilot project, the TIEL framework was not used to place the self-organization strategies within the context of the framework. I taught her how to incorporate decision making, planning, and self-evaluation into her curriculum as isolated skills. She was introduced to the theoretical framework with the other teachers during the official research year. In the final interview, I asked her how using the framework affected her learning. She replied,

> That [the TIEL framework] makes all the difference. You need to have the framework. I need to have it in order to categorize and sort and scaffold and give myself a framework to go back to. I think it's critical.

Erica also felt the TIEL framework helped address Sarason's (1982) concern by providing a language to facilitate the discussion of thinking and learning.

STUDENT PERFORMANCE: REFLECTING TEACHER LEARNING AND TEACHER EDUCATOR'S WORK

Student performance reflected the complex learning and teaching of the teachers and the effect of the teacher education intervention. In each classroom students were empowered by the opportunity to make decisions, plan, and evaluate their own projects. The students' discussions revealed increased motivation, more thoughtful projects, and an expanded capacity to discuss their thinking and learning. In the following examples, the metacognitive discussions with students show evidence of the clear connection between teacher learning and student work and the connection between teacher educator and student performance.

Planning and self-evaluation. As projects increased in complexity, Erica needed a better way to help students plan. I suggested to Erica that she teach the students how to use a blank calendar to plan the dates involved in the study about Mexico. The students were enthusiastic about this planning tool that gave them more control over their work. They stated how they liked the calendar, how it helped them divide their time and work, and how it helped them memorize due dates. They even recalled previous projects without the calendar tool and compared the confusion of those experiences with the current project on Mexico. They were convinced that without the calendar they "would have never been done with the Mexico project."

The students were equally articulate in explaining self-evaluation at the end of projects. S—explained how she had evaluated her presentation on Mexico by referring to the criteria that had been set at the beginning of the project. She explained,

> I thought very hard of what I would do so that my criteria and evaluation would come out good. When we evaluated we got all the questions and everything to do our scores. And I just kind of like looked at my project and everything for some of the questions and I really thought back about the work that I did. And I think it helped me to know the stuff that I really didn't do well.

Metaphors and Patterns. At the final assessment, discussion of decision making, planning, and self-evaluation permeated project work in Stacy's classroom. The students shared their learning with me using colorful phrases to describe the self-organization processes. One student said that without decision making, planning and evaluating, projects would not come together. It would be like "a snake without a spine." Another student described the green thinking (evaluation) as the "seasick thinking." Referring to all five of the thinking operations, he stated that, "Out of all these, the seasick thinking makes you the most . . . SICK!" Another student agreed, "You have to do it over and over and over again." With uncanny accuracy, these descriptions illustrated the back and forth movement of decision making and evaluating, as well as the often unstable process of planning.

The students also told me that they had noticed patterns in how thinking processes were involved in all their projects. One student commented that "the States project was kind of the same as the other projects because we had to do kind of the same things like plan. We had to look up stuff, like in books and inside the computer and encyclopedias." Another student saw the similarities in using criteria for peer editing.

Identifying problems. Even when things did not go well with projects, the students were able to use their articulation skills to identify the problem. One of the projects that Ted planned during the professional learning process involved creating a paper-mâché globe. Using atlases, the students researched the continents and attached cut-outs of each continent onto the globes. In the final interview with the students, D—expressed his frustration with the project. He did not feel the pink planning sheet Ted had given them was adequate in helping him through the process of creating the globe. He was currently redoing his globe because it was upside-down with the continents in the wrong place. To him the positioning of the globe was a very random event, over which he had little control. Even though the planning sheet delineated what the students were to do, it did not give D—enough information on how to do it. N—identified the problem as she saw it, "The plan didn't tell us exactly where everything goes. It just told us the steps. Now put on your pieces. Now paint your globe. Put on your equator."

Student empowerment. Brian wanted his second-grade students to gain a sense of power and control over what they do. He wanted students to become conscious of their choices and responsible for setting their own criteria. He was well aware of how students who feel powerless affect their environment. The student may not be able to meet classroom or academic or family expectations. He may not meet his own expectations, but, according to Brian, the student "can make you (the teacher) go crazy!" A better way was to help students learn to affect themselves and others more positively by explicitly teaching students how responsible choices are made.

At the final assessment, the second-grade students were aware of choice, planning, and evaluating, and becoming more articulate in explaining these processes. One student commented, "If you can make choices, then you can choose what's best for you. Like maybe the teacher says you have to read this big book, but it's too easy for you so you have to pick something yourself." J—, who often struggled in the interviews, transferred the concept of planning to a context outside of school. She said, "When you take the bus or the train you have to plan what stops you're gonna get off in and what stops you're not gonna wait for."

Conclusion and Recommendations

Just as the teachers Sarason (1982) observed had never been prepared to discuss thinking, the findings indicate that the teachers involved in this research were similarly unprepared to teach "the higher order skills that society is calling on schools to teach" (Devaney & Sykes, 1988, p. 19). Historically, this lack of instruction in the complex teaching involved in the project method is not uncommon. Darling-Hammond (1997) points out that in earlier educational reform movements, teachers lacked the "extensive skill" (p. 12) to maintain progressive reforms. While teachers have understood that the intention of using "the project method" is "to make learning relevant," they lacked the knowledge to "fashion work that was both rigorous as well as relevant" (p. 12). While teachers have long been at a disadvantage in bringing complex learning to life in classrooms, change is possible.

SUMMARY OF FINDINGS

Teachers. Through the professional learning process that was part of this research, the teachers learned the complex skills needed to teach self-organization processes to students in the context of the project method. The teachers became more conscious curriculum planners, created materials that supported development of self-organization skills in their students, and led articulate discussions of thinking and learning.

Students. Student performance reflected change in teacher practice. Students in grades two through five showed their capacity for complex learning as they developed and discussed their projects. They showed evidence of intellectual engagement as they became more motivated, more organized, and more responsible in monitoring their own learning. Students showed evidence of "transformational learning" (Clark, 1993, p. 47) as they articulately described their thinking in making decisions, planning, and evaluating their projects.

Teacher educator. The findings indicated clear connections from teacher educator to teacher to student. The TIEL Design Wheel provided visible and verbal connections throughout the professional learning process that transferred explicitly from the teacher educator to the teacher to the student. This conceptual framework, outlining components of complex teaching and learning, provided structural support for both teachers and students as they attained "higher levels of intellectual method" (Dewey, 1964, p. 329). The TIEL framework placed self-organization processes within a context of other intellectual processes and social emotional characteristics. It helped teachers and students develop their capacity to observe and reflect, provided a language for discussing thinking, and scaffolded complex learning for the teachers as well as for the students.

IMPLICATIONS

While this year-long study involved only four inservice teachers, the findings have deep implications for teacher education. First, if we are to have teachers who have the competencies to engage students intellectually, teacher educators must include the explicit teaching of intellectual processes in teacher preparation programs through theory, practical example, and discussion. Second, the study carried out with second through fifth grade students indicates that teacher educators must not underestimate the ability of students to deal with complex learning. Teacher educators must become more determined to prepare teachers who can teach in the complex ways that will support students' capacity to think and understand their thinking. Third, the TIEL Design Wheel provided a strong link from teacher educator to teacher to student. The TIEL conceptual framework must be considered as a potentially "powerful learning opportunit[y] . . . [that can] promote complex learning by teachers [and] students" (Feiman-Nemser, 2001, p. 1014).

FURTHER QUESTIONS

There are many questions to investigate through further research. In the course of teacher education, when can the components of complex teaching and learning be taught most effectively? How can preservice teachers learn and apply the complex processes of decision making, planning, and self-evaluation in the context of project work? Can using the TIEL framework help in "laying a foundation for beginning teaching and preparing novices to learn in and from their practice" (Fieman-Nemser, 2001, p. 1016)? Can using the TIEL framework help induction teachers maintain a commitment to complex teaching and learning, while surviving the first difficult year of teaching and learning to teach? For inservice teachers, can experience be a "pitfall" (Fieman-Nemser & Buchmann, 1985, p. 54) in learning how to teach the strategies of complex teaching and learning?

Currently, I am investigating these questions as I teach Masters Program classes that include preservice, induction, and inservice teachers. Those enrolled in these classes first learn to use the processes of decision making, planning, and self-evaluation explicitly within the context of their own coursework assignments and projects. Next, they learn to design project-based curriculum that includes the teaching of decision making, planning, and self-evaluation to students. The TIEL framework is used throughout to teach thinking processes, scaffold learning, and facilitate metacognitive discussions.

While many questions are under investigation, there are a variety of others to consider. What would be the effect on teacher candidates who experienced complex teaching and learning during their K–12 education? How would this "pre-training" (Fieman-Nemser, 1983, p. 151) affect their teacher education process? Can using TIEL as a structural support for understanding thinking processes help cooperating teachers guide student teachers? Can implementation of complex teaching and learning strategies increase student achievement in basic skills across the curriculum? How can teacher education programs be structured to support the teaching of thinking involved in complex teaching and learning?

Referring to the teaching of thinking, Sigel (as cited in French & Rhoder, 1992) said, "The choice of how best to teach thinking faces the educational community and the public. Nothing is more basic or deserving of prompt attention and resolution" (p. 61). Such knowledge and skills are not optional for teachers who will teach increasingly diverse students living in a shrinking world of bewildering choices caused by ever-shifting social, economic, and political landscapes.

The second grader who explained planning in the context of riding a bus can serve as an example for teacher educators. When this young learner became aware of the concept of planning, her bus riding experience changed. Similarly, as teacher educators become aware that new strategies are required to prepare teachers, we must change our ways of teaching to accommodate this new learning. It is incumbent upon all who educate teachers to explicitly include the pedagogy of complex teaching and learning in the "intervention" (Heuwinkel, 2001, p. 180) that is teacher education.

REFERENCES

Baum, S. M., Renzulli, J. S., & Hébert, T. P. (1995). Reversing under-achievement: Creative productivity as a schematic intervention. *Gifted Child Quarterly, 39*(4), 224–235.

Bogdan, R., & Biklen, S. (1992). *Qualitative research for education: An introduction to theory and methods.* Boston: Allyn and Bacon.

Clark, M. C. (1993). Transformational learning. In S. B. Merriam (Ed.), *An update on adult learning theory: No. 57. New directions for adult and continuing education* (pp. 47–56). San Francisco: Jossey-Bass.

Darling-Hammond, L. (1997). *The right to learn: A blueprint for creating schools that work.* San Francisco: Jossey-Bass.

Devaney, K., & Sykes, G. (1988). Making the case for professionalism. In A. Lieberman (Ed.), *Building a professional culture in schools* (pp. 3–22). New York: Teachers College Press.

Dewey, J. (1964). *John Dewey on education: Selected writings.* In R. D. Archambault (Ed.). Chicago: University of Chicago Press.

Fieman-Nemser, S. (1983). Learning to teach. In L. S. Schulman & G. Sykes (Eds.), *Handbook of teaching and policy* (pp. 150–170). New York: Longman.

Fieman-Nemser, S. (2001). From preparation to practice: Designing a continuum to strengthen and sustain teaching. *Teachers College Record, 103*(6), 1013–1055.

Fieman-Nemser, S., & Buchmann, M. (1985). Pitfalls of experience in teacher preparation. *Teachers College Record, 87*(1), 53–65.

Folsom, C. T. (2000). Managing choice: Helping teachers facilitate decision making, planning, and self-evaluation with students (Doctoral dissertation, Teachers College Columbia University, 2000). *Dissertation Abstracts International, 62,* 1702.

French, J. N., & Rhoder, C. (1992). *Teaching thinking skills: Theory and practice.* New York: Garland.

Fuller, F. F. (1969). Concerns of teachers: A developmental conceptualization. *American Educational Research Journal, 6*(2), 207–226.

Good, T. L. (1990). Building the knowledge base of teaching. In D. D. Dill (Ed.), *What teachers need to know: The knowledge, skills, and values essential to good teaching* (pp. 17–75). San Francisco: Jossey Bass.

Goodlad, J. I. (1990). *Teachers for our nation's schools.* San Francisco: Jossey-Bass.

Goodlad, J. I. (1994). *Educational renewal: Better teachers, better schools.* San Francisco: Jossey Bass.

Guilford, J. P. (1977). *Way Beyond the IQ.* Buffalo, NY: Creative Education Foundation.

Heuwinkel, M.K. (2001). Learning to assess student understanding: An investigation into the role of program. In J. D. Rainer and E.M. Guyton (Eds.) *Research on preparing teachers who can meet the needs of all students, Yearbook, Vol. IX* (pp. 169–182). Dubuque, IA: Kendall/Hunt Publishing.

Holland, J. H. (1995). *Hidden order: How adaptation builds complexity.* New York: Addison-Wesley.

Hollingsworth, S. (1989). Prior beliefs and cognitive change in learning to teach. *American Educational Research Journal, 26*(2), 160–189.

Kilpatrick, W. H. (1921). Dangers and difficulties of the project method and how to overcome them: Introductory statement: Definition of terms. *Teachers College Record 22*(4), 283–288.

Kliebard, H. M. (1995). *The struggle for the American curriculum: 1893-1958.* New York: Routledge.

Marzano, R. J. (1993). How classroom teachers approach the teaching of thinking. *Theory into Practice, 32*(3), 154–160.

National Commission on Teaching and America's Future. (1996, September). *What matters most: Teaching for America's future* (Full report of the commission). New York: Author.

Ogle, D. M. (1997). *Critical issue: Rethinking learning for students at risk.* Retrieved October 28, 2002, from North Central Regional Educational Laboratory Web site: *http://www.ncrel.org/sdrs/areas/issues/students/atrisk/at700.htm.*

Sarason, S. B. (1982). *The culture of the school and the problem of change.* Boston: Allyn & Bacon.

Tom, A. R. (1997). *Redesigning teacher education.* Albany, NY: State University of New York Press.

Learning Styles Preparation Coupled with Teacher Assistance

10.

A Link to Language Arts Achievement Gains for At-risk Hispanic Middle School Students

Jane E. Irons and Nancy Leffel Carlson

Dr. Irons' Educational background includes school psychology, counseling administration, and assessment. She has over 25 years experience in public schools, agencies, and higher education. A major research focus is at-risk children and adults. Publication areas include teen pregnancy, learning styles, teaching strategies, and adults with learning disabilities.

Dr. Carlson has experience as an elementary education teacher, a special education teacher for students with behavior and emotional problems, a school psychologist, and educational diagnostician. Dr. Carlson's area of research and publication is learning styles and strategies.

ABSTRACT

There is extensive literature discussing learning styles from many perspectives, but little research linking learning style teacher preparation with actual student performance outcomes. Project TEACH was implemented in response to middle- school teacher requests for university faculty assistance in motivating at-risk student learners. Over 50 middle-school teachers were provided 6 days of staff development on the Dunn and Dunn Learning Styles Model. Ongoing classroom support was provided by two instructional aides, a project coordinator, and university faculty. School district Stanford 9 Achievement scores were compared for year one and two of the project for 300 students and significant language arts achievement gains appear linked to teacher implementation of learning style strategies. Additionally, 8th-grade language arts gains were substantiated through comparison with students from a school, which did not utilize learning styles methodology. Results of this study have implications for both staff development and teacher training.

P roject TEACH was a 3-year collaborative project between the Texas Woman's University and the Fort Worth Independent School District. The major purpose of the project was to improve student motivation for learning and improve achievement through the provision of learning styles professional development. A multidimensional approach coupled the teacher training with ongoing classroom assistance from the project coordinator, university program director, and two instructional aides. A quasi-experimental research design compared achievement results for year one and year two of the project. A summary of pertinent literature is followed by a description of the project, research methodology, analysis, results, staff development, limitations, and conclusions.

A Summary of Literature

Literature from several areas provided support for development and implementation of project TEACH. The major focus of the study was to investigate linkages among teacher professional development, provision of ongoing classroom assistance, implementation of learning style strategies with at-risk middle-school students, and achievement outcomes. Concern about Hispanic dropout rates and the quality of teachers for at-risk urban students formed a framework for inclusion of the following literature review topics: at-risk students, dropout statistics, learning styles and teaching styles, and professional development issues. At-risk students often do not experience high achievement in public school programs. They frequently are in lower economic groups, have high mobility rates, and are minority with language barriers (Barr & Parrett, 2001). Other contributing factors to at-risk classification include those associated with families and school barriers. At-risk students frequently have disruptive family backgrounds that include poverty, violence, and unstable relationships. Ineffective school curriculum, discipline problems, and untrained teachers who lack experience or expertise to work with at-risk students exemplify school barriers (Barr & Parrett; Bracey, 1989; Johnson, 1997; Pallas, Natriello, & McDill, 1989; Repetto, Pankaskie, DePalma-Hankins, Schwartz, & Perry, 1997).

National dropout rates are found significant for both the South Region with 29% and the Midwest Region with 22% (Kaufman, Klein, & Frase, 1999). At-risk students from minority populations are at greater risk for dropout. Hispanic dropout rates were 26% in the United States (Kaufman et al.). In Texas the highest dropout rate was found in urban districts and rates increase with the size of the district. The graduation rate for Hispanic students in Texas in 1998 was 56% (Texas Education Agency [TEA], 2001).

Literature on learning styles has been extensive during the past 15 years. Authors have been both critical and supportive. Learning styles authors have addressed culture, middle-school students, at-risk students, models/strategies, and teacher issues. Some authors have identified problems with learning style research, particularly the instrument developed to identify learning styles. Ellis and Fouts (1997) are critical of the Dunn and Dunn Model, citing lack of validity and reliability with instruments. In a meta-analysis of 42 studies using the Dunn and Dunn Model, 6 studies were found to contain serious threats to validity (Griggs & Dunn, 1995). The Dunn study also reported that the instruments operationalizing the Dunn and Dunn Model were valid because they measured characteristics used to enhance academic performance and reliability was shown over time.

A study by Nunn (1995) supports learning styles and strategy approaches to improve grade point averages of at-risk middle school students. Comparison of learning styles of culture groups (Griggs & Dunn, 1995, 1996) suggests that children from different culture groups had different learning preferences and associated individual preferences addressing room temperature, auditory and visual stimuli, morning learning time, and external structure with Mexican-American students. Hall and Hyle (1996) examined relationships between achievement and learning styles of middle-school students and recommend teacher staff development to enhance teacher awareness of learning preferences. Griggs and Dunn (1996) suggested that adolescents may not learn when they encounter ineffective teaching. Dunn (1990) reported that learning styles of highly at-risk or dropout students were significantly different than those who remain in school. The body of research conducted on the Dunn and Dunn Model suggests that students who are instructed using teaching strategies and physical setting modifications based on student learning preferences may be expected to achieve significantly higher than those not receiving learning style strategy instruction (Dunn 1996)

The Dunn and Dunn Model uses the Learning Styles Inventory (Price & Dunn, 1997) and the Productivity Environmental Preference Survey (Dunn, Dunn, & Price, 1996) to identify four types of elements that affect learning and comprise a learning style: (a) instructional environment includes sound, light, temperature, and seating; (b) emotionality includes motivation, persistence, and responsibility; (c) social preferences include individual learning, group learning, or learning with peers; and (d) physiological preferences include sensory preferences such as auditory, visual, or tactile, and intake preferences for food or drink (Dunn, 1993).

Some authors suggest that teachers have individual learning style preferences that affect how they teach and that teachers teach like they were taught or how they prefer to learn (Cornett, 1983; Ebeling, 2000; Louisell &

Descamps, 2001). Teaching style areas include instructional settings, use of curriculum, methodology, planning, assessment, and behavior management (Louisell & Descamps, 2001). Literature on effective teachers suggests that these teachers know their own learning styles, recognize the learning styles of their students, and adapt their teaching styles to meet learner needs (Ebeling; Frieberg & Driscoll, 2000; Fullan, 2001).

Current educational reform efforts have identified continuing professional development as critical to improving teacher quality. A number of authors suggest that professional development must provide ongoing continuous support and reinforcement so that teachers are able to understand and apply effective teaching strategies for student learning and behaviors (Fullan, 2001; Goodell, Parker, & Kahle, 2000; Stone & Mata, 2000).

Description of the Project

Project TEACH was a 3-year collaborative effort between the Texas Woman's University and the Fort Worth Independent School District. TEACH was partially funded by the Sid Richardson Foundation. The focus of TEACH was to provide staff development on the Dunn and Dunn Learning Styles Model, provide teacher assistance with implementing learning styles strategies, and investigate the impact of professional development and support on student achievement outcomes. A framework for discussion of TEACH will be provided through the following topics: student characteristics, teacher characteristics, training and teacher assistance, research design, data analysis and results, and conclusions.

STUDENT CHARACTERISTICS

Rosemont Middle School is representative of large urban middle schools with high at-risk student populations. The school serves primarily grades 7 and 8. The school has a low academic accountability rating and was designated as a school with both gang and drug concerns. Nine hundred forty-seven students were enrolled. The major ethnic group was Hispanic with 77%, second was African American with 14%, and third was White with 7%. The mobility rate was 26%; 81% were designated economically disadvantaged, based on free and reduced meal applications; 48% had limited English language proficiency; and disciplinary placements were about 8% of the total population. The ratio of boys to girls was about equally represented (TEA, 2001).

Teacher Characteristics

Fifty-seven teachers and three administrators were assigned to Rosemont. Twenty teachers were assigned to grade 8, 19 were assigned to grade 7, and five were assigned to the language center. All building administrators were Hispanic. The principal was male. One assistant principal was male and one was female. Eighty-four percent of the teachers were female. The majority of the teachers were White (68%), African-American (16%), and Asian (4%). Over one-third (35%) had between 1 and 5 years experience; 14% were beginning teachers; 14% had 11 to 20 years experience; and 16% had over 20 years experience. The mobility rate for Rosemont teachers was similar to that of students, 32% (TEA).

Training and Teacher Assistance

Three full days of training were provided to all teachers and administrators on the Dunn and Dunn Model of Learning Style Preferences at the initiation of the project in November 1999 and January 2000 by an independent consultant. The consultant provided an additional 2 days of training follow-up in August and September 2000 and the project coordinator provided a third day. The training sessions were held on Saturdays and the school district provided teacher stipends for attendance. Twenty-nine teachers and an assistant principal attended the follow-up training. The training focused on the learning styles of teachers, the learning preferences of students, cooperative learning methods, peer learning activities, and making teaching materials to enhance student-learning preferences. The teachers used a training manual based on the Dunn and Dunn Model (Marshall, 1993), and training kits containing manipulative instructional materials and supplies to use in developing teaching activities for students.

Teacher assistance was provided in three ways. Learning preference strategy booklets were developed for each teacher for each class. Individual student learning profiles were merged with class schedules to determine specific class profiles. The dominant learning preference was identified for each class, for each period, and for each teacher. Corresponding teacher strategies were then designed based on the dominant class preference (see Table 1, Example: Recommended Teaching Strategies).

Two Hispanic instructional aides were hired by the project to assist teachers in implementing learning style strategies in the classroom. The aides made photocopies, created and provided manipulative instructional materials, and were available for in-the-classroom instructional assistance to the teachers and students.

TABLE 1

Example: Project TEACH 2000–01 Two Recommended Teaching Strategies for Dominant Class Profile

Learning Preference	Strategy
Noise acceptable	• Allow students to use CD players with earphones during individual working hours. • Provide for conversation and/or activity learning areas in the classroom where students can converse with soft voices during activity times.
Dim lights	• Reduce brightness of lights in the classroom; turn ceiling and overhead projector lights off, use floor lamps, or indirect light from windows. • Use room dividers or classroom furniture to block or diffuse light from windows.
Cool temperature	• Provide a cool temperature classroom environment. • Provide for adequate air circulation; fans, open windows, and ventilation.
Wants to work with peers	• Provide partner and small group work assignments and small group activities. • Use student groups and teams to present lessons to the whole class.
Prefers variety in learning	• Provide a variety of methods for working on assignments and tasks, i.e., multi-media, manipulatives, group study, individual study, student presentations, and learning centers. • Provide for options for completed assignments, e.g., bulletin boards, group presentations, individual presentations, tape-recorded or video-taped presentation, puppet show, skit or play.

University support was provided by the project director on a consultation basis. The project director also served as director for research activities by developing the research design, supervising data collection, and analysis. Two days per week the project coordinator scheduled time in the school to be available to the teachers, assist with training for the instructional aides, collect data for program evaluation, administer learning style inventories to students, and disseminate materials and a newsletter.

RESEARCH DESIGN

A discussion of the research design area includes the participants, instruments, research design, and questions.

Participants. During the initial year of the project, students in grade 7 were selected to take the Learning Styles Inventory (LSI). Grade 7 was selected because these students would be returning to Rosemont the next year in grade 8 and they would be available to continue in the project over a 2-year period. The longitudinal nature of the project was needed to investigate training impact upon achievement. During the first year 423 student learning preferences were identified and 470 were identified in year 2.

Due to the high mobility rate for Rosemont, 88 students who took the LSI in grade 7 did not attend the school for grade 8. This number represents a 21% mortality rate, similar to the 25% mobility rate for this school, leaving a student participant sample of 335 (TEA).

A comparison school, Kirkpatrick Middle School, was selected on the basis of a student demographics data match. The total student population was 579 students in grades 6 through 8. Kirkpatrick student demographics are 79% Hispanic, 15% African-American, and 6% White. The mobility rate for this school was 26%, the lower economic rate was 77%, and 43% were considered to have limited English language proficiency. Disciplinary placements were 4%.

Although all teachers were trained the first year, only 7th-grade teachers participated on a voluntary basis and 12 teachers participated. During the second year 8th-grade students were included and all new 7th-grade students were administered the LSI. Both 7th- and 8th-grade teachers volunteered and 17 participated.

Instruments. The instrument used with students was the Learning Style Inventory (Price & Dunn, 1997). This instrument has 104 questions across 22 domains. Measures of reliability for each of the 22 preference elements on the English version of the instrument are reported and range from .56 to .88. Most of the reliability measures are above .60 (Price & Dunn).

Achievement data were obtained from the Stanford Achievement Test (9th ed., SAT9) (Psychological Corporation, 1996). Achievement results were collected and maintained by Fort Worth ISD Public Education Management System (PEIMS) data bank. Data were provided by the Fort Worth Research Department and obtained under public information procedures. A review by Berk (1998) shows K-R20 reliability coefficients ranging from mid .80s to .90s for most tests and subtests. Extensive and appropriate analysis of bias, reliability, and validity are documented.

The instrument used to measure teacher-learning preferences was the Productivity Environmental Preference Survey (PEPS). This instrument identifies how adults prefer to learn and perform educational activities (Dunn et al., 1996). Reliability is based on factor and content analysis. Reliability coefficients on 20 areas ranged from .39 to .87. A review by Rozecki (1998) indicates information on validity of the PEPS is lacking.

Research Design and Questions. The research design was quasi-experimental causal-comparative (Carlson, 2002). Achievement results were compared for year 1 with those of year 2. Achievement results of Rosemont 8th-grade students were compared to achievement of Kirkpatrick 8th-graders who had not been exposed to learning styles methodology. The following research questions were generated for this study.

1. Is there a statistically significant difference between mean scores in reading, math, and language arts achievement for students in grades 7 and 8 after learning styles teaching strategies have been used?
2. Is there a statistically significant difference between mean scores of students in grade 8 in reading, math, and language arts between Rosemont Middle School and a comparison school, Kirkpatrick Middle School?

Data analysis and results. The results of a paired-sample t test show there was not a significant difference between mean scores on the SAT9 reading achievement test taken in September 2000 and 2001, $t(324) = -.28$, $p = .782$ (Carlson). These results indicate that the score on the second SAT9 test in reading was not significantly different than the first score. Similarly, the results of the paired-sample t test for math achievement was not significant, $t(324) = .45$, $p = .657$). These results suggest that the second SAT9 test in math was not significantly different from the first score.

There was an 81.11 point difference between the mean scores in language arts achievement from year 1 to year 2. The results of the paired-sample *t* test indicate that for the 325 students, there was a significant difference at

($p = .009$) between mean scores for the SAT9 achievement test taken in September 2000 and September 2001 in language arts achievement, $t(324) = -2.63$, $p = .009$. This indicates that the score on the second year SAT9 test in language arts was significantly greater than the first year score (see Table 2).

Mean scores on the SAT9 reading achievement test were compared using an independent t test to determine if there was a significant difference between the reading achievement of Rosemont 8th grade and Kirkpatrick 8th grade. The two-sample independent t test for 127 students from each of the two schools, $t(230.651) = 1.210$, $p = .228$, show that reading achievement does not differ significantly.

Similarly, SAT9 math achievement scores were compared. The two-sample independent t test indicates that the mean scores in math between Rosemont Middle School and Kirkpatrick Middle School do not differ significantly, $t(202.319) = 1.654$, $p = .100$.

Table 3 presents the results of comparing the mean scores of the SAT9 language arts achievement test given to 8th-grade students at Rosemont Middle School and Kirkpatrick Middle School in September 2001. The comparison used an independent t test to determine if there was a significant difference

TABLE 2

Comparison of Mean Scores on SAT9 Language Arts Achievement Tests for Year 1 and Year 2

Paired Sample *t* Tests Statistics

Variables	N	t	Sig	M	SD	SE of Mean
Language Arts 00				560.66	200.08	11.10
	25	.020	.726			
Language Arts 01				599.02	175.41	9.73

Paired Samples Test

Mean	SD	SE Mean	t-value	df	2-tailed Sig.	95% Conf. Interval lower	95% Conf. Interval upper
−38.36	263.49	14.62	−2.625	324	.009	−67.11	−9.61

TABLE 3

Comparison of Mean Scores on SAT9 Language Arts Achievement Test between 8th Grade Students at Rosemont Middle School and Kirkpatrick Middle School in September 2001

Paired Sample *t* Tests Statistics

Dependent Variable	Grouping Variable	N	M	SD	SE of Mean
Language Arts	Rosemont	127	617.37	140.90	12.50
	Kirkpatrick	127	474.56	295.03	26.18

ced *t* test for Equity of Means

Variances	*t*	df	2-tailed Sig.	Mean Diff.	SE of Diff.	95% Confidence Lower	Interval Upper
Unequal	−4.923	180.63	.001	−142.81	29.01	200.06	−85.57

between mean scores for Rosemont Middle School when compared to Kirkpatrick Middle School in language arts achievement scores.

The 127 students from Rosemont Middle School had a mean score of 617.37 total points on the SAT9 language arts test given in September 2001. The 127 students from Kirkpatrick Middle School had a mean score of 474.56 total points on the SAT9 language arts test given in September 2001. There was a 142.81-point difference in the language arts mean scores between Rosemont Middle School and Kirkpatrick Middle School with mean scores higher for Rosemont Middle School.

STAFF DEVELOPMENT

In order to investigate the usefulness of the staff development training, teachers were asked to complete a survey (Parker, 2000). Twenty-eight teachers responded, although not all of them chose to participate in the study. The majority (96%) considered the learning styles workshop important, particularly in identifying their own learning style. Eighty-six percent reported using cooperative learning strategies and 79% reported using small group instruction. Sixty-six percent utilized pairing students for independent work and 52% indicated that they preferred teaching in standard lecture format. Over half (69%) indicated they would like additional use of an instructional aide and more materials provided for implementing instructional strategies. Environmental modifications, which appeared the easiest component to change, were preferred by 52% who requested beanbag chairs or lamps. Forty-three percent of the teachers indicated the greatest assistance from outside resources was in providing ideas and assisting teachers in brainstorming ideas, demonstrating materials, modeling teaching strategies, and provision of make and take materials. Most teachers indicated use of a variety of techniques. In a 90-minute class period, 75% of the teachers reported that they spent between 10 and 30 minutes on individual learning, while 82% spent between 10 and 30 minutes on lecture.

LIMITATIONS OF THE STUDY

A number of limitations were identified for student participation including mortality, instrumentation, maturation, and selection bias. Extensive mortality occurred with a 25% student mobility rate. Researchers had no part in administering achievement tests or maintaining a database. District achievement results were released to the researchers. Maturation may have resulted since students advanced in age over time, while grade level advancement was based on teacher recommendations and accomplishment of grade level expectations. The selection of the comparison school group was not random, but based on a demographic characteristics match. Only Hispanic students were included because they comprised the major student group.

A number of limitations were identified for teacher participants including selection bias, mobility, and history. Teacher participants were volunteers and many were new to the campus or had less than five years experience. The attrition rate for teachers was 17%; some of the teachers were transferred after the first year of the project. History includes events that are not part of the treatment. Although teachers were trained on the Dunn and Dunn Model, there is no way to ensure that strategies were consistently implemented and student-learning increases may have occurred due to other factors.

Conclusions

The literature contains prolific coverage in the area of learning styles. Authors have identified characteristics, developed instruments, developed and implemented strategies, and supported and reported stakeholder satisfaction. However, few researchers have linked learning styles professional development training and strategy implementation directly to achievement gains. Results of project TEACH suggest such a link in the area of language arts for at-risk Hispanic youth. Significant gains were noted when comparing mean Stanford 9 achievement of the treatment school, Rosemont, with a comparison school, Kirkpatrick, for 127 grade-8 students from each school. Additionally, Rosemont students' mean achievement scores were significantly higher in year 2 of the study, when compared to year 1 in the area of language arts.

Significant gains were not found in the areas of reading or mathematics. Reading teachers did not participate in the project, because there was a district reading program implemented to remediate basic skills and increase achievement in that area. Similarly, math teachers were participating in district staff development and associated methodology. Although all the teachers were provided learning styles professional development, participation in the project was voluntary.

A major factor in teacher implementation of learning styles strategies was attributed to the development of a class learning styles profile that was developed in response to teacher requests. When teachers were provided copies of their students' individual learning style profiles, they reported that they were overwhelmed and could not use all the information. When class schedules were merged with the profiles of each individual student and a dominant class profile was identified for each class, the teachers found this information useful and adjusted their teaching strategies to meet the major learning preferences of the whole class.

Teachers found that having instructional aides available for assistance with material development and small group instruction helpful; however, reliance on the project coordinator and program director for professional feedback and generation of ideas and encouragement enabled the teachers to take risks and change their teaching behaviors to meet dominant class preferences. Findings of this study support a multidimensional professional development model, which provides training, ongoing assistance and support for teachers. The practice of including learning styles methodology in both professional development and teacher training programs appears warranted.

Based on the findings of this study, further research is recommended with different ethnic groups, different grade levels, and across content areas.

REFERENCES

Barr, R. D., & Parrett, W. H. (2001). *Hope fulfilled for at-risk and violent youth: K–12 programs that work* (2nd ed.). Needham Heights, MA: Allyn Bacon

Berk, R. A. (1998). In J. C. Impara & B. S. Plake (Eds.). *The thirteenth mental measurements yearbook* (pp. 925–928). Lincoln, NE: The Buros Institute of Mental Measurements, University of Nebraska-Lincoln Press.

Bracey, G. W. (1989). Moving around and dropping out. *Phi Delta Kappan, 70*(5), 407–410.

Carlson, N. L. (2002). *Evaluation of the effectiveness of Dunn & Dunn model of learning styles teacher training on academic performance of at-risk, urban middle-school students: A longitudinal study.* Unpublished doctoral dissertation, Texas Woman's University, Denton, TX.

Cornett, C. E. (1983). *What you should know about teaching and learning styles.* Bloomington, IN: Phi Delta Kappa Educational Foundation.

Dunn, R. S. (1990). Teaching underachievers through their learning style strengths. *Inter-Ed, 16*(52), 5–7.

Dunn, R. S. (1993). Learning styles of the multiculturally diverse. *Emergency Librarian, 20*(4), 24-32.

Dunn, R. S., Dunn, K. J., & Price, G. E. (1996). *Productivity environmental preference survey.* Lawrence, KS: Price Systems.

Dunn, R. S., & Griggs, S. A. (1995). A meta-analytic validation of the Dunn and Dunn model of learning style preferences [Electronic version]. *Journal of Educational Research, 68*(6), 353–363. Retrieved January 2, 2002, from EBSCOhost database.

Ebeling, D. G. (2000). Adapting your teaching to any learning style [Electronic version]. *Phi Delta Kappan, 82*(3), 247–248. Retrieved February 25, 2002, from EBSCOhost database.

Ellis, A. K., & Fouts, J. T. (1997). *Research on educational innovations* (2nd ed.). Larchmont, NY: Eye on Education.

Frieberg, H. J., & Driscoll, A. (2000). *Universal teaching strategies* (3rd ed.). Boston: Allyn & Bacon.

Fullan, M. (2001). *The NEW meaning of educational change.* New York: Teachers College Press.

Goodell, J. E., Parker, L. H., & Kahle, J. B. (2000). Assessing the impact of sustained professional development on middle school mathematics teachers. In D. J. McIntyre & D. M. Byrd (Eds.), *Research on effective models for teacher education* (pp. 203–217). Thousand Oaks, CA: Corwin.

Griggs, S., & Dunn, R. (1995). Hispanic-American students and learning style [Electronic version]. *Emergency Librarian, 23*(2), 11–17. Retrieved January 2, 2002, from EBSCOhost database.

Griggs, S., & Dunn, R. (1996, May). Hispanic-American students and learning styles. *ERIC Digest.* Report No. EDO-PS-96-4. Washington, DC: Office of Educational Research and Improvement (ED). Retrieved January 2, 2002, from *http//:www.ericeece.org/pubs/digests/1996/griggs96.html.*

Hall, L. A., & Hyle, A. E. (1996). Learning styles, achievement and the middle level student: Useful facts or useless fiction? *Research in Middle Level Education Quarterly, 19*(2), 67–88. Retrieved December 26, 2001, from ERIC database.

Johnson, G. M. (1997). Teachers in the inner city: Experienced-based ratings of factors that place students at risk [Electronic version]. *Preventing School Failure, 2*(1), 19–27. Retrieved March 2, 2002, from EBSCOhost database.

Kaufman, P., Klein, S., & Frase, M. (1999, March). *Dropout rates in the United States* [Electronic version]. NCES Reference No. 1999-082. Washington, DC: U.S. Department of Education, National Center for Education Statistics. Retrieved February 2, 2001, from *http://nces.ed.gov/pub-search/pubsinfo.asp?pubid=1999082.*

Louisell, R. D., & Descamps, J. (2001). *Developing a teaching style: Methods for elementary school teachers* (2nd ed.). Prospect Heights, Il: Waveland.

Marshall, C. (1993). *Creating quality in teaching and learning: A learning styles training manual improving educational outcomes for all students.* Richardson, TX: Quality Education Systems.

Nunn, G. D. (1995). Effects of a learning styles and strategies intervention upon at-risk middle school students [Electronic version]. *Journal of Instructional Psychology, 22*(1), 34–40. Retrieved December 26, 2001, from EBSCOhost database.

Pallas, A. M., Natriello, G., & McDill, E. L. (1989). The changing nature of 9 disadvantaged populations: Current dimensions and future trends. *Educational Researcher, 18*(5), 4, 16–22.

Parker, S. D. (2000). *Teacher awareness of learning styles: Implications for teacher behavior change.* Unpublished master's thesis, Texas Woman's University, Denton, TX.

Price, G., & Dunn, R. (1997). *Learning style inventory: An inventory for the identification of how individuals in grades 3 through 12 prefer to learn.* Lawrence, KS: Price Systems.

Psychological Corporation. (1996). *The Stanford Achievement Test* (9th ed.). San Antonio, TX: Author.

Repetto, J. B., Pankaskie, S. C., DePalma-Hankins, A., Schwartz, S. E., & Perry, L. (1997). Promising practices in dropout prevention and transition for students with mild disabilities. *Journal of At-Risk Issues, 4*(1), 19–29.

Rozecki, T. (1998). In J. C. Impara & B. S. Plake (Eds.). *The thirteenth mental measurements yearbook* (pp. 786–790). Lincoln, NE: The Buros Institute of Mental Measurements, University of Nebraska-Lincoln Press.

Stone, B., & Mata, S. (2000). Are we adequately preparing teachers for California's class-size reduction? In D. J. McIntyre & D. M. Byrd (Eds.), *Research on effective models for teacher education* (pp. 203–217). Thousand Oaks, CA: Corwin.

Texas Education Agency. (2001). *Academic excellence indicator system 1999–2000 district performance: Fort Worth Independent School District, Rosemont Middle School* [Electronic version]. Austin, TX: Author. Retrieved December 5, 2001, from *http://www.tea.state.tx.us/cgi/sas8/broke... IS+ Report&level=Campus&campback=220905057.*

Examining the Role of Teacher Involvement in Achieving a Balanced Literacy Program

11.

Pamela Boyd and Pamela Dennis Yandle

Pamela Boyd, Assistant Professor, Curriculum and Teaching, Auburn University, is a dedicated higher education partner collaborating with schools to provide quality professional development. Her research interest in school/university partnerships that promote reform in teaching and learning is reflected in her professional involvements and publications.

Pamela Yandle (Ed.S.) is a teacher at the site of this study. Her intense interest in effective reading strategies is evident from her prolific presentations on this topic, including to The State Department of Education and ARI Regional Principals. She is a professional "making a difference" for literacy statewide.

Abstract

The Alabama Reading Initiative (ARI)'s goal of 100% of Alabama students reading on grade level is linked to improved instructional practices. This study focuses on one of the schools chosen as a Literacy Demonstration Site, Copeland Elementary School. Copeland is an educational setting where examining current practices and initiating improvements related to school reform are priorities. Collaboration with a higher education partner and intensive training provided opportunities for teachers to identify and implement strategies that contribute to a balanced literacy program. Word attack, the area that generated the most questions and concerns among teachers, led to the development of an intervention program. Effectiveness is viewed through two layers of analysis, pre and post-surveying of teachers' attitudes and methods, and pre and post-testing of students participating in the intervention. Evidence from the study revealed a positive link between teacher preparation and student performance.

Introduction

F inding balance in a reading program, or anything else for that matter, is not an easy task. This has never been more apparent than now as the "Great Debate" rages on. On one side is the extreme "drill and fill" approach, still frequently practiced, that focuses on the isolated recitation method of learning the graphophonic patterns in our language (Foorman, Francis, Novy & Liberman, 1991; Morgan, 1995; Snider, 1990). Often this type of instruction results in stable standardized test scores because the instruction matches the testing of skills seen on these tests (Bracey, 1997). On the other side of the debate are those who advocate a more holistic approach to reading instruction with emphasis on the students' personal connection with literature, not direct systematic instruction (Goodman, 1996; Rief, 1992; Routman, 1994; Weaver, 1994). Zemelman, Daniels, and Hyde, authors of *Best Practice in Teaching and Learn* (1998), agree that although most students taught primarily through drill type instruction become functional readers in school, a positive connection with literacy, when it does occur, often happens outside its walls. They point out that improved test scores do not create a nation of mature, effective, voluntary self-motivated readers. A more rational approach, a balanced program, is preferable.

The Alabama Reading Initiative (ARI), sponsored by the Alabama State Department of Education, advocates a balanced approach to literacy. The initiative focuses on teacher education. The goal of the initiative—100% of Alabama's students reading on grade level—is linked to improved instructional practices that provide a balanced literacy approach. Support of dedicated teachers, members of the community, and school administrators is required for successful implementation of this initiative. Summer training for teachers and administrators, employment of a reading specialist, assistance from higher education partners, intensive program evaluation, and evidence of increased student success are required of schools designated as Literacy Demonstration Sites by the ARI.

The ARI defines literate behavior as the students' ability to read on-grade-level materials, fluently and with comprehension. This initiative combines the viewpoints of both the "whole language" and "phonics" camps. ARI's purpose is to design a program that does not promote one best method of teaching reading/language arts. Instead, the curriculum is defined through a thorough review of the research, incorporating recommendations from current research-based studies to meet individual needs of students.

The Copeland faculty and its leaders possess the qualities required to make literacy reform a success. These educators are determined to provide an environment that promotes a positive connection with literacy. They are committed to implementing best practices, those that produce real learning. Even the school building was designed around the idea of creating a community of learners. Arrangements for self-contained, multi-age, and looping classrooms provide varying options for meeting the individual needs of all the students. The language arts/reading curriculum is based on the Alabama Course of Study and reflects standards developed by the International Reading Association and the National Council of Teachers of Reading. These standards provide broad, general guidelines to implement meaning based, individualized instruction. Copeland Elementary School implements these standards based on *Qualities of Best Practice in Teaching Reading* (Zemelmen, Daniels, & Hyde, 1998):

- Reading means getting meaning from print.
- Reading is a process.
- Hearing books read aloud is the beginning of learning to read.
- Beginning reading instruction should provide children with many opportunities to interact with print.
- Reading is the best practice for learning to read.
- An effective reading program exposes students to a wide and rich array of print and goes beyond use of the basal.
- Choice is an integral part of literate behavior.
- Teachers should model reading.
- Effective teachers of reading help children actively use reading and writing as tools for learning.
- Children learn best in a low risk environment.
- Teachers should provide pre-reading, during-reading, and after-reading activities.
- Young children should have well-structured instruction in phonics.
- Teachers should provide daily opportunities for children to share and discuss what they have been reading and writing.
- Schools that are effective in teaching reading have an ethos that supports reading. (p. 30–35)

Creating a community of learners that engages teachers in professional development that enables the development of knowledge and skills leading to an improved learning environment is priority. Student learning is documented and instruction and learning environments are modified accordingly. Copeland faculty work collaboratively with the neighboring university's College of Education. Examining current practices while linking improvements to school reform is an on-going effort of the school/university partnership. This study reports one such effort-implementation of the ARI training and a follow-up study of teacher and student performance.

The Study

CONTEXT

This study focuses on one effort to improve student performance through improving instructional strategies at Copeland Elementary School. Copeland Elementary School is in close proximity to a large research university in the southeast. Copeland houses approximately 375 students in grades one-five. The racial composition is 49% Caucasian, 38% African American, 10% Asian, 2% Hispanic and 1% other. Approximately 44% of the students are eligible for free and reduced lunch.

One hundred percent of Copeland's faculty and staff, the principal, and the higher education partner participated in training provided by the Alabama Reading Initiative in the summer of 1999. ARI modules covering phonemic awareness and phonics, language development, reading comprehension, intervention, reading/writing connection, and formal/informal assessment were the basis for a two-week training period. State selected instructors who were trained in the contents and presentation of the modules provided the training for the Copeland faculty.

The purpose of this study was to explore teachers perceptions of the ARI training and further needs for staff development as well as the effect of the improved instructional strategies on the achievement of struggling readers. More specifically, the study was designed to answer the following questions: How do teachers view the effectiveness of the ARI training and need for additional professional training? What was the affect of the focused professional development (word attack teaching and learning) on the achievement of struggling readers?

DATA COLLECTION AND ANALYSIS

Two layers of analysis were implemented in this study. First, 28 members of the faculty were surveyed concerning the effectiveness of the ARI training and need for additional professional development. In addition, 29 students out of 40 who were identified as struggling readers completed pre- and posttesting on variables of literacy growth to determine if a change in word attack skills occurred.

The Faculty Survey

The researcher participants (the authors) designed the study to document concerns and questions that resulted from the ARI training and to determine continued professional development. As members of the literacy team, the Title I Reading Specialist, the higher education partner, the principal, and teachers reflected on the training and examined student performance. An open-ended survey was developed by the researchers to document the teachers perceptions/feelings toward the ARI training and professional development. The survey questions were structured to gain information concerning the most/least helpful modules, most/least helpful instructional strategies, least/greatest contribution to teachers and students, the perceived teacher and student strengths/weaknesses, and the need for additional professional development. The members of the faculty responded to numerous prompts concerning reading strategies, attitudes toward the reading program, and evaluations of ARI training effectiveness.

FACULTY VIEWS: RESPONSES TO OPEN-ENDED PROMPTS

Most of these prompts were open-ended, allowing for free response from the faculty. The faculty responded to the same overall survey at the beginning and the end of the academic year to determine if attitudes changed over the course of implementation. A total of 28 faculty members responded to the survey at the beginning of the year, representing administration ($N = 1$), counseling ($N = 1$), resource teaching ($N = 6$), and self-contained classroom teaching ($N = 20$). A total of 24 of these faculty members responded again at the end of the year. The professionals responding to the survey represent a wide array of educational backgrounds and teaching experience. The majority have earned master's degrees ($N = 13$), one has an educational specialist degree, and one an associate's degree. Their experience represents an average of 13.2 years, with the range extending from first year of teaching to over 26 years of experience.

According to the faculty responses prior to the academic year, their strengths in teaching included over 28 components, skills, and characteristics. Six of the teachers noted classroom management as a teaching strength

(21%), while five noted their individualization of instruction as a strength (18%). Other patterns included organizational skills and use of guided reading as self-defined subcomponents of teaching effectiveness. Otherwise no clear patterns emerged, with teachers indicating strengths in character areas, such as patience, flexibility and love of children, to strengths in the implementation of teaching strategies such as use of cooperative groups, and hands-on activities. A similar broad distribution of responses occurred for this question on the post-year survey. No patterns emerged on either survey administration, indicating that these teachers view their individualized strengths in a variety of unique and highly personalized ways.

Interestingly, the teachers' awareness of their weaknesses appears to closely parallel the information that teachers found to be most useful from the ARI training sessions on the beginning of the year survey. The training possibly elevated the teachers' understandings of certain reading techniques that they had not used consistently in the classroom, causing them to be more aware of these same components as weaknesses. For instance, 14 of the teachers (50%) indicated that the use of phonemic awareness/phonic strategies as a weakness, with 13 of these same teachers indicating that information regarding phonics was among the most useful information provided through the ARI training. Similarly, two indicated their ability to interpret standardized test scores as a weakness and three indicated the learning of methods to interpret standardized test scores as a strength of ARI training. A theme that emerged among five of the teachers regarding teaching weaknesses was their inability to effectively incorporate reading groups into their classroom instruction.

FOCUSED PROFESSIONAL DEVELOPMENT

Results of the survey provided meaningful conversations, both formal and informal, for faculty meetings and study groups. One area that seemed to generate the most concern and questions was word attack. The faculty decided to assess students in grades 2–5 to determine learning areas requiring supplemental instruction to achieve literacy at their grade level. The faculty was anxious to identify and provide intervention for "struggling readers." At the same time teachers were aware that knowledge and skill in the area of word attack was needed to work with students of all levels. To compliment the training received through the ARI members of the literacy team, including teachers, administrators, and the higher education partner, read about, thought about, and discussed word attack and its place in a balanced reading program. Professional development was embedded into the school day on a regular basis throughout the year. *What Matters for*

Struggling Readers by Richard Allington was selected as a grade level study group text. The ARI Intervention module was revisited for teaching strategies. The Title One Reading Specialist modeled specific intervention strategies for teachers. She often worked with students in the morning one-on-one or in small groups and went into the classrooms in the afternoon. Intervention strategies were utilized, when applicable, by all teachers throughout the day. Small group teacher conferences were held on a regular basis to discuss the student's progress.

The principal provided a resource room supplied with books, appropriate texts, and resources selected by the literacy team. Faculty meetings were organized to allow for discussions on pertinent reading topics such as the integration of reading in the content areas. A book room was established so that all grade level teachers would have access to a variety of trade books at different levels. A student Book Room was established to provide books of interest available for student purchase. The Media Center provided several book swap days for the students. Parent–teacher conferences were required specifically to inform parents about their child's assessment in reading, classroom intervention, and the need to listen to their child read out loud.

STUDENT TESTING

Teachers in grades two through five, identified and referred 40 struggling readers to the Title One Reading Specialist. The criteria for a "struggling reader" was: (1) any student scoring a stanine of 4 or less on the total reading composite of the Stanford Achievement Test (SAT-9); (2) students currently receiving Title I services; (3) students currently receiving special services; (4) teacher referrals; (5) parent referrals; (6) students currently scoring significantly below grade level on the school system reading assessment; and (7) students not achieving potential as denoted by the difference between the School Ability Index score on the Otis Lennon School Ability Test and the total reading composite stanine on the SAT. Twenty-nine identified students were pretested in Fall 2001 and post-tested in Spring 2002 using the Woodcock-Johnson Tests of Achievement-Revised, Form A and Brigance Inventory of Basic Skills.

Specific tests administered were: Letter-Word Identification, Passage Comprehension, and Word Attack. The Letter-Word Identification Test consists of an array of word types including regular words (dog, get), phonetically irregular words (was, you), multi-syllable words with phonetically regular patterns (correctly, experiment), and phonetically irregular patterns (shoulder, island). Other skills assessed were sight word knowledge, affixes, and syllabication. Passage comprehension was assessed using a cloze procedure format. Initially, students were presented with visual clues in conjunction with descriptive words. Eventually, sentences and paragraphs were introduced as the visual cues are faded. Unlike the other standardized testing procedures, the students read this test aloud offering the assessor insight into incorrectly read word types, types of miscues for miscue analysis, and reading strategies used by the students.

The final test administered from the WJ-R assessed the learner's ability to decode pseudo-words starting with consonant-vowel-consonant patterns and continuing in a spiral sequence of word types (CVC, CVC, CVVC, CCVC, CVCC, CCCVC, digraphs, diphthongs, etc.). Decoding has been defined as the ability to read through a word from left to right, generating the sounds that are connected to all the letters or letter patterns in that word and manipulating those sounds until they connect to a word in the student's speaking vocabulary (Honig, 1997). A pseudo-word assessment reflected the learner's true decoding skills. Sight word knowledge seemed to provide information only relative to reading high frequency words learned through repetition rather than by structural analysis skills.

In conjunction with the WJ-R, a diagnostic, criterion referenced test, The Brigance Inventory of Basic Skills was administered to determine a word recognition grade placement equivalency, and assessment of sight word knowledge beginning at a primer level and continuing to a 4.0 grade equivalence (GE). Although the learner may be taught important reading strategies such as contextual cuing a large and stable sight vocabulary continues to be the hallmark of a successful reader (Clay, 1985). The Word Recognition GE Test consists of similar word patterns as the WJ-R Letter-Word ID Test.

Comparison of the pre-post test scores on the WJ-R Test of Letter-Word ID, Test of Word Attack, The Brigance GE Test, and the Basic Sight Word Assessment proved informative. The results of these collaborative assessments yielded insight into the learners' specific areas of strengths and weaknesses. The majority of learners had mastered (90% word recognition accuracy) the 250 basic sight words. Also, the results reflected scores on the WJ-R Letter Word ID and the Brigance GE test which clustered around the current grade placement of the learners. However, the WJ-R Word Attack Test consisting of a systematic, spiral sequence of pseudo-words representing phonetic patterns reflected significantly sub-average scores (i.e., scores reflecting a deficit of at least one year below the learners' current grade placement).

Intervention

The faculty determined that this informative feedback suggested the need for explicit instruction with specific attention given to structural analysis of the words. The discrepancy between identifying basic sight words and pseudo-words affirmed the suspicion that students were reading by sight or visual memory rather than by sound-symbol relations. As students reach the third, fourth, and fifth grades textual reading consists of more multi-syllable words. To identify these word structures the learner must have background knowledge of the skills pertaining to vowel patterns, syllabication techniques, manipulation of affixes, and specific letter combinations. At this instructional level, no longer can the learner depend solely on sight word knowledge. Word attack skills are a prerequisite for decoding multi-syllable words since they must be viewed as 'chunks' or word parts chained together to make a bigger word.

Of the learners assessed in grades two through five, 73% of these students exhibited weaknesses in word attack abilities. These weaknesses had not been previously noted, either formally or informally, largely because of these students' ability to read grade-level connected text relying on their extensive sight word knowledge. However, as stated earlier, these learners, because of their current grade placements, were challenged with vocabulary, both in isolation and connected text, requiring phonological awareness and decoding skills. This led to the question, "Why is phonological knowledge so crucial for the beginning reader?" If children cannot auditorally perceive sounds in spoken words they will have difficulty decoding or "sounding out" words in a rapid and accurate fashion (Lyon, 1998). Also, the words they know in oral language enhance their literary learning. The greater their oral language, the easier it is for the learners to learn new words in written language. Often teachers assume children will learn these skills naturally, but many children do not develop phonemic awareness. They may have the ability to co-articulate the phonemes contained in words but are not able to segment these sounds (i.e., sight word/whole word recognition is implicit, as opposed to explicit identification). In these cases, explicit, systematic instruction in phonemic awareness should be implemented daily, as an early intervention strategy. Examples of phonological awareness tasks:

Phoneme Deletion	What word would be left if the /k/ sound were taken away from *cat*?
Word to Word Matching	Do *pen* and *pipe* begin with the same sound?
Blending	What word would you have if you put these sounds together? (/b//a//t/)
Sound Isolation	What is the first sound in *rose*?

Phoneme Segmentation	What sounds do you hear in the word *hot*?
Phoneme Counting	How many sounds do you hear in the word *cake*?
Deleted Phoneme	What sound do you hear in meat that is missing in *eat*?
Odd Word Out	What word starts with a different sound: *bag, nine. Beach, bike*?
Sound to Word Matching	Is there a /k/ in *bike*? (Stanovich, 1999)

To accommodate the needs of these learners intervention strategies were designed using feedback derived from formal and informal assessments and teacher observation. Word attack or decoding was the targeted skill for intervention since this was the assessed interference with comprehension for these learners. Carnine (1997) defines decoding as the translating of printed words into a representation similar to oral language. Understanding the representation is comprehension. A successful reader must be proficient in decoding to comprehend. Honig (1997) stated that first grade decoding ability predicts 80–90% of reading comprehension in 2nd and 3rd grade, and it still accounts for nearly 40% of reading comprehension by 9th grade. Four aspects of a decoding model include: decoding units, processing skills, knowledge base, and strategic knowledge (Carnine, 1997).

"Regular" word study was of equal importance. A regular word is a word in which each letter represents its most common sound, making the word phonetically decodable. The instruction for regular word study incorporated blending or "sounding out" but only after mastery of the individual letter sounds with emphasis on short and long vowels. The blending strategy can apply to many different words. Carnine (1977) reported that teaching letter-sound correspondences and sounding out resulted in students correctly identifying more unfamiliar words than when students were trained using a whole word approach. Implementation of a systematic, code-based format of instruction was instrumental in students learning to decode words. Also important was understanding how to correctly sound-blend words with special emphasis on blending both continuous and stop sounds. Regular word presentation followed a systematic scope and sequence (Carnine, 1997). A sample of this follows.

(V = vowel, C = consonant)

VC and CVC that begin with a continuous sound, e.g., at, Sam

CVCC that begin with continuous sounds, e.g., runs, lamp, fist

CVC that begin with stop sounds, e.g., hot, cap

CVCC that begin with stop sounds, e.g., cast, hand

CVCC in which both the initial consonants are continuous sounds, e.g., slap, frog

CVCC in which one of the initial sounds is a stop sound, e.g., crib, stop

CCVCC, e.g., brand, clump

CCCVC and CCCVCC, e.g., split, sprint

Base words with affixes

Intersperse irregular sight words and irregular words

The faculty believed that a crucial element for success was the teacher's ability to assess the learners in order to determine current levels of functioning, the learner's knowledge base, and understanding of skills. This feedback allowed the teacher to begin instruction at the appropriate level in the spiral scope and sequence format and focused on specific strengths and weaknesses.

In conjunction with adherence to a systematic scope and sequence, teachers used modeling and pacing of word types, first in isolation, then in context. To promote generalization of these skills, targeted word patterns were practiced in connected text formats using decodable text correlated to the appropriate level of instruction. Decodable text is recognized as stories that have a significant proportion of decodable words (70–95%). Also, the sequencing of stories is such that the letter-sound relations the children have learned are cumulatively reviewed in the words of the stories. These stories were comprehensible and the words in the stories contained in the children's spoken language. This approach was used in the general education and reading resource settings and included oral reading practice at home. Consistency, professional collaboration across the instructional settings, and repetitious practice were all key factors that promoted the success of learners. Not only did practice build competence, but competence enhanced interest, and stimulated continued motivation to practice.

For further exposure to targeted word patterns in context, literature-based trade books were used in a guided reading format across educational settings. To facilitate incidental learning, these trade books were matched to the learner based on the learner's instructional reading level. Guided reading, with the use of trade books, was an effective component of this mixed instructional agenda. Reciprocal teaching provided guided practice in the use of strategies such as predicting, question generating, summarizing, and clarifying. These enhanced children's ability to construct meaning from text.

Intervention Steps

1. Phonological/phonemic awareness
2. Systematic explicit instruction in phonics
3. Word attack strategies
4. Regular word study
5. Formal and informal assessment
6. Modeling and pacing of word types (decodable texts)

Findings

Regarding participation in the ARI training, none of the teachers felt forced, 32% felt strongly encouraged by someone else, and 68% participated due to a personal decision. The faculty ratings regarding the ARI training fell into a clearly positive distribution, both prior to the actual teaching year, and then again at the end of the year. Table 1 provides data from the ratings of the ARI training.

From the frequency of positive responses listed in Table 1 it is obvious that the teachers found the ARI training worthwhile. At the end of the year, though percentages were based on fewer respondents, rating of ARI training increased with an additional 14% indicating that the training was extremely worthwhile. Following a year of implementation, teachers seemed better able to identify their strengths and weaknesses. Regarding what was most useful about ARI training, three patterns emerged: appreciation of the embedding of current research and updating of educational philosophy; valuing a variety of ideas and methods, and recognizing the importance of instruction in phonemic awareness and phonics, emphasizing work attack strategies

STUDENTS: CHANGES IN LITERACY SKILLS

Early in the academic year, using previously stated criteria; forty students from grades 2, 3, 4, and 5 were pretested on a number of literacy skills. Included were The Woodcock-Johnson Word Identification, The Woodcock-Johnson Reading Passage Comprehension, Word Attack Skills, and The

TABLE 1		
Reactions to ARI Training		
	Extremely Worthwhile	**Moderately Worthwhile**	**Not Applicable to Teaching**
Pre	21 (78%)	5 (19%)	1 (4%)
Post	22 (92%)	2 (8%)	

Brigance Word Grade Equivalent Assessment. Later in the year (range = 3 to 7 months after completing the pretests), 29 of these students were posttested on these same instruments. Unequal numbers of students from varying grades completed the posttests. Representative numbers per grade level for the students who completed both pre and posttesting fell into the following distribution: Grade 2 (N = 1), Grade 3 (N = 8), Grade 4 (N = 13), and Grade 5 (N = 7). Table 2 displays the pre and posttest mean scores and the statistical results of a paired sample t-test for each of the variables of literacy for all the students, regardless of grade level, involved in the posttesting.

From viewing Table 2 it can be observed that the posttest scores increased on all four measures of literacy skills. From pre to post intervention, students increased their ability to complete letter and word identifications correctly. They increased their reading comprehension skills, and their word attack skills. Their grade equivalency regarding word recognition also increased. These gains were all significant at the .00 alpha levels suggesting that these differences in means could not be due to any element of chance but rather caused by a definite external intervention.

Some of the constraints of the research design must be recognized. Because no group of students was randomly selected as a control, no causal or inferential statements can truly be applied to this data. Randomly selecting a comparable control group of students with similar needs and withholding additional literacy instruction would, of course, be unethical. Some of the increases could possibly be due to the regular reading curriculum rather than the intervention strategies used with this group of students. However, the pattern of increases on literacy outcomes does suggest that effective instruction is taking place at this ARI site. This is due to teachers' emphasis on reading and literacy skills embedded within all areas of instruction, as well as positive gains resulting from the teacher initiated intervention program described in this study.

TABLE 2

Pre and Posttest Means and Statistics .
for T Literacy Outcomes of Yarbrough Elementary
School Students (N = 29)

	Letter-Word ID	Compre hension	Word Attack	GE
PreM	3.46	3.67	2.68	4.10
PostM	8.54	5.52	6.10	4.88
t	8.54	8.10	5.74	8.81
alpha	.00	.00	.00	.00

An unexpected and interesting finding from this data is an apparent relationship between word attack skills and word recognition ability. At first consideration, it would be expected that no relationship would exist between these two variables. In fact, these are practically contradictory literacy skills. Word attack skills are methods of decoding that require time to cognitively process, whereas sight word recognition implies immediate responses to words that are instantly recognized and retrieved from an individual's memory bank. Surprisingly, in this particular study, these two pre intervention variables positively and significantly correlated (correlation = .324; significant at the .05 level). This finding suggests that students who excel in one literacy skill also excel at other literacy skills, even though the particular skills are seemingly unrelated. Students whose abilities increase in word attack skills also become more effective at sight word recognition.

Conclusions and Implications

Practice in the decoding of pseudo-words reinforces specific structural analysis strategies crucial to reading success. At these aforementioned grade levels, if the learners have not become automatic with a large number of words, and proficient at decoding new words, reading connected text becomes increasingly difficult, both conceptually and structurally (Honig, 1997). For these students the losses accumulate, and the opportunities for them to advance or catch up diminish over time (Kameenui, 1993). Without explicit, systematic intervention procedures, a "Matthew Effect" is created (Stanovich, 1986). This is a phenomenon in which the "rich get richer" (i.e., the children who learn early to decode continue to improve in reading), and the "poor get poorer" (i.e., the children who do not learn to decode early become increasingly distanced from the "rich" in reading ability).

"When children learn to read they must acquire two different kinds of skills. They must learn how to identify printed words, and they must learn how to comprehend written material" (Torgeson & Mathes, 1999). This catapults us back into "The Great Debate," code-based instruction or meaning-based instruction? Research now supports a blend of the two, creating a balanced literacy approach. Using a balanced approach to literacy instruction moves beyond the endless debates and returns us to a common sense approach to teaching and learning.

Prior to comprehending printed text, the learner must become phonologically aware. Defined, phonological awareness involves learning two concepts related to language. The first concept is learning that words can be divided into segments of sound smaller than a syllable. The second concept includes learning about individual phonemes (Torgeson & Mathes, 1999). This knowledge is crucial for the acquisition of "sounding out " skills needed to become fluent, accurate readers. Instruction in phonological awareness should be part of the reading curriculum K–2. We learn to walk before we learn to run. In the same way, we acquire the alphabetic principle before we can read fluently. This calls for direct, systematic, explicit instruction in phonics, not through a single procedure, but by using a variety of strategies to provide individual learners with tools for "cracking the code" and bringing meaning to print.

This study provides critical insights and implications for schools engaged in initiating and sustaining school reform in literacy. Examining and reflecting on the effect of teaching strategies on student performance is essential. Copeland faculty provided students with opportunities for all students to engage in meaningful reading experiences that reflect Best Practice. However, through participation in an intense reading initiative, reflection of instructional strategies, and examination of struggling readers the faculty discovered and addressed an area of need in their literacy program. It is important to note that this intervention program grew out of these teachers' perceived need for increased emphasis on word attack teaching and learning and follow-up professional development. Evidence gathered from this study makes it apparent that the ARI training, and the reading intervention program inspired by it, had a positive effect on reading achievement at this school. A number of literacy related variables (word and letter identification, word attack skills, reading comprehension, and word grade level equivalents) could be cited. The intervention strategies that were implemented made a positive contribution towards the literacy goal stated by the Alabama Reading Initiative, 100% of all students reading at their grade level. This goal could be considered unrealistic and unattainable, but as this study indicates it is an achievable goal, given a dedicated faculty working in collaboration with a partner university.

REFERENCES

Bracey, G. W. (1997). *The truth about America's schools: The Bracey reports, 1991-97.* Bloomington, IN: Phi Delta Kappa Educational Foundation.

Carnine, D. (1997). How do children learn to read? Evidence from decades of Research. *Voices on Word Matters,* 188–197.

Clay, M. M. (1985). *The early detection of reading difficulties* (3rd ed.). Portsmouth, NH: Heinemann.

Foorman, B., Francis, D., Novy, D., & Liberman, D. (1991). How letter-sound instruction mediates progress in first-grade reading and spelling. *Journal of Educational Psychology, 83*(December), 456–469.

Goodman, K. (1996). *On Reading.* Portsmouth, NH: Heinemann.

Honig, B. (1997). Reading the right way. *CORE Reading Research Anthology,* 7–12.

Kameenui, K. J. (1993). Commentary—Diverse learners and the tyranny of time: Don't fix blame; Fix the leaky roof. *CORE Reading Research Anthology,* 218–225.

Lyon, G. R. (1998). Overview of reading and literacy initiatives. *CORE Reading Research Anthology,* 13–23.

Morgan, K. (1995). Creative phonics: A meaning-oriented reading program. *Intervention in School and Clinic, 30*(May), 287–291.

Rief, L. 1992. *Seeking Diversity: Language Arts with Adolescents.* Portsmouth, NH: Heinemann.

Routman, R. 1994. *Invitations: Changing as teachers and learners K–12.* Portsmouth, NH: Heinemann.

Snider, V. E. (1990). Direct instruction reading with average first-graders. *Reading Improvement, 27*(Summer), 143–148.

Stanovich, K. E. (1986). Matthew effects on reading: Some consequences of individual differences in the acquisition of literacy. *Reading Research Quarterly, 21,* 360–406.

Stanovich, K. E. (1999). Romance and reality. *CORE Reading Research Anthology,* 24–35.

Torgeson, J. K., & Mathes, P. (1999). What every teacher should know about phonological awareness. *CORE Reading Research Anthology,* 54–61.

Weaver, C. (1994). *Reading process and practice: From socio-psycholiguistics to whole language.* Portsmouth, NH: Heinemann.

Zelmelmen, S., Daniels, H., & Hyde, A. (1998). *Best practices: New standards for teaching and learning in American schools* (2nd ed.). Portsmouth, NH: Heinemann.

Summary

Linda Quinn

"The only way to increase the learning of pupils is to augment the quantity and quality of real teaching" (Dewey, 1939, 614–615).

The chapters in this division provide four views of the ways in which teacher education interventions can have an effect on student learning. Each research report addresses the complexity of teaching, the benefit of forming partnerships, the need for continued support from peers, and the importance of conversations with fellow teachers and students.

Historically, teachers have always been capable of doing more than one thing at a time in more than one way. They have to. Doyle's (1986), description of the "multidimensionality" of classrooms demonstrates that teaching is a complex act.

In the first chapter in this Division, Wendy Burke provides a framework for the complexity of learning to teach through a discussion of the processes of learning. This connection underscores the link between what teachers know and are able to do and the achievement of their students.

In Burke's chapter, the introduction of teacher work sampling during student teaching provides a basis for beginning teachers to use information about teaching contexts and differences among students to facilitate learning. Reflection in action (Schon, 1987) is seen as fundamental to the development of professional practice and the use of work samples serves as a way to engage in an inner professional dialogue that can lead to a fully developed teacher identity. Knowles, Cole and Presswood (1994) discuss reflection as ideas and thoughts that are "bent back" (p. 9), to help teacher candidates through a circular process from personal experience and practice, to information gathering and documentation, to reflection and analysis, to the formulation of personal theories, and finally to informed action (9-10). This process is clearly evident in the work study practices of Burke's teachers.

During student teaching, the Renaissance Teacher Quality project in Burke's study provided collaborative support from content area professors, teacher education methods professors, and cooperating teachers. Burke's "semi-structured" and open-ended interviews during the study provided the teachers, professors and candidates involved in the project the opportunity to articulate impressions they had gained from the experience. During the first year of teaching support shifted from the project to school sites, mentor teachers and district professional development. One question raised from Mary's description of her first-year experiences is the possible conflict between the perception of "a good teacher" that exists in a given school, and a beginning teacher's perception acquired from teacher education coursework. New teachers get worn down. In Heidi's words, "Teaching is tough." Understanding the importance of helping beginning teachers prepare for their first year brings up coherency issues between teacher education programs and schools' expectations for teachers. Do teacher education programs improve schooling or do schools change the teachers who emerge from teacher education programs?

In the second chapter of this Division, Christy Folsom also uses the construct of complex teaching and learning to frame her study. A discovery that "something important was missing in the interactions between teachers and students," led Folsom to implement a professional-development intervention on the intellectual processes involved in project work. Her report highlights a "glaring gap" in teacher preparation, and focuses at least one educator's attention on the fact that in the rush to fill classrooms with well-prepared teachers, perhaps a most important element of quality teaching has been left behind. According to Folsom, what is left behind is what Dewey describes as "higher levels of intellectual method"(Dewey, 1964, p.329).

Findings from this teacher education intervention are examined and analyzed in relationship to changes in the thinking and practice of four teachers and the learning of their students. The intellectual process was clearly at work as both teachers and students grew in ability to discuss thinking and learning. Folsom's description of the effect of this intervention is inspiring, and the questions she ends her report with substantiate the need to reexamine the content of teacher education programs. Only a small number of teachers and learners benefited from this intervention. The question teacher educators should answer is how to make the advantages of intellectual growth this intervention provides available to all teachers and learners.

Jane Irons and Nancy Leffel Carlson report a staff-development project initiated through a request for help from middle school teachers. Support from a team of educators spanned a two-year teacher education intervention designed to help teachers motivate at-risk learners through an increased understanding of learning styles. The project unfolded within a three-year collaboration between university and school district partners involving training, ongoing assistance and teacher support. The study highlights issues that contribute to the complexity of teaching and ways that changing teachers' perceptions of reasons behind student learning can change the student learning. The authors state that the support for teachers afforded by the project encouraged them to experiment with teaching strategies they didn't commonly use. A concern often expressed by beginning teachers is the sense of isolation they experience in teaching. Partnerships and professional development can foster a sense of belonging as educators and teachers work together to grow professionally.

The final chapter in this division, by Pamela Boyd, discusses a state wide reading initiative, its implementation in a site "designed around the idea of creating a community of learners," and an intervention program that emerged from teacher preparation. Boyd states a priority of the project was "Creating a community of learners that engages teachers in professional development that enables the development of knowledge and skills leading to an improved learning environment." Improving instructional strategies was key to this intervention and documenting the effect of the focused professional development on reading achievement supported the effort. Teachers in this study appeared to recognize their own weaknesses and expressed a desire for information that would enhance their knowledge base. In my experience, teachers usually know a great deal about teaching and learning, and they have a fairly good idea of what they don't know.

Boyd cites the "Matthew Effect" as it relates to children learning to read, but it could also be applied to teacher education interventions and the case of learning to teach in programs that incorporates meaningful "activities" that help teacher education candidate acquire skills of critical reflection, the ability to assess student performance as a result of teaching interventions, and the consequences of their personal-professional beliefs for their students. Such programs would require a community of teachers and learners engaged in improving student learning.

While the four research reports in this section add to the knowledge base of the effect of teacher interventions on student learning, they also provide insight into the processes and partnerships necessary to set the stage for such interventions. Teamwork and collaboration are elements seen as essential to facilitating continuing professional development. Successful efforts in this regard provide regular opportunities for participants to share perspectives and seek solutions to common problems in an atmosphere of collegiality and professional respect (Fullan, Bennet, & Rolheiser-Bennet, 1989; Little, 1982). Teachers engaged in the study of teaching and learning become aware of research and its implications for the school and classroom (Sparks & Hirsch, 1997, p. 63). Effective programs require commitment, training and hard work, and the support of the teacher education community

Forty-six percent of newly hired teachers in public schools are first-time teachers (Bolich, 2003, p4), which implies that they were recently enrolled in teacher education programs, that they may be overwhelmed by the complexity of their teaching placements, and that they are eager for help and support. Some may have been fortunate enough to graduate from programs implementing interventions that they can transfer to their classrooms, some may be working in sites that have collaborative agreements with institutions of higher education, some may be engaged in staff development related to a specific need of their school, and some may be part of a larger research study begun when they were teacher education candidates. If any of the thousands of first-time teachers have the experiences described in the four chapters in this division of the Yearbook, they may already be well on the way to becoming master teachers.